COLIN CHAPMAN
WAYWARD GENIUS

Colin Chapman, stop watch and
lap chart in hand. *(PN)*

COLIN CHAPMAN
WAYWARD GENIUS

MIKE LAWRENCE

breedon **books**
PUBLISHING

First published in Great Britain in 2002 by
The Breedon Books Publishing Company Limited
Breedon House, 3 The Parker Centre,
Derby, DE21 4SZ.

ISBN 1 85983 278 4

Printed and bound by Butler & Tanner, Frome,
Somerset, England.

Cover printing by Lawrence-Allen Colour Printers,
Weston-super-Mare, Somerset, England

CONTENTS

ACKNOWLEDGEMENTS

Everyone quoted in this book contributed to it and to each and every one I can only say 'Thank you'.

Special mention, however, must be extended to a number of people who did more than generously share their stories. They are, in alphabetical order:

Michael and Nigel Allen, who were in at the start of Lotus (Michael was an equal partner in the first Lotus company) and who read my early drafts and commented on them in detail. This account of the early days of Lotus tells a different story to any other because of their patient cooperation.

Mike Bennett, an Australian Lotus enthusiast, who found me stories from people Down Under and who sent me a video of a talk delivered by Derek Jolly (an important early player), which he had arranged. Through Mike, I was able to telephone Derek and obtain the letter of Derek's which is quoted.

Frank Costin who, many times, had me up to the small hours as a bottle of amber liquor went down. Music, poetry, the Meaning of Life, nothing was beyond Frank.

Ron Hickman, who invited me to stay at his house and who gave me access to his considerable, unsurpassed, data files on Lotus and also his address book. Somehow, staying with Ron did not seem like work. Ron was also exceptionally helpful on the phone with all the many detail questions I had after my visit.

Gilbert 'Mac' McIntosh, whose role in the early days of Lotus has never been properly recognised, but whose contribution was incalculable.

Tony Reeves, a man not known to motor racing, but who runs the the website of Colin Chapman's school, the Stationers' Company's School. Through Tony I was able to assemble the first portrait of the young Chapman.

Peter Ross, who corrected numerous mistakes in my early drafts, and who generously shared research he has done for his own forthcoming book on the early days of Lotus. Peter is one of the unsung heroes of the Lotus story.

Picture Credits

(FF)	Ted Walker/Ferret Photographic
(LAT)	Tim Wright/LAT
(PN)	Peter Nygaard/Grand Prix Photos
(DJ)	Derek Jolly
(FMC)	Fran Chamberlain/Ford Motor Company
(IMC)	Indianapolis Motor Speedway

AUTHOR'S NOTE: NUMBERS

In the early days, Lotus had no coherent policy when it came to numbering cars. Indeed, what is now called the Lotus Mk I was never called Lotus at all: the name was first applied to Chapman's second special. The third car was called the Lotus Mk III and Colin used Roman numerals up to the Mk XI, which was anyway usually called the Eleven. Subsequent Lotus road cars have always had names beginning with 'E', even those which, like the 'Etna', never got beyond the mock-up stage.

The first Lotus single-seaters, the 12 and 16, had Arabic numerals, and the Elite was designated the Mk 14 (Mk 13 is is missing from Lotus as it is from most maker's lists), but it was never known as anything but the Elite. The Mk XV had Roman numerals, but everyone called it the Fifteen. At about that time, Colin gave up on the Latin. In the early 1960s, 'Mark' became 'Type', so the original Elan was the Type 26 though it was known only as the Elan.

Lotus Mk XXVI is not a handy title, especially when set down against Elan. Lotus T49 or LXIX? No contest, I think.

To avoid confusion, I have used Arabic numerals throughout. Most other books refer to the Mk III, I call it the Mk 3. Since what is known as the Mk I did not carry the Lotus name at all, there never was a Lotus Mk I, I think that's fair.

PREFACE

ONE word sums up Colin Chapman and it is 'star'. A star is larger than life. A star is someone we would all like to be. A star is someone who lights up a room.

Colin Chapman had star quality, which is why he was able to attract so many people to his side. Their contribution to his success was not always acknowledged, but that is often the way with stars. The public needs stars, which is why they are placed on pedestals, but the public does not necessarily need to be reminded that the star needs a make-up artist, a lighting technician and a sound engineer.

Chapman was a star, but he was also no saint. He had been a chancer from his earliest days, but the motor racing media does not like to mention such things. Many successful men have mistresses but, according to a close associate, Chapman liked to parade them as though they were medals, confident that he could get away with it.

Colin Chapman was the most charismatic and brilliant engineer in the history of motor racing. He, and his team, innovated the majority of the most important design parameters of the modern Grand Prix car and, more than anyone else, he was responsible for the establishment of the British motor racing industry. Chapman was often credited for things he did not do, but he is rarely credited for the creation of the British motor racing industry which currently directly employs 50,000 people, indirectly employs a further 50,000 and has an annual turnover of more than a billion pounds.

Consider that, in just 30 months, from autumn 1955 to spring 1958, Chapman and his band of helpers did the following while working from a converted stable block near his father's pub in North London.

1. Guided the design of the chassis of the Vanwall, the first British car to win a world championship Grand Prix, and the winner of the 1958 Constructors' Championship, the first occasion that the trophy was awarded.
2. Revised the BRM P25 so that instead of being a dangerous flop, it became a Grand Prix winner.
3. Designed the Lotus Eleven, which won more races than any car to that point.
4. Designed the Lotus Seven, which is still in production as the Caterham Seven. It is a cult car which has been copied all over the world.
5. Designed the Elite, which dominated its class in international racing and took Lotus into the mainstream car industry.

6. Proved that he was a formidable racing driver, a driver of Formula 1 standard, and then retired from racing.
7. Took Lotus into Formula 2 and Formula 1.
8. Advanced the careers of numerous drivers, which is one reason why British drivers were dominant in the 1960s.
9. More or less founded the British motor racing industry.

Most people would be proud to be linked to one of these achievements in a lifetime.

From Lotus sprang numerous other companies because Chapman attracted the brightest and the best, and he demonstrated to them what they could achieve. Lotus was not so much a company, as a movement. Today, we live in an entrepreneurial society, but it was not like that in the late 1940s and early 1950s. Colin Chapman was more than just an innovator in motor racing, he was a social innovator as well. He had enormous charm and charisma, people liked him and believed in him and even as a schoolboy he had stood out as a leader.

Chapman inspired people. Keith Duckworth and Mike Costin met at Lotus and went on to found Cosworth Engineering, the most successful engine maker in Grand Prix history. Mike Costin's older brother, Frank, was drawn into motor racing by Chapman, and he went on to become a distinguished freelance designer. Others went on to found chassis works, body shops and one, Ron Hickman, invented the Black & Decker Workmate.

While Chapman was alive, Lotus was the most exciting car company in the world. The Lotus Elan of 1962 set such standards of excellence that Mazda was happy to acknowledge that its highly successful MX-5 sports car, introduced more than a quarter of a century later, was inspired by the Elan. One difference is that the Mazda did not break new ground, but another is that it did not break down.

I can remember the excitement I felt when Ian H. Smith's book, *Lotus: The First Ten Years* was published. I was first in line to slap in a book request at my local public library. I devoured Ian's book. I was aged 16 and Colin Chapman was my hero. Much later, when I could afford such things, I bought the updated version, *The Story Of Lotus, 1947–1960, Birth Of a Legend*, but I have never had a reason to read it. I have referred to it frequently, but I have never re-read it because the book is branded on my memory.

I can say precisely when I became dedicated to motor racing. It was 1 February 1957, when I bought a copy of *Motor Sport*. I had been reading race reports and such, and buying the odd magazine, but the moment I bought that copy of *Motor Sport* was the deciding factor. I devoured every word that DSJ, Denis Jenkinson, wrote. It was not a bad time for an English schoolboy to become interested in motor racing. In 1957 Vanwall (with a chassis by Chapman) became the first British car to win a world championship race. Cooper dominated Formula 2 and Formula 3. The BRM P25 (modified by Chapman) won two Formula 1 races. They were non-championship events, sure, and the opposition did not amount to much, but the P25 had been dangerous before Chapman got his hands on it.

Aston Martin took a magnificent win in the Nürburgring 1,000km. Five Jaguar D-types started at Le Mans and they finished 1-2-3-4-6. Equally as important, Team Lotus won two classes at Le Mans and finished 1-2 in the parallel handicap race, the Index of Performance.

The Lotus Eleven carried all before it in the important 1100cc sports car class which then was the equivalent of today's Formula 3, the major stepping-stone for the serious young driver with his eye on higher things. Driving for Team Lotus were Cliff Allison, Graham Hill, Innes Ireland and Alan Stacey, all of whom went on to Formula 1. In addition there was the immensely talented Keith Hall and Peter Ashdown. Hall retired from racing for family reasons while Ashdown became Lola's first works driver.

That is not a bad strike rate for a little team, but then Chapman was a superb racing driver in his own right and he knew talent when he saw it. It became a joke in Formula 1 that the number two seat at Lotus was a short ride to oblivion, but the following all made their F1 debuts in a *number three* Lotus: Mario Andretti, Jim Clark, Emerson Fittipaldi, Nigel Mansell and John Surtees, and they are only the world champions who began that way. No other team has ever given so many opportunities to so many drivers as Lotus did with Chapman at the helm.

That, then, is one aspect of the man: Colin Chapman was in every way at the forefront of motor sport. However, he also had his dark side. He cut corners in business, and did so from his earliest years. He charmed people to his side and he exploited them. The crunch came with the involvement with John Z. DeLorean. When Lord Justice Murray handed down a prison sentence to Fred Bushell, Chapman's chief accountant and right-hand man, for a scam which lifted nearly $18 million from the British government, he did something that is most unusual for a British judge. He said that if Chapman had been in the dock he would have received a sentence of at least 10 years.

So Colin Chapman could have died in prison with his reputation in tatters. The man who had once received a Young Businessman of the Year award, who had been made a Fellow of University College, London, who had received a CBE from the Queen, who has often been nominated the the most brilliant racing car designer there has ever been, could have ended his life a convicted criminal. As it was he died suddenly of heart attack just as everything was beginning to unravel around him.

I grew up with Chapman as my hero and he never ceased to be my hero, even when I began to hear about his feet of clay. That is the problem in telling Chapman's story. He achieved so much, yet writing about him 20 years after his death, one does so with the knowledge that, had he lived, he would have been disgraced.

You measure a man's life by the space he leaves behind when he departs. By any reckoning, Chapman left a huge space.

Mike Lawrence
Chichester
July 2002

CHAPTER ONE
THE YOUNG RASCAL

ANTHONY Colin Bruce Chapman was born on 19 May 1928. His father, Stanley, owned the Orange Tree pub in Richmond, on the outskirts of London, where Colin's mother Mary had once been a barmaid. By all accounts she was very pretty, which has never been a handicap for any barmaid. This fact may not be unconnected to the fact that she married her boss. Stan Chapman was no run-of-the-mill publican. He was a personable man who also ran a successful catering business, but in those days you had to be a publican to be able to hold a licence to sell liquor. Stan had ideas about upward social mobility, which he passed on to his son, and he hated being referred to as a publican.

Stan Chapman was an entrepreneur and, not long after Colin's birth, he bought the Railway Hotel, a large pub in Hornsey, North London. Thanks to the catering business, Stan did so well that he was able to install a manager in the Railway Hotel while he looked after business in the wider sense. It seems that Mary Chapman was both thrilled by this elevation in status and also discomfited by it – she became excessively house-proud as she found herself in a splendid home which was way beyond the dreams of most women of her class.

Stan Chapman was a man who knew how to make contacts, and secure contracts, and he was, in his own small pond, a fairly big fish. The landlord of a popular pub has always been a special figure in a community and although not overly wealthy, the Chapman family was comfortably off. Stan even owned a sailing boat, *L'Assiette*, which at the time was a rare achievement for anyone.

During World War Two, publicans were not often affected by rationing. While there were many shortages, on the whole beer flowed freely and publicans were in an excellent position to hear of special, if not completely legal, deals. Stan is long dead, so it is impossible to check, but given his entrepreneurial instincts it would have been very unusual indeed if he had not dabbled in the black market. Almost everyone else who could, did, and it makes one wonder whether doing dodgy deals was another characteristic Stan passed down to his son.

Stan, short and compact like his son, appears as a spear carrier in many an account of Colin's life, but Mary Chapman, when she is mentioned at all, is merely a name. The pretty, vivacious barmaid is invisible. Not even Colin's friends from his earliest years can shed much light on her, though she must have offered them orange squash and biscuits. There must also have been birthday parties and the like, but nobody can remember anything about Colin's mother except that she was so house-proud that Colin had to take his shoes off when he entered the front door, and put on slippers.

Perhaps the first indications of the path that Colin's life would take came when he was very young. At the age of seven, he built a soap-box cart with independent front suspension. He had acquired an old pram and had sawn one of the axles in two. Unfortunately, although he recorded the fact, he left no details of the machine. The story sounds like typical Chapman myth-making.

Geoffrey Teychenne knew Colin from the age of five. The two boys attended St Mary's Infants School, Hornsey, and played with their model train sets together. Geoffrey, who gave up science to become a sculptor, is the cousin of John Teychenne, who played an important part in the Lotus story, and he recalls Colin coming back from the test which won him the place at the preparatory school attached to the Stationers' Company's School. He said 'Colin was very pleased with himself. The interviewing board had asked him how many farthings there were to a pound, he'd worked it out in his head and then took the board through his thinking. That was pretty remarkable for a kid of eight, but Colin was always exceptional at maths.'

The Stationers' Company's School in Hornsey was a free grammar school, founded in 1858 by one of the City of London's ancient guilds. The attached preparatory school accepted only about 12 boys a year so to win a place there was a special event. It more or less guaranteed a place in the main school, where Colin duly went. The young Chapman thus had a very good start in life. After the war, a grammar school education would become available to a quarter of all children, but a place in a grammar school in 1939 pointed to an exceptional future. The education may have been free, but parents had to provide a school uniform, games kit and a lot of other extras. There was also the expectation that a pupil would stay at school until at least the age of 16, whereas most children left school aged 14 to become breadwinners. Many a bright child could not even contemplate sitting the examination for a place, but Stan Chapman had the wherewithal and Colin's success reflected well on him. No doubt Colin's attendance at the best grammar school in the area was used to broaden Stan's social contacts.

Colin was an excellent pupil, who sometimes came top of his class, but he was as likely to receive a detention as a gold star. His teachers thought him bright but impulsive, and that was the pattern of his life. John Astrop, now an illustrator of children's books, was one of four boys at the grammar school, including Geoffrey Teychenne and Chapman, who formed a little gang. John recalls:

Colin was very handsome. The girls all loved him and he was always one for the girls.

He was brilliant at lessons, but he was forever getting into trouble. What you have to remember is that because of the war, we only got half an education. If there had been an air raid the previous night, and there were many, we got the morning off. This was supposed to allow us to sleep but, of course, we spent the morning searching for shrapnel.

The school was on top of a very steep hill, Denton Hill, and Colin used to dare us to follow him downhill on our bicycles. He was totally mad. He'd go down the hill with his hands off the handlebars and his feet off the pedals. Even when it snowed and Denton Hill was a sheet of ice, he was out there. He was a real dare-devil.

Because it was wartime, our teachers tended to be elderly, the fit young ones were in the armed forces. Our teachers had been hauled out of retirement and many of them used their World War One army ranks, so we had Colonel this and Major that, while corporal punishment was an everyday event.

Colin and I had 'Fluff' Woolley as our form master and he favoured a thwack on the bottom with a cricket bat for any infringement. Colin received his fair share. Eventually our little gang clubbed together and bought 'Fluff' a miniature cricket bat, but the ploy backfired on us when he said, 'Let's see how well it works, bend over.'

Geoffrey Teychenne recalls that Colin was always looking for new challenges: I once went round to his house and in his garden he had constructed a track for his bicycle. He'd put down plant pots, cans, whatever he could find, and laid planks on the top of them. He rode his bicycle on this track and dared me to do the same. He just had to make things more difficult for himself.

We shared a desk through the seven years we were at the Stationers' Company's School. We were friends and also rivals since we competed for the science prizes. I was better at science than he was, but he was better at maths. I won the major science prize, and he won the prize for being the best all-rounder. We both obtained places at London University, but at different colleges, and we drifted apart.

One small thing I recall. When Colin was about 11, Stan Chapman proudly showed me a pistol that Colin had made from matches. It was beautifully made and it fired matchsticks.

For a year or so after the outbreak of war, the entire school was evacuated to Wisbech, deep in the Fenlands, and Colin, already crazy about aircraft, loved the huge skies and the frequent sighting of RAF fighters and bombers.

Keith Hewett, who also attended St Mary's Primary School with Colin, and who knew him well at the grammar school, recalls that all the other pupils looked up to Colin. Keith says:

He had a very attractive personality. There was a slide at the local swimming pool and most dare-devils thought they had done everything when they went down on their bellies, but Colin used to go down on his feet. He was always immaculately turned out, he took a great deal of pride in his personal appearance, but he was also kind. When I got punctures on my bicycle, it was Colin who would mend them for me.

Keith recalls hearing a story that, on VE day, Colin 'borrowed' a London double-decker bus to celebrate. Keith is at pains to stress that it was only a story, but the story would not have circulated unless people believed that that it was something Colin was likely to have done.

Colin would never be a tall man and perhaps this caused him to compensate in other ways. The boy who becomes an agitator in his class at school, especially when he is clearly among the brightest, is usually a boy who is wants to prove something to himself, and others. Keith Hewett says, 'I was even shorter than Colin which is perhaps why I was keen to emulate him down Denton Hill.'

Another schoolfriend, Peter Stopford, recalls being in a woodwork class with Colin. He says:

We were set the exercise of planing a block of wood until it was perfectly square when set against a try square. Colin simply could not get his block square. The answer to him was simple, he adjusted the try square to fit the block.

It was an early example of Chapman's attitude to rules. The rule said that the wooden block had to fit the try square and Colin's block did fit his try square. One view says that he cheated, because a try square is supposed to be a true measure and the block should have fitted it. Another view says that the stated aim of the exercise was to align the block and the try square and that he did.

In 1959 at Le Mans, the cockpit of the works Lotus 15 was marginally too narrow to comply with the rules. Colin solved the problem by arriving at scrutineering with a measuring rule that 'proved' that the car was legal.

John Astrop recalls that, aged about 15, Colin had an Austin Seven with which he used to tinker, though he was too young to drive on the road. John says, 'We got the impression that Stan indulged Colin, nothing was too good for him.' Ken Meredith, two years Chapman's junior, remembers that Colin rode a Claude Butler bicycle, which then was every schoolboy's dream. Once, when Colin wrecked his bike, Stan bought him another. That was indulgence above the usual level.

Outside school Colin used to hang around with a gang of a dozen or so youths, including John Teychenne. John remembered:

We used to get up to all sorts of mischief. Colin's Dad used to do the catering for the Saturday night dances at Hornsey Town Hall. It was half a crown to get in, and that was a lot of money in those days. Colin got in free, naturally, but I would go over a high wall and Colin would let me in through a side door.

All round the dance floor were Art Deco ash trays mounted on chromed metal columns. We got some large bangers and once, it was during the war, we dropped the bangers into the ash tray columns. They made a huge noise and everyone dropped to the floor, thinking it was an air raid.

We both liked swimming and would often go to Hampstead Park Pond where the top diving board must have been about 35ft high so, of course, that was the one we had to dive off.

A picture is emerging of a young man who was a charismatic dare-devil, indulged by his parents, who was unusually intelligent, but also something of a tearaway. That is not the stereotype of a Boy Scout, but Ken Meredith confirms that they were both members of the 79th North London Air Scout Troop and that they went camping together. Colin, of course, was the Troop Leader, and Ken says, 'He was also a King's Scout, so he was like a god to me.'

To become a King's Scout you first had to be 14 years old, to have gained your First Class badge and then achieve a further 12 badges within 18 months. Among them were Camper, Forester, Naturalist, Pathfinder, Ambulanceman and Signaller. Few people in Chapman's later life ever associated him with tracking the spoor of a badger through woods and noticing plants, but not only could Colin do that, but he also remained an advocate of the Scout movement throughout his life.

In 1945, aged 17, Chapman won a place at University College, London, to study civil engineering. Stan Chapman fondly imagined his son building bridges and skyscrapers, and it was not a misplaced dream. Colin had sailed through school, and won prizes, and in the aftermath of war and the destruction it had brought, civil engineers were in demand. Stan could be satisfied with his son.

By the time that Colin won his place at University College, he had met Hazel Williams, at a Saturday night dance in Hornsey Town Hall in 1944. Hazel's parents also lived in Muswell Hill and her school was at the bottom of Denton Hill. Bob Hester, a life-long friend, remembered:

In his later life, Colin became very much a ladies' man, which surprised me, and upset Hazel, but each morning Colin would walk Hazel to school with his arm around her.

I remember that Colin once had a girl in his car, it was many years later, when Lotus was established. To his horror he was passed by Hazel, driving in the opposite direction. Colin told her that she was the girlfriend of John Doe, a senior man at Lotus, and Doe had taken so much drink that he was flat out on the back seat. Colin was merely making sure that the poor girl got home safely.

Hazel swallowed the story and, soon afterwards, Mr Doe came to dinner at the Chapman home. Hazel turned on him and said that she thought it was disgusting that a senior executive had been legless, that Lotus deserved better. By that time everyone knew about Colin's peccadilloes and Doe was quick to take the blame.

I think it was in the 1960s that he changed because I can remember Jim Clark once joking that when they went away to race, Jim would be at a party and Colin would be in his hotel room with a book.

Perhaps Jimmy's comment was politic rather than definitive, and perhaps Bob was behind with the news. Robin Read, sales manager at Lotus 1959–62, recalls that Colin was known to have been playing away from home long before he, Robin, joined Lotus. Some lurid stories have been told.

The issue might as well be tackled at at this point to get it out of the way. Bob Hester's story about John Doe and the girl in the car is paralleled by similar tales, until Hazel did find out and Colin's associates were spared the task of covering up for him. Colin had several long-term mistresses, and he cheated on them as well. Some of those ladies are now grandmothers and it would be cheap to rake the past too thoroughly. Besides, nobody has ever suggested that the name of Colin Chapman does not still bring a smile to their faces.

It is impossible to know the real Colin Chapman because he presented so many faces to the world. Perhaps the real Colin Chapman is the engineer. No engineer who worked with him has a bad word to say about Colin as an engineer. Ron Hickman, who designed the Lotus Elan, was ripped off by Colin in financial transactions, yet maintains that Colin was absolutely straight when it came to engineering. Every other engineer says the same.

The following story has been published and the attributed source is Hazel. Stan Chapman was too old to join the armed forces when war broke out, but he was active in Civil Defence. In 1944, Colin and his father created a device which could plot the course of a V1 flying bomb so that they would know whether it was coming in their direction. If it was, runs the tale, Stan would order evacuation of the area. In fact, Stan had no such authority.

It's one of those 'boy genius' stories which are beloved by Hollywood biopics but it is hogwash, as anyone who has been on the receiving end of a V1 will know. When it came to a doodlebug, if you could see one, and doodlebugs were not very large, you could see what direction it was taking. If it was coming your way, it was coming at about 350mph, which means at best you could see one for 10 seconds. The crucial factor was when the engine cut out because, between 10 and 30 seconds later, the V1 would hit the ground and explode. It was impossible to tell from the ground when the engine would cut out, so there never was a 'boy wonder' gizmo.

The story illustrates a problem of writing about Chapman. He was a man to whom myths accrued and he was not averse to massaging his own mythology. It was a characteristic he shared with Enzo Ferrari, along with a passion for women and motor racing.

CHAPTER 2

FOUNDATION YEARS

A T UNIVERSITY, Colin did not work unduly hard. Hagiographers have written that he found the work easy, but he did not. He struggled because, for first time in his life, he was in an environment where everyone was bright. He had to work rather than breeze through, and he wasn't too keen on work.

Colin bought a 350cc Panther motorcycle and would roar between home and university, riding with verve until he rammed a London taxi. The elderly ladies who had booked the cab were surprised when Colin sailed through the window. Stan and Mary Chapman decided that four wheels were safer than two, and Colin was soon making the journey in a Morris Eight.

Colin attended university rather than being involved in it. The only student organisation which interested him was the University Air Squadron, which gave him the opportunity to learn how to fly and to earn his private pilot's licence. Flying would be a major part of Colin's life and he learned lessons from aircraft technology. Because he did not expend much energy studying, Colin had lots of spare time. He also had an eye for the main chance and began to deal in second hand cars with a fellow student, Colin Dare. Colin was involved in the car trade from his second term at university, which gives some idea of his priorities.

Wednesday and Saturday afternoons would see the two Colins, Chapman and Dare, in Warren Street, a few hundred yards from University College and London's notorious meeting place for used car traders. Colin was only 17 when he entered a pool of sharks and he survived. He didn't just survive, he prospered, and you only prosper in a pool of sharks if you are a shark yourself.

Dealers would would arrive in Warren Street, park their cars, and trade. Used cars were all that there were in Britain in 1946. At the time, there were no consumer protection laws, let alone laws regulating roadworthiness, and many cars which came to the market in 1946 had been laid up since 1939 so their condition was often ropey. Dealers got up to all sort of tricks. A lady's stocking forced down the dipstick opening would wrap itself around the crankshaft and deaden the sound of worn big ends. Extra thick oil would do the same for the few miles that the engine lasted. A noisy back axle or gearbox could be subdued with sawdust.

Whether Colin ever employed such ruses or not, he must have known of them, and he certainly learned how to demonstrate a car so that the potential customer did not pick up faults. There was the MG Tourer which belched smoke when driven normally, but did not when nursed by Colin. Warren Street was not for the fastidious. Colin was mingling with sharp characters and the fact that he made a success of his trading says that he was no innocent. The Warren Street experience was an important part of his background. In his later career, Chapman often cut corners and employed the mentality of the Warren Street spivs. To be accepted in Warren Street, you had to be a spiv.

Before long, Chapman and Dare had had built up quite a stock of cars. Some were kept at the Chapman home, some in a lock-up garage behind Hazel's house. Stan Chapman was not enthusiastic about his son's enterprise, but indulged him anyway. It is hard today to appreciate how much status there then was to having a son at university. While Stan Chapman disapproved of his son's wheeling and dealing in Warren Street, Hazel's father indulged the young man who, as time went by, he began to see as his future son-in-law. A university man was a good catch, a university man who could also trade was even better – there would always be meat on the table and the children would not go without shoes. There were times when Hazel's father would lend Colin money to clinch a deal, although Colin never did get round to paying him the agreed 10 shillings a week for use of the lock-up garage.

Within a few months, Colin was trading in Warren Street on his own because Colin Dare failed his exams and had to leave. By 1947 he had stock valued at £900, a remarkable achievement for a student trading as a sideline and competing against seasoned professionals. During 1947 Colin began to do extra work on his cars, improving them and adding value. That meant time and trouble, but he had plenty of spare time. His college records show that his lecturers were expressing concern about his progress and, indeed, he failed the maths element of his second-year exams. This doesn't square with accounts which say that he found university a breeze.

All Colin's spare cash went into his trading and Hazel, who figured that this was a young man who would go far, supported him. Colin and Hazel's social outings became restricted to the Hornsey Town Hall dances, where they did not have to pay to get in and where, for them, the drinks were free. Otherwise they went on trips to the local cinemas where entry through an emergency exit was not unknown. Colin always expected someone else to pay.

In December 1947, the British government dropped a bombshell. The meagre petrol ration for private cars was cut entirely save for those in certain professions. Worse, there was no indication of how long the regulation would stay in force. Overnight the bottom dropped out of the used car market and the value of Colin's stock halved. He managed to sell all his cars save for an Austin Seven which he neither he, nor anyone else, wanted. On the other hand, he had become involved with cars and he reckoned that there would be petrol in the future. He had also tinkered with an Austin Seven aged 15, so he knew the model inside out. Colin decided to make something of the car. It was a 1930 model with a fabric body which was easily removed. He then began to apply academic theory plus a fair measure of trial and error.

At the time, the esoteric art of trials driving, or mud plugging, was popular. You had to drive to the top of a muddy hill with your passenger acting as ballast, bouncing when necessary, or hanging out of the car to distribute weight. When Chapman began to build his car, trials driving was no backwater, it was mainstream motor sport. Mainland Britain had no circuits, though there had been two race meetings held on an ex-military airfield, one in 1946 and one in 1947, slim pickings there. Actually, when Chapman began to build his car there was no petrol and therefore no motor sport of any description.

Colin began by flattening the quarter-elliptical rear springs, then he swapped the back axle round, left to right, so that he could mount the springs above the axle, instead of below, which meant that he maintained the ground clearance essential for a trials car. It also eliminated the oversteer which was endemic among Austin Sevens. The body was constructed from sheet aluminium, easily obtainable from any scrap yard that handled ex-military stock, over plywood, and that created a strong sandwich. It was a lot stronger than the 1930s body. Colin was no metal-basher, but his attention to detail was exacting so, though the body was angular, and not pretty, it was neatly made. One of the perils of trials driving was being caught by trees or shrubs, so the mudguards on Colin's car were secured by Rawlplugs and screws. If they encountered an unyielding object, the mudguards would detach from the body and it was a simple matter to put them back on.

Every part of the car received meticulous attention. The engine was rebuilt with new manifolds, and a Ford downdraught carburettor, and the cable brakes were were modified with new linkages. All this sounds as though there was an original mind at work, but everything described was common practice. It shows, however, that Colin had done his homework and had exercised the ability, which he would demonstrate throughout his life, to separate the wheat from the chaff.

The car's completion coincided with Colin's final exams, when he failed his maths part one for the second time, and he left university without a degree. Every other account of Chapman's life speaks of celebrations when he was awarded his degree in 1948, but it did not happen. One assumes that Colin told the story of the celebration to cover what must have been a humiliating failure. He had taken his eye off the ball, trading in cars, and he had failed, whereas until then he had succeeded at every level.

The little car to which Colin devoted so much care and attention was a superior Austin Seven Special. Only a small proportion of specials which were started were ever finished and few were finished with the attention to detail that Colin brought to his car. Once the car was finished, so runs the legend, Chapman did a remarkable thing. He re-registered his car (PK 3494 became OX 9292) and so it ceased to be an Austin Seven and it became, officially, a Lotus. Or did it?

If Colin had done that, then it would be one of the most revealing details of his story. Virtually everyone else who had built an Austin Special registered their cars as an Austin. Instead, Colin created a new marque name for his car as a marker for the future – or so it has been written. Why is it then that when Chapman entered the car in trials, he entered it as 'Austin Seven Special'? Why is it that when he sold the car, he sold it as 'Austin Seven Special'? He sold the Austin after he had sold his second special, which was billed as 'Lotus'. Not Lotus Mk 2, the second car was sold as plain 'Lotus'. The Chapman 'Austin Seven Special' (we'll call it Lotus Mk 1 for convenience since everyone else does) disappeared a long time ago. Despite the best efforts of Lotus enthusiasts, not a single nut or bolt has been found.

The basic petrol ration was restored on 1 June 1948, and a few motorsport events were organised. That winter the Austin Special performed quite well in trials and Colin picked up a couple of awards. He was always looking for improvements and before long he had split the Austin front axle to create independent suspension. Split-axle front suspension would be a Lotus hallmark right up to 1956. It was a simple solution, and one which worked well, but such conversions had been around since the 1930s. It was not an example of brilliance, it merely showed that Colin had observed and absorbed.

Chapman did not suddenly burst on the scene through strokes of genius, but he was on an upward learning curve, and he had the sense to realise that. A positive thing was that Colin knew that you never stop learning. After leaving university, he could have been called to National Service – two years in the military whether you wanted to serve or not. With his background in the London University Air Squadron, and his private pilot's licence, Colin did the smart thing and applied for service in the RAF. He was accepted as an officer-cadet, which meant considerably more pay than he would have received as a conscript. On top of all that, he could resign his commission, whereas a conscripted 'oick' could not. Stan Chapman still wanted to see his son building bridges and skyscrapers, and he worried that the armed forces lose status very quickly once a peace treaty has been signed. To Colin, however, it was a chance to clock up flying hours while someone else picked up the bills.

From October 1948, Colin was in the RAF. He trained on Tiger Moths and Harvards and had his Austin Special to play with at weekends. Several of his fellow trainees were so impressed by the little car that they began to build their own specials, or so the story goes. One wonders how many, if any, were completed.

Colin was stationed at Ternhill in Shropshire, not far from the Welsh border, and a long haul from Muswell Hill in the days before motorways. It took five or six hours to make the journey in an Austin Seven Special and none of the photographs of the car shows any sign of weather protection. Michael Allen (who would play a pivotal part in the formative days of Lotus) tells the following story:

Petrol was rationed, but there was red fuel. This was for farmers and tradesman and was dyed red – anyone else who used red fuel could receive a hefty fine. On the other hand, there were people prepared to sell it. Colin built a second fuel tank under the scuttle which held red fuel and made what looked like a brass box which had a regular side carburettor and also a downdraught carb., each servicing one of the two tanks.

Colin could drive on red fuel and if the police became suspicious, a pull on a wire would swap the fuel supply, without missing a beat. If the police demanded to inspect the fuel, which they would do by poking a stick into the fuel tank, they would go to the obvious place, the rear fuel tank.

Before long Colin was at work on his second special. He joined the 750 Motor Club, which was to breed a generation of racing car designers, and he read everything he could about car design. The Austin Special was okay, but the best one could hope for with it was a minor award in a mud plugging event. There had been a time when trials were dominated by big cars with American V8 engines, but smaller, more nimble cars were taking over. A favoured combination was a Ford Ten engine in an Austin Seven frame and such a car was within Colin's grasp. He began to build one in Muswell Hill during his leave periods and weekend passes.

Hazel was not courted conventionally. She and Colin were an item and she went along with him because she trusted that he was hers and he was going to do remarkable things. The one constant in Chapman's life, for 38 years, was Hazel. Theirs was never a conventional relationship, but it endured. Colin's second car used Ford running gear in an Austin chassis and, since Colin was in the RAF, it progressed slowly. He would arrive at Muswell Hill when he could, work on his car, and when he returned to camp, he would leave Hazel with a job list. This could range from her painting or filing bits of the chassis to buying parts for the next stage. Nigel Allen recalls: 'Hazel was then managing her mother's wool shop in Muswell Hill and it used to drive her mad that she could never get her hands completely clean.'

Colin charmed a fellow airman, John Hall, to assist him. Hall therefore became the first of many people who helped Chapman's career and who then slipped from notice. John Teychenne also helped and, apart from being a long-time friend, John's father owned a garage in Hornsey. Percy Teychenne had many contacts at Ford and was able to obtain parts for the project. Colin bought a Ford Eight and put the engine in his chassis, having devised a system to mate a Ford engine to a four-speed Austin gearbox. The chassis used split-axle independent front suspension and Ford pressed steel wheels were fitted. Even at this stage of his career, Colin understood the importance of stiff wheels, something which would one day see the famous Lotus 'wobbly web' magnesium alloy wheels for which Colin received all the credit, although he had little to do with the design.

A Ford Eight engine was not ideal, but funds were low. Then Colin discovered a burned-out Ford Ten in a scrap yard. The engine seemed fine, however, and further enquiries (nobody has ever accused Colin of not doing his homework) indicated that it was virtually new, with only about 1,000 miles on the clock. The trouble was that the insurance company which owned the wreck wanted £30 for it. His time spent dealing in Warren Street had not been wasted. Colin knew that there was a market for his old Ford Eight car, even if its engine was in his new special. The important thing was that he had the car's log book and, among the sharp guys who dealt in used cars, that mattered more than an engine. He sold the Ford Eight and used the money to buy the engine and gearbox from the Ford Ten. Colin now had a nearly new engine and gearbox, and had offloaded his old Ford Eight chassis. He also had the Ford Eight engine, surplus to requirements, on which he made £5 clear profit. He told the whole story in a four-part series in the magazine *Motor Racing* in late 1954. The fact that a monthly magazine was happy to feature a four-part series by a 26-year-old maker of specials and kit cars tells its own story. From very early in his career, Colin was regarded as a phenomenon.

On 5 August 1949, after another re-sit of the maths element of his course, and more than a year after he left University College, Colin was finally awarded his degree, a BSc (Engineering) at the lowest level, Pass. Today nobody would even be considered as a trainee engineer with any Formula 1 team with such a poor qualification, especially one which was in civil, not mechanical, engineering. Colin is not the only one: some of the greatest designers in history could not get a job today in Formula 1.

In September 1949, Colin received his RAF 'wings' and was offered a full-time career in the service. He declined the offer and resigned. He had spent less than a year in uniform, whereas most of his contemporaries spent two doing National Service. He also came away an experienced pilot. He later wrote, 'I had made up my mind to be a fighter pilot... I was to learn subsequently that the RAF had no real flying opportunities to offer.' Stan Chapman was pleased that Colin was back in Civvy Street and he arranged a job with a building company for his son. This was typical – Stan loved to be able to use his contacts. He was not a secure man, socially, but using what influence he had meant a lot to him.

Before the end of 1949, the new car, named Lotus, had appeared in trials although it was still unfinished. A present of cash at Christmas allowed Colin to complete the job and soon Lotus had an aluminium nose cowl with twin headlights behind the grille. That was another Chapman touch: putting the headlights in the nosecone reduced drag.

In his new job, Colin had to be up at five to be at work by seven and, since he was working late into the night on his car, and still courting Hazel, it soon became too much. He gave up the job with the building company, joined Laystall Engineering for a short time and, in April 1950, joined the British Aluminium Company. His brief was to persuade builders to incorporate aluminium in their structures, particularly in the roofs. One can imagine that Colin was pretty good at that because he had all the right credentials. He was handsome, personable and well turned out – even in casual dress, Colin was smart. Since he was also reading a lot about metallurgy (which, one day, would be useful for his cars) he began to know his subject inside out. Also, and very important at the time, he had a service record. An ex-RAF pilot was a man to be reckoned with and by then he did have a university degree. Colin's business card could open any door. Since Stan had arranged Colin's first job, using his network of contacts, he was not thrilled when his son moved on. Tension clouded their relationship for a time.

During 1950 Chapman drove Lotus in one event or another most weekends. In September 1950 he put it up for sale in *Motor Sport* and, a telling detail, he paid extra to buy a display advertisement complete with photograph, something which few outside of the motor trade did. Two months later he offered his Austin Seven Special for sale, also in a display advertisement complete with photograph. Why the name Lotus for the second car? Chapman was smart enough never to say why it was called Lotus, he kept everyone guessing. He never publicly revealed the reason for the name so it has tantalised people ever since. One theory is that his pet name for Hazel was 'my little lotus blossom', but according to Nigel Allen, his nickname for Hazel was 'Razzle Dazzle' because she lit up his life. Another theory is that Colin had become intrigued by eastern mysticism and that is not as odd as it may seem. Chapman's mind was open to all sorts of ideas and at university he must have encountered all manner of people. Another theory, concentrating on more basic matters, says that Chapman got many of his best ideas while sitting above a porcelain bowl with his trousers round his ankles – he did hold a diploma in Hygiene Sanitation – and a company called Lotus made such fundamental requirements. Lotus also made bath tubs and Chapman liked to soak in a bath thinking up new ideas, so that theory has it adherents. Yet another theory is that it relates to 'Lot U/S' or Lot Unsold, but that would have only related to his first car, which became Lotus Mk 1 only in retrospect. Besides, Colin sold his cars direct, there were no car auctions at the time. Many years later, cynics would say it stood for 'Lots Of Trouble, Usually Serious.' In fact, none of the above is anywhere near the mark. In 1951, after an expensive meal paid for by Derek Jolly, who has yet to appear in the narrative, Colin was sufficiently relaxed to disclose the origin of the name. However, since Colin did not want it to be widely known, his wish should be respected.

In September 1950, Colin and Hazel flew to Jersey for a holiday and returned to England with rain lashing down. This focused Colin's attention on comfort with winter looming. Ian H. Smith's *The Story of Lotus, 1947-60* tells that Colin was thinking through all the possibilities and reckoned that the ideal car would be an Austin Seven with an aluminium body. No sooner had he reached that conclusion than he saw one in superb condition in a pub car park. Leaving Hazel in Lotus he went into the pub, found the owner of the Austin and went into overdrive. Smith says that he even bought his own pint of beer for the first, and only, time in his life. According to the story, Colin discussed Austin Sevens and pointed out all their faults. Before long the poor owner had serious doubts about his car. Colin then spoke of the Korean War and predicted that there would be another suspension of the petrol ration. Then he mentioned the money to be made from breeding budgerigars, he had read a magazine article about it. The long and short of the story is that £45 changed hands and the former owner went looking for the nearest pet shop to buy budgies.

Or so the story goes.

Ian H. Smith suggests that Colin buying a pint was a rare occasion and so it may have been at the time. Bob Hester said, 'Colin could be pretty brash in his younger days but, as he matured, he grew into a thoughtful and generous man. I think he realised it was the right thing to be and I can recall many acts of personal kindness he performed for many people.'

According to Michael Allen, Colin found a pub with a large car park near the offices of British Aluminium and used to park his car there. The landlord of the pub got fed up with seeing it, while never being able to catch the owner. One evening Colin went to collect his car and discovered that the publican had removed the rotor arm from its distributor. He was soon on the phone to Michael, who brought a replacement. After that he used to park on the street. Tony McAffrey recalls that he worked near to British Aluminium's offices and would often arrive to park his car at the same time as Colin. Tony said, 'Colin had a favourite parking place which he regarded as his own. If someone else got there first, and this was a public road, remember, he would be furious. You could always tell by the way he slammed his car door.'

In June 1950, Colin drove Lotus in his first motor race meeting, a clubbie at Silverstone. He won a five-lap scratch race and came third in a handicap. That was a turning point in his life. Colin realised that his future was in racing, not in trials. Besides, he had demonstrated that he was an accomplished racing driver. Trials had become a fairly specialised activity, its innocent days were ending, and circuit racing was going from strength to strength. By 1950 there were circuits springing up all round the country largely because there were so many ex-military airfields everywhere. Airfields were used as an expedient, and some British motor racing purists sneered at them. Racing round a circuit marked out by straw bales was not the same as road racing on the Continent, it was not Monaco or the Mille Miglia. On the other hand, Colin learned about designing cars for circuits which were smooth and open and they were the circuits of the future, as considerations of safety closed many of the traditional road courses.

Lotus was sold to the well-known trials specialist, Mike Lawson, who was very successful with it. In 1957, Lotus featured in the Boulting Brothers' comedy film about the legal profession, *Brothers In Law*. By then, it was a comic feature, a quaint old banger on a par with the cars that circus clowns use, but it had been a formidable machine in its time. It had been the car which had established Colin as a young man to be watched.

CHAPTER 3

BORROWED ROBES

HAVING sold the Austin Special and Lotus, Colin embarked on Lotus Mk 3, which was built for the burgeoning 750cc (Austin) Championship. A 1930 Austin Seven saloon was bought for £15 and work began. No sooner had the project started than Colin met the Allen brothers, Nigel and Michael, who also lived in Muswell Hill. Nigel recalls that he and his brother dabbled with second-hand cars and had an extremely well-equipped workshop. 'Colin would drive by and he noted what equipment we had. At the time he had only the usual tool box plus a small electric drill. He introduced himself and, before long, asked whether we'd be interested in building a racing car. He was a very likeable fellow and we thought, "Why not?" Through him we became members of the 750 Motor Club, which used to hold its meetings at The Red Cow, Hammersmith.'

The brothers were impressed by Colin's charm and ideas, though the suspicion lingers that he had noted their facilities, the size of their family home, the fact that the Allens employed a maid, and had approached them as a con-man plays a 'mark'. Colin persuaded them that they should each build a Lotus Mk 3. The centre of operations soon moved from from Vic Williams's lock-up garage to the Allens' spacious and well-equipped workshop.

The registration number of the new car was LMU 3 and Michael Allen says that Colin reckoned that LMU stood for 'Lotus Motor Unit' and tried to obtain LMU 1 and LMU 2. It's a small point, but the fad for special number plates was then in its infancy.

The rules of the 750 Formula required the use of the major components of the Austin Seven, but there was virtually no limit as to how they could be modified. The chassis could be drilled to lighten it, the beam front axle could be split to create independent suspension and so far as the engine was concerned, just about the only restriction was the use of an original block and crankcase.

Most Austin Seven specials were fairly crude, but the Mk 3 set new standards. It could compete with, and beat, cars of twice the engine size and, in what was then the very small world of British motor racing, it caused a sensation. It established the Lotus legend and Chapman's reputation as a designer and driver.

When writing about the Mk 3, two aspects have caught most people's attention. One is the triangulated tubular bracing, which has been called the 'first Lotus spaceframe', and the other is the engine. Less often remarked on was the soft springing, controlled by very effective hydraulic strut dampers. This was Chapman's one original contribution to the design: the headline elements were the work of other people.

In order to reduce manufacturing costs, Austin used a 'siamesed' inlet system, which is to say that two cylinders shared one branch of the inlet manifold, a system which is inherently inefficient. Austin knew, as did every manufacturer, that one port per cylinder was ideal, but the Austin Seven was built down to a price, not up to a standard. Besides, if the engine became more efficient, the brakes would have to be upgraded, there would have to be better suspension, and so on. Austin sold the Seven to people who were simply proud to own a new car.

According to orthodoxy, it was a stroke of Chapman genius to 'de-siamese' the engine by creating an inlet manifold where each branch was divided into two passages by welding a steel partition down the centre of each branch. That effectively created a a four-branch manifold which meant that the adjacent cylinders in the firing order no longer had to compete. Not only was this a simple ruse, but it worked brilliantly. Indeed, it was so good that, from the end of the season, it was banned from the formula. With one stroke Colin had proved himself so far ahead of anyone else that rules had to be changed to give everyone else a chance. The implication was that Chapman was a man you'd only box if he had one hand tied behind his back.

That is the stuff of legend, but unfortunately it is just that, a legend. The real story is somewhat different.

For a start, the Mk 3 actually had several engines. The method to 'de-siamese' the engine just described was used on one of them. It was also the method which was revealed to the press and and so it is the method which has passed into motoring racing lore. It worked well enough, but that was not how it was done on the main engine that Chapman used during 1951 and that was reserved for future use.

Chapman's 'stroke of genius' was not actually his idea. Colin had struck up a friendship with Derek Jolly, an Australian who was heir to the Penfold wine business, which became very big indeed. Derek was so wealthy that he rebuilt part of Adelaide to suit himself. He wanted a restaurant where he could entertain friends, so he built one, The Magic Flute, on Melbourne Street. He wanted a theatre, so he built one, the Sheridan, on the same street. Melbourne Street was run-down, so Derek bought 44 ramshackle houses and rebuilt the street, which is now one of the swankiest in Australia. Derek was seriously rich. *The Sunday Mail* (Adelaide) ran a piece on him in December 2001, which claimed that he was 'a man so rich he bought items three at at time.'

Unfortunately, time was not kind to Derek, who lost heavily in the world economic downturn of the later 1980s, so the profile was in a series called 'Where Are They Now?' Derek died, in reduced circumstances, in 2002.

However, back in the early 1950s Derek had let slip to Colin that he had done something special with his engine. Colin was on the case at once. Derek had been running an Austin Special in Australia and had written to the 750 Motor Club with a view to bringing his car over when he visited Europe. His senior manager had told him to go to Europe because, as he said, 'Let's face it, our wines are crap.' As a member of the club's committee, Colin was given the job of replying and their friendship grew from there.

Derek was perhaps the first cosmopolitan person Chapman had ever met. Certainly, Derek was the first person to be able to take Colin and Hazel to expensive West End restaurants, which left them wide-eyed. A friend of Jolly's, Mike Bennett, believes that Chapman saw Jolly not only as a fellow racing enthusiast, and a fascinating man in his own right, but also as someone who might be tapped for money.

There is no doubt, however, that there was genuine friendship between Derek and Colin. Colin would write Derek long letters when Derek was in Australia and, when Derek was in England, he frequently wrote to his mother. Here is an extract from one such letter, written on 20 February 1951:

> After dinner, I rang Colin up (he is the one who has been writing 10 page letters to me in Adelaide) and he and his two friends (Michael and Nigel Allen) turned up in a Chummy Austin 7, and whizzed me off to East Finchley.
>
> He is building 3 identical Austins which are very advanced in design – he is the nicest & kindest most helpful person one could wish to meet. He seems to know everyone, and about everything worth knowing.
>
> He used to work for Laystall's (and therefore got everything at price) – he now works for the British Aluminium Co. (and therefore gets all his alloys and sheeting for free).
>
> He says he is building the 3rd Austin for me [that would have come as news to Michael Allen, whose car it would have been, had Colin told him, which he never did] which will be ready in time for the Austin 7 engine I brought with me on the Otranto.
>
> We went inside the house, and guess what was there – a TELEVISION set – I was fascinated and they couldn't tear me away for two hours! He showed me films in colour of his racing career, and he loved my photos, and after an enormous supper, we all drove back to St. John's Wood.
>
> What a start to my trip!

It was Derek Jolly who first 'de-siamesed' an Austin engine, which he did at the suggestion of an Australian special builder, Ron Uffindel. Derek said, 'Once I'd de-siamesed the ports, the top speed of my car went up from 70mph to 90mph. If I had been setting a time of 40 seconds for a hill climb, suddenly my time was 32 seconds.' Derek shipped his engine to England with the intention of installing it in one of the Mk 3s then under construction. The deal was that Derek would work on the cars when his business commitments permitted. It appears that this was not often, and Chapman took charge of the engine until Derek arrived. Although Colin had promised not to do so, he opened the crate, removed the engine, and set about learning all its secrets.

Despite this betrayal of trust, Colin's charm was such that Derek remained his friend. Derek said of him:

Colin and I were great mates, we both had the ability to visualise. As soon as Colin saw what was taking shape, immediately a new idea arrived which led him off in a new direction.

He had such driving ambition, his mind was racing ahead, he was dismissive of people he felt were not going to contribute to the the the cause.

Colin associated with the Allen brothers as they were useful to him, they had the premises and the tools, their mother providing copious amounts of tea and cake.

He and I would both go to the ends of the earth to get something done, neither of us would tolerate people who were less than adequate.

Derek later won the Australian Sports Car Championship in a Lotus; he shared a works Lotus with Graham Hill at Le Mans in 1959 – Derek put up the car, of course – and he was appointed the first Lotus importer for Australia. Derek Jolly certainly played his part in Colin's story. Like so many other people, Derek was under the Chapman spell. People tended to see Colin as a 'loveable rogue' and many didn't mind even when they knew that he was ripping them off. The fact is that without these two sides of him, Colin might have spent his life selling British Aluminium's fine products, climbing the company ladder, and dabbling in club racing at weekends. As it was, Derek recalled that Colin would visit a scrapyard by day, identify something he wanted and then they would make a raid at night. Derek could have bought the entire scrapyard, but that wasn't as much fun.

The Lotus engine, so often hailed as an example of Chapman's genius, used Jolly's principles. It was not a straight copy because Nigel and Michael Allen were too sophisticated for that. Nigel was studying to be a dentist at the time but went on to patent precision cutting instruments using air bearings. One application was a turbine drill for dentists where the drive shaft (which carries the cutting head) was supported by air within its casing. Millions of people have reason to be grateful. Other applications of the principle have included the gyroscopes in nuclear submarines and the cutting of computer chips – we speak here of a remarkable engineer. Nigel says:

I didn't feel that I needed to go into college every single day and Colin was exciting to be with. He had his day job and Stan insisted that he stuck to it. Sometimes, we did not see him all week, but he kept in touch by phone.

Colin had read Ricardo's book on gas-flow and he had absorbed it. The lessons learned from Ricardo were his chief contribution, and he had learned them properly. He also knew Austin Seven engines inside out – Austin had developed the unit over many years and Colin knew the best combination of components.

I did most of the work on the chassis, Michael did most of the work on the engine. I remember that once Colin decided that we needed a bracket to hold the steering box and I asked him for a drawing. He had not got one so I devised a model from cardboard, which I could trim, and we proceeded like that. I even went on a welding course run by the British Oxygen Company.

We were so bound up with everything, it took us some time to realise that we were doing all the actual building and he would sit on his backside all evening, on a crate known as the 'meditation box', making sketches.

Once it was the evening when the meeting of the 750 Motor Club was taking place at The Red Cow. Michael and I suggested that we should all drop work and go. Colin was against that, but he said he had to attend because he was on the committee. He'd love to be working with us into the night, he said, but we should carry on while he did his duty. It sounded reasonable at the time.

Eventually Michael and I decided to pack it in for the night and go to the meeting ourselves. We arrived to find Colin at the bar telling people how he had done this and that, but it was nonsense, he'd done none of it.

Michael Allen concurs: 'When Colin addressed a meeting of the 750 Motor Club, it was always "I did this and that", never "We did this and that."' Nigel continues: According to Colin, it was Hazel who had bound the steering wheel of the Mk 3 with leather to get a better grip. The steering wheel was in fact cut, using an abrafile, from high tensile aluminium by my fiancée, now my wife, Pauline. She then padded it and bound it with leather. Colin took credit for everything.

We were not only working late into the night, we were providing the workshop, the tools, the gas for the welding and, on top of that, we were annoying the neighbours. Several refused to pay their council rates because of the noise we were making, so we had that to contend with on top of everything else.

Eventually I commented to someone that wasn't it about time Stan Chapman made a contribution? My remark got back to Colin and he was absolutely furious. It is noticeable, however, that not long afterwards Stan made available the stable block adjacent to the Railway Hotel.

The stable block had been used by Stan to store beer crates and barrels.

In the four-part series which was run in *Motor Racing* from November 1954 to February 1955, neither of the Allen brothers was mentioned in connection with design or build. Instead, Colin wrote, 'I built the Mark III during the winter of 1950-1... ' He also wrote, 'It wasn't until I was enjoying a Christmas party in 1950 that the solution to the problem suddenly struck me. I seem to get my best ideas after Christmas parties, probably because I have time to sit back and think. Anyway, the idea was to de-siamese the inlet ports.'

Is this a case of Colin spinning a tale to assist in the creation of a myth, or should it be called a bare-faced lie? Colin was a consummate liar (did he really, aged seven, make a soap-box cart with independent front suspension? If so, how? How could it be done using an old pram?) He was also a myth-maker and was loathe to let others take any credit.

The engine which the Allen brothers built did not have a dividing strip welded through the middle of a twin-branch manifold. It had a four-branch manifold, though nobody knew it. In order to disguise the fact that there were four pipes leading to the engine, they were made to appear as two. A proprietary brand of metal filler, Loy, was used to fill the gaps and then the pipes were bound with asbestos tape to disguise the ploy. Hey presto! Four inlet pipes took on the appearance of two and nobody was the wiser.

Though the idea had been to build three cars, it was soon clear that only one would be ready for the start of the season. It was decided to concentrate on that one, while building the other two. Colin would concentrate on the 750 Championship and Nigel and Michael would also get races until their cars were ready. The problem was that Colin was always coming up with new modifications for his car and, to keep car number one going, parts were lifted from the other two. Though the Allen brothers did compete in 1951 (as did Hazel, Stan Chapman, Derek Jolly and Derek's girlfriend) they never took delivery of their cars.

Many races at club level had tiny entries, and quite a few were run as handicaps. Organisers were grateful for any entry, so Lotus Mk 3 once raced five times, with five different drivers, at the same meeting. It was the star of the meeting because it not only performed extremely well, but it also actually lasted five races. The record, of six entries for the one car, was set in a sprint at Ternhill, where Colin had trained as an RAF pilot. On that occasion LMU 3 was driven by Colin and Hazel, the Allen brothers, Derek Jolly and Derek's girlfriend.

LMU 3 was the quickest 750cc car of the time, due to the meticulous engine preparation by Michael Allen, but it was not reliable at first. Many modifications were made to it: the engine mounting bushes were changed, the original two-bearing crankshaft was replaced by a three-bearing crankshaft and a forced lubrication system was created. It was Nigel Allen, however, who identified a major problem. The Austin chassis flexed and that strained the crankcase. One night Nigel sketched a triangulated frame which was bolted over the top of the engine. That cured chassis flexing and not only relieved the strain on the engine block, but greatly improved the car's handling. Nigel had made the 'first Lotus spaceframe' that Saturday night and Colin had nothing to do with the idea, although hagiographers often cite it as early evidence of his genius. Colin, however, immediately realised the potential of a light, triangulated, tubular structure. He may not have thought of it, but he was not slow on the uptake.

Spaceframes had long been used in aircraft, but at the time Nigel created his structure it was almost unknown in the automotive world. There had been multi-tubular chassis but no properly triangulated frames. Jaguar had one on the C-type but, when Nigel created his structure, the C-type had not been announced. The Mk 3 would lead directly to the spaceframed Mk 6, and the design of that was a team effort.

Once Nigel's frame had cured the engine problems, and also improved the handling, the Lotus simply flew, but the 750 Championship was actually won by a chap named Lionel West who piled up points all season. The Lotus Mk 3 did not win the 1951 750 Championship. Colin subsequently claimed that the Mk 3 won eight of the ten 750 Championship races that year, but if this was correct, how did Lionel West manage to take the title?

The idea behind the special engine(s) had been lifted from Derek Jolly, Nigel Allen had built the tubular structure, and Colin was happy to steal their limelight. On the other hand, he did make positive contributions. One was an insistance on lightness, something which would become a Lotus trademark. Components were weighed and as much weight as possible was removed. The Mk 3 had a tight 'slipper' body with the mandatory headlights incorporated in the car's nose cone in order to reduce drag. Although it was Nigel Allen who had hit on the tubular structure, it was Colin who had gone for soft springing with relatively long travel.

Even at that early stage in his career, Colin could not bear to be beaten. Bill Morris, well-known in historic racing, says:

> I remember one race at Snetterton when Arthur Mallock [later the maker of the successful Mallock U2 Clubman's cars] beat Colin into second place. Colin immediately protested about Arthur on the grounds that he was not carrying a spare wheel as the rules demanded. Arthur showed the scrutineer the spare wheel he was carrying, and it was just that, a wheel, with no tyre. Colin wasn't the only person to read the rules.

Colin was also not slow to latch on to the power of the press. At the time, the specialist motor racing press in Britain consisted of *Motor Sport* (monthly) and *Autosport* (weekly) while *The Motor* and *The Autocar* devoted a couple of pages to the sport each week. That meant that Colin had to charm no more than seven or eight writers, all of whom were grateful for stories to fill their pages. Friendly, available and quotable, Colin was a dream for the handful of motor sport journalists of the early 1950s. He was a university graduate, he had won his RAF 'wings', he had won motor races, he had built cars which had won races and he had pulled off a number of groundbreaking strokes in engineering, or so he said. A hack would have had to have been insensible not to have realised that here, in the phrase of the time, was a 'coming man'.

Before long, other people began to ask the Lotus team to make bits and pieces for them, and there were even enquiries for cars. Then, in November 1951, a firm order came from Mike Lawson, who had bought Lotus. Trials had become more and more competitive and Lawson needed a more specialised car. This would be called Lotus Mk 4.

At the end of the year, Nigel Allen decided to focus on his dentistry, though he would continue to race Lotus cars and help out for three or four years more. Nigel had become tired of being taken for granted. He would help, because it was fun to help, but he decided to ration his fun.

Michael Allen and Colin decided to go into partnership and they formed the Lotus Engineering Company. The deal was that Michael would work full-time and Colin would help in the evenings and at weekends. The partnership began formally on 1 January 1952 and Michael recalls that part of the deal was a verbal agreement that Colin would give up his job with British Aluminium as soon as the workshop was up and running. It was an agreement which was conveniently forgotten.

CHAPTER 4

A CHANGE OF GEAR

T HE YEAR 1952 is a significant one in the history of British motoring and motor sport. A Conservative government had been returned late in 1951 and, before long, it had lifted many of the restrictions which had rationed the supply of new cars on the home market. The floodgates were opened and two significant things happened. The first was that the sales of most small British companies (Allard, Dellow, HRG, Lea-Francis, and so on) took a nose-dive as the seller's market became a buyer's market. The second was that British motor sport became more specialised. The days when one car could be used for races, rallies, trials and hillclimbs, and stand a chance of success in all, evaporated very quickly. Competitors had used one car from necessity, now they were beginning to have choice. A third, unrelated factor, was that by 1952 Britain had three permanent circuits, at Brands Hatch, Silverstone and Goodwood. These were backed up by a host of temporary airfield circuits. If you bought a car for racing alone, you could now plan a full season.

So 1952 was a landmark year. The world championship was run to the 2-litre Formula 2 and that meant that outfits such as Cooper and Connaught were competing in Grands Prix. The small motor racing community in Britain stepped up a gear and Lotus stepped up a gear with it.

There were other elements at work. King George VI died and was succeeded by his daughter, the pretty and vivacious Elizabeth. The effect that Queen Elizabeth II had on Britain, then emerging from bleak days of shortages and rationing, is easily forgotten, but it cannot be understated. When a pretty young woman came to the throne, with a dashing and handsome consort, it made an impact impossible to imagine unless you lived through that time. The phrase 'New Elizabethan' became current, harking back to a Golden Age. There was a sense that times were changing, and a general feeling that Britain was emerging into the sunlight and the new

Queen symbolised that. There were better days ahead, an ideal environment for men like Colin, men who were going to play a part in a national transformation. Lotus could not have been founded at a more auspicious moment in post-war Britain.

Furthermore, the 750 Motor Club had announced that, from 1953, it would organise a racing series for cars using the 1172cc Ford range of engines. That announcement created a new market and Lotus had reached a point in its development where it was ideally poised to exploit the possibilities of the new market. Of course, as a member of the committee of the 750 Motor Club, Colin had played a role in forming the category. One is not suggesting that Colin had manipulated the club. The 1172 formula was a logical progression, and was a brilliant success, but Colin was in on the ground floor.

On the back of the many successes of the Mk 3, advertisements appeared in the specialist press which boasted that the Lotus Engineering Company could offer a full range of components and services for the special builder. In fact, almost all the services had to be subcontracted because Lotus did not have the machinery to do things like grind crankshafts, and Michael Allen did need to sleep at some time. The advertisements, however, suggested that Lotus was a well-founded and bustling company.

Other companies, like LMB and Buckler, offered items such as split front axle conversions, but they were not fronted by Colin Chapman. Colin was the crucial factor. Colin was the well set up young man who spoke at meetings of the 750 Motor Club. Nigel Allen says:

My brother, Michael, was actually carrying Lotus. Colin was simply not up to it.

I have no regrets about my time with Lotus. Colin was likeable and, through him, I was able to race all over the place, including on classic circuits such as the Nürburgring. It was fun.

I made my final split from Lotus in 1955 when I qualified as a dentist and married. At least I thought I had made my final split. In 1955, I set up my dental practice in Cheshunt, close to the country's largest secondary school. A few years later, Lotus moved to Cheshunt and I found myself looking after the teeth of a lot of Lotus personnel and also Colin and Hazel's children.

Colin has been credited for many things which were actually the work of other men, but it was his personality that attracted those men to the stable block. Even when he used them shamelessly, they tend to remember him with affection. Nigel and Michael Allen, for example, may have been responsible for much which made the Mk 3 so successful, but it was Colin who drew them to motor racing.

The new company's first product was a trials car (Mk 4) for Mike Lawson. The Mk 5 was to have been a radical Austin-engined car using Colin's 'de-siamised' Mk 3 engine in a new, low-slung chassis. It was never built but, many years later, the major components of the engine were acquired by Colin's son, Clive. Clive runs

Classic Team Lotus (CTL) from the small factory in Norfolk from which cars that won world championships emerged. CTL supplies spare parts to owners of Lotus racing cars and enters some in historic racing on behalf of patrons who pay to use cars from what was Colin's private collection.

Adam Currie put in a bid for one of the two incomplete Mk 3 chassis which, eventually, would be fitted with a Ford engine and become the Lotus Mk 3B. Currie won races with the car and then moved to Kenya as Dunlop's manager in East Africa. The third Mk 3 chassis was eventually sold, in 1955, to a Mr Weston, who paid £5 for it.

Over the winter of 1951/52, a friend of John Teychenne, Clive Clairmonte, decided that he wanted a single-seat Formula Two car from this exciting new outfit which had won races and whose advertising was so plausible. The Clairmonte car was designated the Lotus Mk 7, Clive handed over £250, and work began. Though the Mk 7 was to some extent a distraction, as Colin was raring to finish the Mk 6, it did give him an opportunity to explore new ideas.

The Mk 7 was intended to have a Riley or ERA engine, depending which account you believe, and Chapman's design was bold. The chassis was a simple, but rigid, spaceframe, front suspension was by coil springs and double wishbones while a de Dion axle was used at the rear. The rear brakes were mounted inboard, to reduce unsprung weight, and the front springs were inboard at the end of rocker arms. That was a system previously seen only on a Maserati and would not be seen again at a serious level for many years, when it would be revived by Lotus.

The Mk 7 showed an original mind at work. A lot of its features were very advanced for the day, and the de Dion rear axle would appear on other Lotus cars before long. The trouble was that the little company was stretched to its limit as it was also preparing the Mk 6, so progress was very slow. Eventually, Clive Clairmonte took away what had been made and the car was completed by his mechanic, who added side extensions to the chassis and turned it into a sports car with a Lea-Francis engine. As the Clairmonte, it first raced in June 1953, enjoyed a long career in British club racing, and exists to this day. Because the car had never been publicly known as the Mk 7, the designation was deemed available when naming the spiritual successor to the Mk 6. As it happens, 'Seven' is a number resonant from myth and legend and 'Lotus Seven' has a pleasing rhythm.

Adam Currie may have bought the second Mk 3 chassis, but it was always going to be finished next week, or the week after, because all the attention was being given to the top priority, the Mk 6. Lodging with the parents of Adam Currie was an old family friend, Peter Ross. Peter was completing an engineering apprenticeship at de Havilland, then one of the greatest of the world's aircraft companies, which was based in Hatfield, and Muswell Hill was a short drive down the A1, the Great North Road, from Hatfield.

Peter had first met Colin in 1948 when riding as the bouncing ballast for a mutual friend, Derek Wootton, and had met him again at the 750 Motor Club's meetings at The Red Cow. One evening, Peter turned up at the stable block, got stuck in, and helped Adam Currie to complete the rolling chassis. Not only did Peter, a very capable engineer, get drawn in, but it was he who spread the word at de Havilland and that was the connection which would assure the success of Lotus. Among those from de Havilland who were drawn to Lotus was Gilbert 'Mac' McIntosh, who says, 'The aviation business was changing as the accountants moved in. It was not the industry we joined. If you want to know what that meant, look at BMW and Rover. BMW is a company run by engineers, Rover was run by accountants.'

The turning point in the Chapman, and the Lotus, story was the Mk 6, which was a basic two-seat road/race car, and a logical development of the Mk 3. It was wider than the Mk 3 both because it was designed around Ford axles and because it needed to be wider to give it a roomier cockpit – the Mk 3 was too narrow to be a practical road car. Central to the Mk 6 was a very light, rigid, and properly triangulated spaceframe, and it was finished with a tight 'slipper' body. The frame of the Mk 6 demonstrated Colin's relative inexperience because the bottom tubes were unnecessarily large, as though they were replicating a conventional chassis with the other tubes forming a substructure above. Colin had yet to learn how to stress a frame to its optimum. To most eyes, however, the Mk 6 was a very advanced design.

Though most examples of the Lotus Mk 6 were destined for the 750 Motor Club's new Ford 1172cc series, Colin was more ambitious and decided that the 1508cc engine from the Ford Consul showed promise, provided it could be reduced to under 1500cc. Colin had his eyes set above club racing: he was interested in national racing. Michael Allen said, 'Colin approached the Ford Motor Company with a request to back him. Ford turned him down on the grounds that motor racing was a risky business and they did not want their new engine to be associated with failure.' Not even John Teychenne's father could get his hands on a Consul engine.

Colin's response was to go around Ford dealerships, buying components, until he had assembled all the parts needed to build a complete engine. He then had the engine brought under the 1500cc ceiling by grinding metal from the big end journals eccentrically and fitting smaller bearings, so shortening the stroke. Subcontract work was undertaken by an engine reconditioning shop, Johnson Roberts, which was run by Murray Hall Buckler, the brother of Derek Buckler. Michael Allen actually built the Consul engine, while it was Mr Allen Sr who picked up the bills. Nigel Allen reckons that his father contributed at least £1,200 to the Lotus Engineering Company during 1952, which included the cost of assembling the Ford Consul engine, and to put that into perspective, at the time that money could buy a semi-detached house in most parts of Britain.

The prototype Mk 6 showed immense promise in the few races in which it appeared in 1952 and there were soon enquiries for replicas – Lotus did not stint on the claims it made in its advertisements. Nigel Allen did most of the driving, but Colin had the odd outing in it. Given that Colin was a very gifted racing driver, in a different class to anyone else connected to Lotus, he showed remarkable restraint. If he did not always appear to pull his weight in the workshop in the early days, he was determined that Lotus would be a success and if that meant taking a back seat as a driver, that was the price he paid. Peter Ross says:

> I think that Colin worked as hard as Nigel and Michael did, but it appeared otherwise because he was not always in the workshop. When you're building a car, a great deal of time and effort goes into chasing components and the time spent doing that is not always apparent.
>
> On the other hand, Colin never did give the Allen brothers the credit they deserved. I don't think that he realised what a goldmine of talent they were and had he treated them better I think they would have stuck with him.

The Mk 6 was clearly a cut above most sports cars of its time, but then came calamity when the prototype was written off in a road accident. Nigel Allen was driving the car when a bread van, coming in the opposite direction, took a right turn across Nigel's bows. The car was wrecked, but Nigel was unharmed, which speaks volumes for the strength of its structure. The prototype had been comprehensively insured, however, and the driver of the bread van admitted he had been at fault. Even so, it took time for the insurance company to pay and that meant a very precarious few weeks for Lotus which, after all, had little work apart from making parts for special builders, and that work was largely subcontracted.

Michael Allen, who was an equal partner, had become disgruntled with the way that he felt he'd been used. He had done most of the work and Colin claimed all of the credit. Eventually it became too much for him and he left Lotus. When the insurance money came through, Michael was paid for his share of the business. It has been written that Michael's share of Lotus's assets amounted to the wreck of the prototype, but when Nigel Allen bought his first production Mk 6 he transferred the registration of the prototype, which was a write-off though the remains were sold on, to his new car. Many years later, when the prototype of the first production Lotus became an historically important car, and was therefore valuable, two examples of the one prototype appeared.

After Michael Allen left, and with a loan from Hazel of £25, Colin established Lotus as a limited company with Hazel and himself as the directors, but Michael Allen was the only shareholder, apart from Colin, for the first year, right up to the time that the first share dividend was paid. Michael Allen then severed his ties with Lotus. The letterhead of the new company's stationery included the lines, 'Automobile and component manufacturers. Racing and competition car design and development.' Every claim was just about true, even if none was backed by much capital. There is no point, however, in selling oneself short, and Colin never did.

During 1952, several people had approached Chapman to build them a car and in the December 1952 issue of *Motor Sport* an advertisement appeared that offered 'The Lotus Chassis Frame' (the Mk 6, by any other name) for just £110. That was enough to grab anyone's attention, though of course you would also need odd items such as a body, engine, wheels, seats and so on. Lotus, however, could supply most of the components, even if that meant buying in and using subcontractors, though the engine and transmission were the responsibility of the customer.

The advertisement was designed by Patrick Stephens, who was then working in Stonchams, a shop specialising in books and magazines on cars and motor racing. Colin had called in one day and the inevitable happened. Patrick had built his own Austin Special (and wrote a newsletter on its progress) and knew Colin from the meetings at The Red Cow. Naturally, he just had to be involved. The same Patrick Stephens later became a distinguished publisher.

Colin did not have to place 'Situation Vacant' ads to find the right people for his projects, they dropped into his lap. The Allen brothers lived close to him. John Teychenne was an old friend and he would not only do work for Lotus, but would make important introductions.

Colin had first met Peter Ross when Peter was bouncing for Derek Wootton and, by 1953, Derek was working for Tony Vandervell's racing team and urging his boss to call on Colin as a designer. Peter Ross, in turn, made other crucial introductions and they also passed on the news. People arrived at Hornsey like homing pigeons, as though guided by some genetic instinct. North London seemed to be teeming with motor racing enthusiasts, many of them very gifted, who were looking for an outlet. Colin and Lotus supplied that outlet.

When Napoleon interviewed generals, he did not ask 'Are you successful', he asked, 'Are you lucky?' Colin was lucky and it is better to have be born lucky than to have been born rich.

CHAPTER 5

MOTOR MANUFACTURER

T HE LOTUS Mk 6 was essentially a kit car, though the term, 'kit car' had yet to be coined. In fact, many Lotus cars sold in Britain until 1973 were sold as kits for the simple reason that a self-assembled car escaped purchase tax which, at one point, reached 60 percent. The year 1973 is key, because that was when Value Added Tax (VAT) was introduced, with the result that many kit car makers went to the wall, while Lotus responded by moving up-market. In the early 1950s, so far as the Mk 6 was concerned, there was not only relief from purchase tax, there could be a considerable saving in labour costs, and besides, Lotus could not supply the running gear.

In later years, Lotus cars would arrive at your house on a trailer, having been almost completely assembled at the factory. The advertisements claimed that two people with a basic tool kit could assemble an Elan, say, over a weekend; though if you bought one, and didn't know a spanner from a mallet, Lotus could always direct you to someone who did.

Many a Lotus employee benefited from a tax-free wad of banknotes. That happened from the earliest days and Nigel Allen recalls assembling two Mk 6 kits for customers who, it may be safely assumed, told the Customs and Excise people that they'd built them themselves. There is also the matter of cars which went through the back door. Anecdotes abound of Lotus cars which never went through the company books and many of the stories are likely to be true. Lotus was not the only company doing that: in the pre-1973 days of purchase tax, it was a practice not entirely unknown in the specialist car community.

Since the Mk 6 could be bought with body panels, and just about all were bought as a chassis/body unit, it has a claim to being the world's first complete kit car. An exception was the Mk 6 bought by Peter Kirwan-Taylor, a merchant banker, who had an enveloping body, but he was a rarity. Derek Buckler had pioneered the kit car, but Buckler did not supply bodies. Not only did the Mk 6 have an aluminium body, made by Williams & Pritchard, but the quality of finish was so high that many owners did not bother to paint it.

It was John Teychenne who recommended Williams & Pritchard, who were then based in nearby Enfield. They had built the body for a trials car, the JVT Special, which John had made, and he was so pleased with the result that he made the introduction to Colin. Charlie Williams and Len Pritchard were artists in metal. It is no exaggeration to say that they worked to Rolls-Royce standards (they had both worked for subcontractors supplying leading coachbuilders before the war) or that they worked to aircraft standards, since they had both spent the war making parts for Spitfires. Len Pritchard recalls:

> Colin brought us a bare frame, told us roughly what he wanted, and left us to get on with it. We took a great deal of care over it, not only in the way it was put together but the way it looked, because we virtually styled it. We also had to work out things like brackets on the chassis.
>
> From the beginning, Charlie and I decided that we would only do our best work. A lot of competition cars at the time looked awful, with the body added as an after-thought. We felt that the body was important. It was an integral part of the car, its looks established the car, and we weren't prepared just to 'skin' a frame, a term of the time which I detested.

Chapman was delighted with what he saw and, three months later, another frame appeared at the Williams & Pritchard workshop, and then another, and another. All the frames were made by John Teychenne's new Progress Chassis Company. John had been working for Arnott Superchargers, another North London firm. Arnott specialised in superchargers (naturally) and tuning kits and had also diversified into making a batch of 500cc racing cars, which were not very successful. In truth, Arnott's greatest distinction was that the team principal was a young woman. 'Daphne Arnott – Girl Builds Car!' was the gist of the headlines, and when she built a sports car, also unsuccessful, it made the national press.

In his spare time, John worked for Lotus, helping to make the first examples of the Mk 6. Then, when it seemed that there could be steady work, he and a colleague, Dave Kelsey, left Arnott to set up Progress in a small workshop not far from the Hornsey stable block. Lotus was Progress's chief customer, but Progress was open to other work and the same went for Williams & Pritchard. Before long, orders for the Mk 6 meant that Williams & Pritchard was bulging at the seams and Colin found them space in the stable block.

Under the umbrella of Lotus, therefore, were the world's finest maker of aluminium bodies, Williams & Pritchard, and Progress, then the finest independent maker of chassis frames. John Teychenne and Dave Kelsey soon recruited others, like Frank Coltman, who was a genius with a welding torch. John Teychenne and Colin Chapman went back a long way and John knew that Colin could charm the birds from the trees. Thus, if John arrived at Hornsey with a Mk 6 spaceframe, and there was not cash to hand – £30 per frame, painted – he took the frame away until the cash was on the table. Friendship was fine, but the rent had to be paid.

Len Pritchard says:

> We spent a lot of time chasing up invoices, but that was usual at the time. The one person who did pay promptly was Brian Lister, but then Brian is a gentleman, unlike many people in motor racing.
>
> With all the work we were getting from Lotus, we needed to expand and Colin offered to lease us a section of the stable block. For a few years we occupied about three-quarters of the stables and Colin had the rest. Ours was purely a business arrangement, we did not get close to Colin on a personal or social level.

The contribution that Williams & Pritchard made to the Lotus story cannot be underestimated. When one unpainted car (not a Lotus) with a Williams & Pritchard body went to race in Italy, the Italians could not believe the standard of its finish. They were used to hammering metal and then applying filler, lots of filler, and none of their work could stand being unpainted. The Italians made some lovely shapes, but their craftsmanship was actually of a fairly crude level. Charlie and Len did everything with no more than a guillotine, a welding torch and a wheel on which to roll the panels. The templates for the bodywork were cut from cardboard boxes and hung on meat hooks. The tools were primitive, but the product was superb.

In addition to Williams & Pritchard, and Progress, there were many volunteer helpers. Motor racing enthusiasts read about Lotus and wanted to be involved. There was not much to do of an evening in 1952, except to go to a pub, and for some people, Colin was a role model. He was doing something, he was going somewhere, and lots of people wanted to be touched by the twinkle dust. Len Pritchard recalls: 'They [the volunteers] arrived from nowhere, maybe six or a dozen every night. Lotus had that effect on people, there was always a buzz of excitement – and the odd flare-up – but Lotus attracted fans.'

Bob Hester, Colin's friend from school, was among the volunteers. Bob says:

> Everything was basic, but that's how things were then. There was a sink where you could wash your hands, but I never saw a first aid kit. There wasn't much in the way of heating, either, and in the winter it could be bitterly cold, but we just got on with things, we had different expectations then. Today, the place would have been closed under Health and Safety regulations.
>
> None of us had much money and down the street you'd see all these pre-war Austin Sevens. They were all we could afford to run.
>
> Colin could lose his temper, he could really explode, but he was always perfectly civil to me. I was, after all, working for nothing, so I could come

and go as I pleased. The reward for people like me came when Lotus ran works cars and the engines had to be run in. We'd take it in turns to run them round the North Circular Road.

That was surely more fun for a motor racing enthusiast than any of the options at the time. You could listen to the wireless, go to a pub or cinema, or you could pursue a hobby – courting a girl was different in those days. Spending an evening at Lotus, where you met like-minded blokes, was an exciting alternative because, even if you were only filing a piece of metal, you were at least doing something in tune with the changing times.

The Lotus Mk 6 was an instant success, both commercially and in competition, and approximately 100 would be sold before production ceased in 1956. Forty or fifty cars a year sounds not a lot today, but Ferrari got nowhere near that figure in its early days. In fact, the vast majority of kit car makers have folded before reaching much beyond double figures as a total production run. It was not long into 1953 that customer examples of the Lotus Mk 6 were racing, which suggests that owners had little difficulty in assembling their kits. The same cannot be said of many subsequent kit cars, which too often have been sold as a dream rather than practical reality. Between them, the Lotus extended family got everything right at their first attempt – and they were breaking new ground.

Customers included a number of drivers who would carve distinguished careers, plus Frank Nichols. Nichols raced a Mk 6 in 1954 but, before the end of the year, had replaced it with the CSM, built for him by Mike Chapman (no relation). The CSM bore an uncanny resemblance to Frank's Lotus Mk 6 and Colin was not best pleased when Nichols put the CSM into production as the 'Elva'. Heated words were exchanged, and Colin threatened legal action. Frank knew that Colin could not afford to take the case to court and besides, he could always point to the fact that he was offering replicas of the CSM and that, in particular, the Elva's bodywork was different. Nichols went on to carve out a niche for himself as a manufacturer and Elva sometimes rivalled Lotus in some classes.

Michael Allen's departure, and Nigel Allen's increasing distance from Lotus, left a gap in the organisation. That gap was filled by Mike Costin. Mike had been doing National Service in the RAF until November 1952 and then had resumed work at de Havilland. Peter Ross says:

> By then I knew that Colin was going to lose Michael Allen and needed help. I told Mike all about Lotus and introduced him to Colin. Mike was impressed by Colin and by the air of excitement at Hornsey. On the basis of that meeting and what I had already told him, Mike began working for Lotus on 1 January 1953. It was on a part-time basis which meant every waking moment he was not working for de Havilland.

Lotus was swept along by the heady, optimistic atmosphere of Coronation Year, but also had its own impetus and a rapidly growing reputation. The Mk 6 was not only appearing on the circuits in ever increasing numbers, but was winning races.

Colin's own career as a racing driver was put on hold while Lotus dealt with the orders which were flooding in. 'Flooding' is a relative term, but when you are working from a stable block, it does not require many orders to create a tidal wave. Orders even began to arrive from abroad.

Everything had to be rearranged in order get the cars out of the door. Len Pritchard says, 'We were working seven days a week. I can't speak for Charlie (Williams) but I think my wife came close to the point of saying "goodbye" to me, and she might have done if she could have remembered what I looked like.'

It was not until the end of July 1953 that Colin had a Mk 6 of his own, fitted with a Ford Ten engine, reduced in size to 1098cc so it could run both in the 1172 Formula and also in the 1100cc class. Colin did more than simply reduce the engine's capacity, he added original features of his own, among them special cam followers. With his new car he won a five-lap scratch race at Goodwood, beating Philip Desoutter's Mk 6 by three seconds. Then, at Silverstone, Desoutter won.

Colin's deal with Mike Costin was that Mike would drive in all the 1172 Formula races and the first was at Silverstone. It was Mike's first race and Colin told him, 'Get behind Phil Desoutter and he will teach you all about cornering. Do NOT overtake him.' Mike could have won, he was a very good driver, but he did as he was told and followed Desoutter. In the press, which means the report in *Autosport*, the result generated good publicity because it seemed to show that a customer could beat the works car. Even though only the 10,000 or so people who took *Autosport* each week could read about these Lotus 1-2 finishes, that included everyone in the tiny motor racing community.

It was actually not that difficult to raise excitement at the time. The *Autosport* report of the Goodwood meeting did not mention that the two Lotus Mk 6 entries were up against pre-war Fiats and Rileys and a couple of Morris Minors. Only when you go through the entry lists of the time do you realise just how thin British motor racing was. In 1953, it was not difficult to create a stir in British racing, although most who tried still failed.

There were dozens of workshops turning out racing cars at the time. Many people will be amazed by the number of makes of 500cc Formula 3 cars, for example, because not many are remembered. In the main, these cars were built by over-ambitious mechanics, and most were failures. By contrast, the people attracted to Lotus were engineers, as Colin was an engineer, and many had the aircraft industry as their background. Some engineers want more from life than a secure job as a member of a team charged with designing an airliner's cockpit. Colin gave such people an opportunity to step out from the crowd and create something which bore their own signatures. It is not coincidental that so many racing car designers of the 1950s and 1960s came from aviation. These days, they arrive at a racing car maker straight from university and, perhaps, become a member of the team designing the cockpit of a Formula 1 car.

Eric Broadley, founder of Lola Cars and a non-graduate, once told the author that if the young Broadley knocked on his door looking for a job he wouldn't be taken on. 'I couldn't take the risk,' he said. If Colin Chapman, in his early twenties, were alive today, Lotus could not have happened. Nobody today can progress from a special to world championships, because the way is blocked. To enter Formula 1, you first have to buy one of the 12 franchises and to do that you need to post a bond of $48 million. Below Formula 1 is Formula 3000, and the chassis and engines for that are set. The regulations which govern Formula 3 are so tight that no new maker has a realistic chance of entering the category except by making a huge investment. There are similar scenarios across the globe.

Just as Colin and his crew hit the right moment to introduce the first proper kit car, so Lotus came on the scene at the one moment in British post-war history when anything seemed possible. Furthermore, the motor racing community, reeling from the abject failure of the BRM project, needed a star on which to hang its hopes. Colin was that star. The Mk 6 could hold its own in any company at the time, provided that the customer installed a decent engine. Even fitted with a Ford Ten engine it could could hold its own against cars such as the 1500cc Cooper-MG, so before long orders from continental Europe, North America and Australia began to trickle in.

Colin wasn't selfish with his Mk 6. Mike Costin had drives in it, as did Hazel, and even Stan Chapman had a drive in a handicap race at Silverstone. Colin, however, was an exceptional driver and he took the wheel at the more important races. At that point, however, he probably did not know how good he was. Colin's career as a racing driver would only really begin in 1954 and it would be brief.

CHAPTER 6

FROM CLUB RACING TO LE MANS

D URING 1953 Lotus became a force in British motor racing, even if only at club level. The 750 Motor Club's new Ford-based category took off splendidly, within its modest terms, and the Lotus Mk 6 was the car to have. Colin was still holding down his day job with British Aluminium, but in the summer of 1953 a priceless volunteer helper arrived in the person of 'Nobby' Clarke. Clarke ran a small electrical business with his brother, but got hooked by Lotus and throughout the rest of 1953 he ran the factory. It was supposed to be a part-time job – Nobby was paid by the hour – but he was putting in full-time hours before he officially joined Lotus full-time on 1 January 1954. Nobby is no longer with us, but by all accounts he was absolutely the right man for the job.

A modern manager, trained in the conventional way, the way laid down for people of middling ability to follow, would have nightmares over Nobby's job description: how would a modern manager cope with enthusiastic, but sometimes misguided, volunteers who turned up to work for nothing? Nobby coped and found them something to do. Out of the blue, Colin had found the right man and one whose job application would not be given a second glance these days. With that weight of responsibility taken from his shoulders, Colin set up a separate department, Team Lotus, whose first brief was to design the Mk 8.

Like Colin, Adam Currie worked from St James's Square, London and they would sometimes take lunch together. One day, in late 1953, Adam lent Colin a book he had discovered, about creating and stressing tubular structures. Like Ricardo's work on gas-flow, it was a book which Colin digested thoroughly.

Colin set to work on the Mk 8 with Peter Ross and Gilbert 'Mac' Macintosh. Mac

was a stress engineer who worked on many of de Havilland's great aircraft of the
early 1950s. Peter and Mac have never received the full credit they deserve for their
part in the Lotus story. Indeed Mac, who later became chief designer for JCB, is
rarely mentioned. Frank Costin (Mike's elder brother) always maintained that Peter
and Mac were the main designers of the Mk 8, but Peter denies this strongly and
Mac says:

> You cannot cannot point a finger and say that so-and-so was responsible
> for this or that. Things emerged from discussion.
>
> In broad terms, Colin sketched the layout, Peter produced full-scale
> detailed drawings and I did the stressing. That was the way the drawings
> were done, but before the drawings was the discussion.
>
> Colin is the one of the best engineers I've ever known. He had a very
> basic approach, best summed up by his constant question, in that flat North
> London accent, 'What are we trying to do?' He brought everything back to
> that fundamental question, 'What are we trying to do?'
>
> I would spend Sundays with him and it is impossible to say who was the
> father or mother of any given idea. I unearthed a paper on the principles of
> roadholding, written by Maurice Olley, former chief designer at Vauxhall,
> and Colin absorbed it.
>
> Colin used Olley's principles to answer another simple question, which is
> how to make a car go through a corner as quickly as possible. It seems
> ludicrously basic, but not everyone asked the question. At the 1954 British
> Grand Prix meeting, Colin got into discussion with Rudolf Uhlenhaut, chief
> designer of Mercedes-Benz, and he discovered that they were of the same
> mind and worked to the same principles.

Endorsement came no higher – Uhlenhaut was the last word.

Mac continues:

> My main input was to calculate the stresses, which I did according to
> aviation principles. Frank Costin and I both urged the use of a monocoque
> chassis, because monocoque construction was what we used in aviation. We
> even made preliminary drawings for one in 1954, but Colin demurred. He
> said that if it was such a good idea, someone would have done had it before,
> and besides, he had John Teychenne to build his spaceframes, but there was
> nobody to build him a monocoque. Frank and I even considered building a
> monocoque from wood.

Frank Costin recalled the same scenario: 'Mac and I urged Colin to use a monocoque
and to put the engine behind the driver. He wouldn't go the mid-engined route
because he didn't want people to think that he was copying Cooper.'

The story of Colin having a flash of inspiration over lunch and sketching the first
Lotus monocoque on a paper napkin in 1961 is a myth, one which Colin engineered.
Drawings for a monocoque chassis were made in 1954. That, incidentally, was the
year that Jaguar presented the D-type, which had a monocoque central section, but

there had been monocoque racing cars long before that. Colin was not averse to creating and nurturing his own legend, and there were times when he did so shamelessly, as with the first Lotus monocoque sketched over lunch, but Mac McIntosh makes an important point:

> In technical matters, Colin was absolutely honest. I remember people saying to him that so-and-so was getting away with this or that. His response was that he could not see the point of the exercise if it meant breaking the rules.
>
> If a golfer picks his ball out of a bunker when nobody is looking, he loses the reason for playing and that is what it was like with Colin. He refused to break the rules, he always took the pure line.

When it came to the bodywork for the Mk 8, Dave Kelsey built a model which resembled the Jaguar C-type. That was not a bad example to follow since the C-type was unique at the time in that it employed aerodynamics rather than streamlining. Mike Costin took one look at the model, instinctively felt that it was not the way to go, and suggested to Colin that he consulted his older brother, Frank. At the time, Frank Costin headed de Havilland's Aerodynamic Rectification Department at Chester. Frank had met Colin once and Colin had not been very happy when Frank told him that the Mk 6 was overweight and that he should apply aviation principles of engineering.

It was typical of Frank to wind Colin up like that. Frank loved an argument and he was an open and generous opponent. He was in love with aviation and, to his dying day, claimed that he did not think very much of cars, though he was to design many. Frank was older than the guys at Lotus and that was something which Colin found slightly intimidating. He need not have worried, however, because at that first meeting Frank detected in Colin not only an original mind, but the same love of engineering that he had himself.

Frank had no connection with motor racing, and he would later claim that at the time he had never even seen a motor race, but this may be selective memory. Be that as it may, when Mike made his proposal, he could see an interesting problem. Low drag was relatively easy to achieve, but Frank was acutely aware that the final shape also had to be stable because drivers' lives would depend on it. The problem gave him some sleepless nights.

Using a slide-rule and the principles of hydrodynamics, Frank made calculations, added bits of plasticine to Dave Kelsey's model and returned it. Dave was upset that his proposal had been rejected, but Colin was very impressed with Frank's work, particularly when Frank explained the thinking behind it. Of course, when the Mk 8 was first shown to the press, Colin spread the story that the body had been developed in a wind tunnel, but no car designed by Frank Costin was ever developed in a wind tunnel.

Furthermore, Frank's proposal was positively futuristic with its sweeping rear fins, and that was just the sort of image Colin wanted to project. Colin was always aware of image. He was not a tall man, but he walked tall, on the balls of his feet.

He wore clothes well and was aware of the effect his personality had on others. Frank's design was everything that Colin wanted.

According to Nigel Allen, Colin still did not always pull his weight and, while working on the Mk 8, Nigel recalls one evening when Colin said, 'Must have everything finished tonight.' He then disappeared into the office with a friend, Colin Bennett. While the volunteers worked late into the night they saw no sign of Colin but worked to peals of laughter coming from the office. Peter Ross puts a slightly different spin on the occasion:

> It was not a case of Colin not pulling his weight, because he was doing administration work with Bennett. Bennett used to do work on sales, especially dealing with overseas enquiries. He refused to get his hands dirty, which did not make him the most popular person among the volunteers, but the two Colins were actually working, though on the business and not the car.
>
> The trouble was that it was just three days before the Mk 8 had its first race and we were working flat out. Sometimes Colin could be a bit insensitive.

There was a major snag with the prototype Mk 8, which was that in order to remove the engine, it was first necessary to remove the cylinder head in situ, which was a long job. It took 12 man-hours to remove the engine and it took 24 man-hours to replace. The design of the frame was modified for customer cars, which is just as well, since customers did not have a host of volunteer helpers to call on.

The Mk 8's first race was to be the British Empire Trophy at Oulton Park and Mike and Colin shared the driving on the long haul north, having put in gruelling hours to complete the car on time. Colin took the first stint of driving, then Mike took over, but he was caught out by the fact that the body was so aerodynamically efficient that it did not convey the sense of speed he had been used to, driving an Austin Seven. Mike wondered why a police car suddenly took interest and a glance at the rev counter showed that he was doing 70mph in a built-up area.

Mike slowed, but typically Colin told him to lose the police. Mike put his foot down and was soon hitting 115mph, a remarkable speed for a car with a modified 1500cc MG engine. At that speed the airflow made his eyes water and, too late, he saw a roundabout looming. The Lotus left black tyre marks on the road as Mike braked desperately, and it launched into the centre of the roundabout. The front end of the car was damaged, but Mike and Colin managed to push the car into a side turning. The police car was too busy trying to negotiate the same roundabout to notice them. The rest of the team eventually caught up in their Morris Minor and saw Colin and Mike waving to them. Using the Morris, the team towed the Lotus to a nearby garage and began to repair it. They had just gone through three nights without sleep, but there was no way they were going to miss the race. Parts were taken north from Hornsey by more volunteers who stayed to repair the prototype, which required new tubes in the spaceframe. They worked on the car non-stop and slept in shifts at a hotel in Chester, much to the surprise of the staff, who served twice as many breakfasts as there were rooms. The car itself was completed at the circuit on the day of the race.

The British Empire Trophy was run as a handicap and Colin finished fifth. That signified little, because the result depended on the handicap – the important thing was that so many people wanted the car to race. That was the edge which Lotus had.

Colin's first win came at the International Trophy Meeting at Silverstone where he also drove in the Formula 1 International Trophy itself. It was the only time that he started an F1 race and it was to be no dream debut. He sat on the back of the grid having qualified 39 seconds behind the next slowest competitor and he finished in last place in his heat. He was also last in the final, eight laps down and unclassified. The reason was simple: Colin was driving the Emeryson, a special built by Paul Emery. Emery achieved some amazing things in his career considering that he was always strapped for cash. On this occasion Paul had bought a rejected Aston Martin DB2 engine, reduced its capacity, and ended up with a fairly feeble unit. In fact, Emery had bought half a dozen Aston Martin engines and sold some to the other special builders. The trouble was that they were all engines rejected by the factory for being substandard and Paul had bought them from a scrapyard. When Aston Martin discovered they had become the unofficial supplier of engines to the North London special building community they took a sledge hammer to the block of any subsequent engine they sent for scrap.

The prototype Mk 8, registered SAR 5, was soon making its mark, and other drivers placed their orders. If SAR 5 didn't always finish a race it at least tended to have the grace to retire after Colin had set a new lap record and lap records were then important since retirements were many.

Then came a major landmark in Lotus history. SAR 5 was entered in the 1500cc class in one of the support races at the British Grand Prix. Nobody expected Colin to win because Porsche had sent a works 550 Spyder with its new dohc engine, which then produced around 125bhp. Furthermore, it was to be driven by the very gifted Hans Herrmann who was a member of the Mercedes-Benz Grand Prix team. Not long before, Herrmann had won his class in the Mille Miglia by a clear 20 minutes and, at a time when there was no upper capacity limit for sports racing cars, had brought his little Porsche home sixth overall. All the indications were that it would be a walkover for Herrmann and Porsche. How wrong can you be.

Not only did Colin win the 1500cc class, but Peter Gammon in an MG-powered Lotus Mk 6 was second, while Herrmann's Porsche trailed in third. It is impossible to cite a modern parallel to this achievement. Two cars built in a stable block had defeated what was considered to be the outstanding 1500cc machine in international racing. Of course it helped that Lotuses were designed for smooth circuits such as Silverstone, but it remains a landmark not only in the history of Lotus, and of Colin himself, but in the history of British motor racing. People began to see Colin not only as an exceptional designer, but as an exceptional driver.

Colin continued to race SAR 5 with variable success for the rest of the season. When SAR 5 was on song, it was the fastest 1500cc car in Britain and it even made a couple of forays to races at the Nürburgring. Lotus had begun to compete at international level. However, it was not only SAR 5 that won races; customers were winning as well. Much depended on the engine that was fitted, but any Mk 8 was clearly in a class of its own.

In the middle of 1954, another major character in the story appeared: Fred Bushell. Fred was a junior accountant with a top City firm. He lived in North London and had often walked past the Lotus works, which was between his local tube station and his home. One evening, in a public toilet close to the stable block, Fred was relieving himself and Colin, in his mechanic's overalls, was doing the same. A chance remark led to Fred being invited to see the Lotus works.

Fred saw at once that he could make a contribution to what was clearly an exciting if disorganised young outfit. There was something else in Fred's case. He worked in the City of London when it was pin-striped trousers and bowler hats, when commuter trains would disgorge thousands of penguins, each with a briefcase and a furled umbrella. From this anonymous horde, the only ones who could reasonably hope to reach a truly senior level were those wearing the right Old School or Regimental ties, or who played golf, rode to hounds, or married the boss's daughter. Fred was not among their number. But Colin, the son of a publican, seemed to show another way to the future. Fred was never interested in motor racing, but he was a brilliant accountant who knew that his brilliance was unlikely to receive due credit treading a conventional path. He began by doing basic accounting for Colin in his spare time, and then began to build a group of companies under the umbrella of Lotus. There were advantages with tax and also the fact that separating the various elements protected the whole operation.

Within two years of introducing the Mk 6, Lotus had become major player in British motor racing. Colin now made two major decisions: he would give up his job with British Aluminium and, after a 10-year courtship, he would make Hazel his wife.

On 16 October 1954, Colin and Hazel married in Northaw Church. Hazel had dressed in a house nearby and thought that she should let the church bells stop ringing before before she made her appearance. The bell ringers thought they should carry on ringing until the bride appeared. The upshot was that the bride was 15 minutes late.

The newly-weds set up home in Monken Hadley, a village just north of London and a short drive from Hornsey. Not only did Colin become a full-time employee of Lotus on 1 January 1955, but so also did Mike Costin. Mike looked after development work and a separate company, Racing Engines Ltd, was established with Mike as a director. Racing Engines Ltd looked after engine tuning and work on brakes, gearboxes and so on, while the general service element of Lotus Engineering, grinding crankshafts and so on for special builders, was quietly dropped.

During 1954, two developments occurred which were to have a profound effect on future activity. Firstly, Frank Costin had been worried that he had designed the body of the Mk 8 solely from aircraft principles and he wanted to check the aerodynamics under real conditions. SAR 5 was taken to a disused airfield and tufts of wool were attached to the body so that Frank could see how they behaved at speed. He even had himself strapped to the bonnet of the car so he could see how the tufts acted immediately behind the front wheels. That hair-raising exercise would influence Frank's future designs and make Lotus into a world-beater.

Secondly, Kieft Cars ran a car at Le Mans fitted with an 1100cc Coventry Climax FWA engine. The FWA (Featherweight Automotive) was a modified version of the the 1020cc 'FW' (Featherweight) engine which was originally designed to meet a government contract for fire pumps. Cyril Kieft, a businessman with wide connections and his own workshops, worked with Coventry Climax to make it a viable car engine. There was more to it than enlarging the engine by increasing the bore, there was also the matter of replacing the standard cast iron crankshaft with one of forged steel, increasing the compression ratio, adding twin SU carburettors and paying attention to the porting.

The Coventry Climax FWA was light, powerful, reliable, readily obtainable and, at £250, not unduly expensive. There was nothing in the world to touch the FWA at any price and the rule at the time was that when such an engine appeared, a class of racing would grow around it. Cyril Kieft received little from his investment in the Coventry Climax FWA, leaving motor racing at the end of 1954 to rejoin the steel industry when it returned to private ownership. Colin was the main beneficiary of Cyril's initiative: he pounced on the FWA.

For years the accepted learning class for the serious young driver had been the 500cc Formula 3, but that was in decline. The 1100cc sports car class would take its place and Lotus was ready with the Mk 9. Again Frank Costin had produced an eye-catching and very efficient body, while the underpinnings remained much the same as before. In Britain, Lotus's chief rival was Cooper, which had produced a mid-engined, central-seat car with the Coventry Climax FWA engine.

Cooper had made more racing cars post-war than any other maker, mainly in the 500cc class. The two companies met head-to-head for the first time in 1955 and it was the beginning of a clash which would last for several years. Cooper's approach was pragmatic, and they used large diameter curved tubes to build their frames, whereas Colin insisted on properly triangulated spaceframes. Colin would sometimes refer to the Coopers as 'those bloody blacksmiths' and John Cooper would smile and say that when you bought a Lotus, you'd better buy a welding kit as well. In later years, John Cooper could also point to the fact that Cooper had won two world championships before Team Lotus won its first world championship Grand Prix. John, the most sweet natured of men, would say that as a matter of fact, he had the greatest respect for his rival, though he did admit to calling Lotus 'That crazy lot from Hornsey.'

John Cooper and his father, Charlie, were exceptional mechanics rather than pure engineers. This riled Colin more than a little when they beat him and though Frank Costin and others at Lotus urged him to place the engine behind the driver, he resisted the idea in case he was accused of copying the 'blacksmiths'. In the future, Lotus's biggest disasters tended to occur when Colin was reacting to rival outfits.

Cooper was marginally on top in 1100cc racing in 1955, due largely to the fact that Cooper had excellent relationships with a lot of young drivers who had started in the 500cc Formula 3, where Cooper was the dominant marque. Thus Cooper was able to sell cars to some very good young drivers and, in addition, run stars such as Salvadori and Brabham. However, Lotus Nines still took a lot of wins in Britain and word soon got round that they were better than the Coopers.

Some Nines ran in SCCA racing in America, where they proved superior to the Italian imports which usually had a touch of Fiat around their engines. Specialist Italian makers built cars to race on European roads, so their philosophy was 'Tune the engine, make the chassis strong, make the body pretty and paint it red.' Most American sports car racing took place on ex-military airfields or bespoke circuits, as in Britain. These were the types of track for which Lotuses were designed, so naturally Lotus made a bridgehead. Before long there was an American Lotus importer, Jay Chamberlain, who won the concession for California.

Lotus Nines also ran in major events such as the Sebring 12-Hours, Le Mans, the Goodwood Nine Hours and the Tourist Trophy, but though they were quick, they often failed to finish. If there was any bad luck going around it tended to settle on a Lotus. At Sebring, Lotus was heading for a 1-2 in class when one of the drivers was blinded by the sun and crashed. The other car would not start after a pit stop. It was close to the end of the race so the driver pushed it to a point just shy of the finishing line and when the flag dropped, he crossed the line on his starter motor and was promptly disqualified.

At Le Mans Colin was suffering a slipping clutch but was holding second in class when he slid off the road at Arnage, reversed, and continued. He was disqualified for reversing. Most times he would have got away with it, but this was in the aftermath of the worst accident in motor racing history, when more than 80 spectators had been killed. In the Tourist Trophy, Cliff Allison and Colin led their class by a country mile (and even led the leading 2-litre runner by nine minutes) when an oil pipe fractured. That meant a very long pit stop and a drive through the field, but a Cooper took the class by seven seconds. Still, there were plenty of minor wins on both sides of the Atlantic.

As well as 28 examples of the Mk 9, Lotus also made a version of the Mk 8 to accept the 2-litre Bristol engine. To achieve this, the frame had to be extensively reworked and so the car was designated the Mk 10. Six were made (one was delivered to the movie star, James Dean, who died before he could race it) and they achieved no great success.

One of the six buyers was the late Cliff Davis, who had been very successful with his Tojeiro-Bristol. He regretted the move because the heavy Bristol engine upset the delicate balance of the chassis. Cliff once said, 'I was carried away by the publicity. It was the worst move I ever made.' By contrast, Mike Anthony frequently showed well, but the class was a fading category which was dominated by the remarkable Archie Scott Brown in a works Lister-Bristol. Furthermore, Coventry Climax had released the 1500cc FWB engine and one of those fitted in a Mk 9 made the Mk 10 redundant.

The real point was that within three years of the first appearance of an advertisement for the Mk 6, Lotus had become the world's most prolific and successful maker of small capacity racing sports cars.

CHAPTER 7

YOUNG, GIFTED AND IN AN ELEVEN

N ITS seasonal review at the beginning of 1956, *Autosport* commented on the 'phenomenally successful season that Lotus enjoyed in 1955, particularly in the hands of its designer'. With unsolicited tributes like that coming in, Colin was no longer placing many advertisements. He had learned how to work the press and had taken a journalist, Alfred Woolf, on board as a part-time PR consultant.

At the end of 1955, both works cars were loaned to *Autosport* for a road test. John Bolster, the magazine's technical editor, gave the cars glowing reports: 'The whole cornering process is so effortless, with no rolling, bouncing, or tyre scream to give an air of urgency to the proceedings... ' On the Continent, the Paris-based Swiss journalist, Gérard 'Jabby' Crombac was racing a Mk 6 and that generated further publicity. Jabby would become a close friend of Colin's.

G.A.V. 'Tony' Vandervell, a.k.a. 'the Guv'nor', now enters the story. Vandervell had made a fortune through manufacturing engine bearings. He had been a supporter of the BRM project, had resigned in disgust, and had run Ferrari Formula 1 cars before starting his own Vanwall Grand Prix project. The Vanwall engine was sound. It was based on the cylinder design of the Norton 'double-knocker' motorcycle engine and nothing was better than that at the time. The original Vanwall chassis was a direct copy of a Ferrari Tipo 375 – Vandervell simply sent a chassis to Cooper who ran up a copy. The body was more or less a cover thrown over the car.

Vandervell approached Frank Costin to make suggestions to improve the body and Frank came up with a couple of minor aerodynamic modifications for the Italian Grand Prix. They worked. The Guv'nor then invited Frank to the International Gold Cup at Oulton Park where the one Vanwall finished third, a lap down. Frank recalled: 'After the race, Vandervell and I got stuck into the scotch and he asked me to look at his car and tell him what I thought. I said that the engine was fine, but the rest was a load of crap. I told him that what he needed was a chassis designed by Colin Chapman and a body designed by me.' Vandervell had been hearing much the same from members of his team, among them Derek Wootton, Vanwall's truck driver and an old friend of Colin's. Derek and Colin went back to the days when they shared an Austin Seven 'Chummy'. Vandervell had begun to suspect that his team members might be right, and, being a very shrewd man, probably invited Frank to Oulton Park just to have it confirmed.

According to *Vanwall*, by Denis Jenkinson and Cyril Posthumous, Colin was invited to the Vanwall headquarters at Acton. He was shown the proposed 1956 chassis and began his assessment with comments such as, 'I wouldn't have put that tube there.' He was being diplomatic, but crunch-time was inevitable and, when it came, Colin told Vandervell what he really thought. Vandervell liked men who spoke their minds and he was delighted. Colin clearly knew his stuff and he held a master class in chassis design for the Vanwall team. He didn't design the new car so much as show Vanwall the way it should go. It did not end there, because Peter Ross remembers drawing a jig for the Vanwall de Dion rear axle and visiting Vanwall with Colin to do other detail work. The de Dion rear axle layout of the 1956 Vanwall was pure Lotus Mk 9 which, in turn, derived from the Mk 7 'Clairmonte'.

Peter reckons that the Vanwall chassis was, at heart, very similar to the Clairmonte car. He thinks that it is even possible that Colin passed over copies of drawings he made for the Mk 7. He said: 'Colin had two sets of numbers. One set referred to projects, they were the "P" numbers, but when a project became a car, it was given a mark number. I know for a fact that the Lotus Mk 8 developed from P3, and I suspect that P5 was the Vanwall chassis.'

Colin did not design the Vanwall in the sense that he drew a complete layout, but his input was rather more substantial than giving a talk around a table with a few 'back of envelope' sketches. Furthermore, Colin followed the design during its evolution and construction and he and Peter Ross worked with Vandervell's own team on it. Colin made the difference between Vanwall being another British no-hoper, like a British heavyweight boxer, and Vanwall becoming a world-beater. Frank Costin made up the rest of the difference. His body for the car was probably the first true aerodynamic body in Grand Prix racing. There had been 'streamlining' before, but no pure aerodynamics.

In 1957, Vanwall would become the first British car to win a world championship race, three races in fact, and, in 1958, Vanwall would win the first Formula 1 Constructor's Cup. Vandervell fulfilled his ambition to beat 'those bloody red cars' (he and Enzo Ferrari had a long and prickly relationship, underlined by mutual respect) and the reason Vandervell was able to do so was because of Colin and Colin's knack of attracting the best.

It is not known how much Colin was paid for his contribution to Vanwall – he kept that secret – but Tony Vandervell took Frank Costin to the Vandervell company car park and invited him to pick a car. Frank was flabbergasted, he'd received nothing for designing bodies for Lotus, and he chose modestly, a Ford Anglia. He didn't ask for payment, he was on the ride for the sheer fun of it, but eventually Colin did buy him a car, another Anglia. There was a minor rebellion at Lotus when Colin bought Hazel a fur coat. Colin had laid up trouble for himself by assuming too much of those who had worked their fingers to the bone to make Lotus what it was. When trouble arrived, he was sensible enough to take note. He was jolted, but he learned. The Hornsey workshop was buzzing. Estimates for Mk 6 production range between 90 and 110.

The Lotus Nine was even featured as a cutaway illustration in the centrespread of *The Eagle*, a comic very popular with schoolboys. For Colin to have one of his cars featured in *The Eagle* was a major occasion and one with no contemporary equivalent. Before long, *The Eagle* featured a cutaway illustration of the Vanwall and there was Colin's name again.

You had to live through these times as an impressionable youngster to grasp the impact. Colin became a hero in a way which is now impossible to imagine, let alone achieve. Colin was taking on the world, he was excitement personified. Few knew the names of his lieutenants, but aviation engineers are self-effacing. Frank Costin once said, 'The happiest moment of my life was when I had my first drawing passed. Down at the bottom were my initials, F.A.C., and that meant everything to me. It meant that I had the approval of a bloke I respected.'

Everyone expected Colin simply to continue with his successful range of models for 1956, but he decided to scrap them all and concentrate on a single car, a brand new design called the 'Eleven'. It was officially the Lotus Mk XI, but everyone called it the Eleven. As a result, all Lotus road cars would have names beginning with the letter 'E', even prototypes which did not make it to production.

The winter of 1955/56 was severe, and the stable block was not the most pleasant place to be since the main source of heat was body warmth, but work went on with people putting in impossible, non-union, hours. None of them can remember the discomfort, they only remember the enthusiasm. There are tales of Austin Sevens, everyone drove an Austin Seven, or they seem to remember they did, tipped on their sides with welding torches applied to their brake drums so that their owners could get home to their mum's cooking. Many a father drew on his pipe and predicted, 'Mark my words, no good will come of it'.

The cover of *Autosport*, 10 February 1956, showed Colin seated in the new Eleven and the magazine devoted two pages to the new car. Two pages may not seem much, but there were only 10 editorial pages in the issue since there was not much motor sport to report in February. The timing was crucial, the Monte Carlo Rally was over, and so was the post mortem, which had filled most of the pages of the previous issue of *Autosport*. The timing of the launch showed the influence of

Alfred Woolf, Colin's PR man: only a journalist would have known to time the piece so precisely.

At the time, few competition cars were given a press launch, finding their way into print more or less by accident when they appeared at a test session or a race, but the launch of the Eleven was a masterstroke of PR. Colin wore a tie and a two-piece suit for the occasion, not his 'lucky' checked shirt. It's an apparently trivial detail, but in 1956 a suit marked Colin as a professional businessman and, by implication, showed that Lotus was a thoroughly professional operation.

The Eleven was not so much a model as a range. It began with the 'Sports' which had a Ford Ten engine and rudimentary weather equipment including a windscreen with wipers. The Sports was for the person who would use it as his everyday transport and perhaps run in the 1172 Championship. One of the mechanics at Lotus persuaded Colin to allow him to build an Eleven Sports (nicknamed the *Yellow Peril*) and he did very well with his car. His name was Graham Hill. It was Hill's car which was released for road testing at the end of the year – *Motor Sport* recorded a top speed of a shade under 90mph. Since Graham had little money, certainly not enough to have bought *Yellow Peril* outright, he must have charmed Colin into some sort of deal.

Next up in the Lotus Eleven range was the 'Club', which had a Coventry Climax engine, an Austin A30 gearbox with bespoke ratios, and a solid BMC rear axle with drum brakes. Again, the Club was supposed to be a dual-purpose car, and buyers did drive them to meetings, and sometimes even won races. There was, however, no attempt at making the Club weatherproof.

Finally there was the 'Le Mans' which was a pure competition machine with Girling disc brakes all round, a de Dion rear axle and an optional tail fin with a wrap-round windscreen. There was no pretence that this was a viable road car, although, like all sports racing cars of the time, it was road-legal and had to be registered for the road. The chassis was a further refinement of the Lotus Mk 8 spaceframe, but Frank Costin's body was completely new and featured a tiny radiator intake, something which would become a Costin trademark. Frank later said, 'I had made a mistake with the Nine by giving it large rear fins to improve its stability. What I hadn't realised was that racing drivers prefer a car to be slightly nervous because it responds better.'

The Eleven was launched in a way that no previous competition car had been launched, which sent a wave of excitement through the motor racing community. In the future, Lotus would arrange test days for potential customers and more than one bought a Lotus because Colin had laid on an event.

In terms of performance, the first Eleven was not big advance. A well-driven Nine was not overshadowed by the newcomer, as Peter Ashdown, who would become Lola's first works driver, demonstrated on many occasions. Peter said, 'The drum brakes on the Nine gave better overall performance in most races. Early disc brake systems were not always consistent and, in particular, the brake discs were prone to distortion.'

Most of Lotus's many new customers did not know that, and would probably not have believed it. Disc brakes were all the rage and, then as now, every ambitious driver must have the latest 'demon tweak'. It's the Purple Pole Principle. The Purple Pole Principle, an idea coined by Alistair Caldwell, states that if a car wins a race and a purple pole is found in the cockpit, come the next race every car will have a purple pole in the cockpit.

Lotus simply carried everything before it in the 1100cc class, which was growing in stature all the time. The reason was that Lotus was attracting better drivers. Cooper was still competitive, but was losing the battle for drivers' heads and hearts. Colin's working of the motor racing media was paying off. Colin launched his new car, and wore a suit, while Charlie and John Cooper merely let journalists into their workshop, where a chap called Brabham could be glimpsed in his mechanic's overalls.

Colin himself had a highly successful driving season, and he trounced Mike Hawthorn driving Ivor Bueb's Lotus Eleven on more than one occasion. The fact that Ivor had given up on Cooper for his sports cars tells its own story, because Ivor Bueb had made his name driving Coopers.

Before long, Esso became very interested in Lotus, and a long relationship was founded. Reg Tanner, then Esso's competition manager, introduced a young driver called Cliff Allison, who became the first true Lotus works driver. Cliff, a qualified engineer, had been racing in the 500cc Formula 3 with a Cooper that he had modified, and he was under contract to Esso. A test day was arranged at Snetterton and Cliff set a quick time, but not as quick as Colin. Cliff was asked if he could go quicker, said that he could, and did. Cliff recalls:

> I've never owned a Lotus, I was a works driver. Most people who raced under the banner of Team Lotus bought their own cars and received assistance from the factory because in those days there was usually a team prize for the important events. In sports cars, the only true works drivers were Graham Hill and myself.
>
> Because we were both engineers, Colin and I spoke a common language. He was a very good driver who might have gone far had he not had Lotus to run. I was usually quicker than he was, but it was not by much.

Cliff, it should be noted, would later be headhunted by Ferrari.

Cliff received a retainer from Esso (it peaked at £2,000), and he paid his own expenses. He received half of any prize money and half of the starting money, when it was paid. He also had a share of trade bonuses which were paid by such as tyre companies when cars did well. The figures seem risible today, but in 1956 a professional footballer had his basic wage capped at £750 a year and cricketers were classified as either Gentlemen (amateurs) or Players (professionals) and they had separate entrances at Lord's. In 1956, no England cricket team had ever been skippered by a Player. Athletics was purely amateur without even a sniff of a manila envelope stuffed with cash, let alone funny medication.

One of the drivers who raced under the umbrella of Team Lotus was Keith Hall. Keith, who comes from Northumbria, was driving by Cliff Allison's garage in Cumbria and caught a glimpse of Cliff's Cooper. He stopped, made enquiries and pretty soon had one himself. He switched to a Lotus Eleven in 1956 and soon had a run-in with Colin. He recalls:

We nearly had fisticuffs. We were racing at Crystal Palace and Colin drew alongside and kept banging into me. At the end of the race, I said it was all right for him, if his car got dented, he could just put it into the workshop and forget about it, while I had to get mine repaired. I told him that if he ever did that to me again, I'd have him off the track.

Apart from that, we got on okay. I had bought an Eleven and had carried out a number of modifications, most of which worked. I'd been a mechanic in the RAF during my National Service and got pretty interested in engineering, though I was actually running the family business, wholesale clothing, a million miles from motor racing.

Among the modifications I made was the addition of vents to cool the front brakes, which were prone to fade through overheating, and that was something which Lotus copied. I put washers in the de Dion rear axle to give negative camber on the back wheels and I was also the first person to fit Weber carburettors on an FWA engine. For a long time I was fairly reluctant to lift the bonnet of my car.

I was doing okay as a privateer, and was regularly beating the works cars. Colin then approached me and asked if I would like to race with Team Lotus. I told him that I couldn't see the point since I was beating his cars. Colin said that Team Lotus could negotiate better starting money and I would have access to all the spares they took to meetings. That sounded fine by me, but I stipulated that I should prepare my own car because I reckoned that I did a better job than Lotus did.

With the exception of Cliff Allison and Graham Hill, drivers under the Team Lotus banner had a similar deal to the one offered to Keith Hall. The difference was that most of them were based in the south so they had easy access to the Lotus spares department, while Keith lived in the distant north. 'I would turn up to meetings and that was really the only contact I had with Colin or my teammates,' Keith said. 'At the end of a meeting at Crystal Palace, say, I had a six-hour drive north.'

Team Lotus, then, was largely a loose-knit group of privateers. The public perception was different – the public perception was of a large works organisation. In 1958, for example, Team Lotus included Cliff Allison, Peter Ashdown, Keith Hall, Graham Hill, Innes Ireland and Alan Stacey. Keith, who was among the best of the bunch, retired at the end of 1958 under pressure to concentrate on the family business, which did not excite him at all. Peter Ashdown was offered a genuine works drive with Lola at the same time, and the other four went on to Formula 1, initially all with Lotus. The six-car Team Lotus squad of 1958 may have been more illusion than substance, but Colin could pick drivers.

To add to the excitement growing around Lotus in 1956, a monthly magazine appeared called *Sports Car and Lotus Owner*. It was edited by David Phipps, a young Oxford graduate who would stay close to Colin for the rest of Chapman's life. David had a huge, largely unacknowledged, influence on Colin's choice of drivers, for example. *Sports Car and Lotus Owner* was the idea of Roy Pearl, who also published *Motor Racing*. Aficionados recall *Motor Racing* with a great deal of fondness as the first British magazine with an international outlook. A look through the advertising section of either journal suggests that neither could have been making much money, but *Sports Car and Lotus Owner* was nicely produced with good quality paper and photography, much the work of David Phipps.

Sports Car and Lotus Owner remained in production for three or four years, which was good going considering there weren't actually very many owners of Lotus cars. David Phipps said, 'The magazine survived more than just a few issues due to the amount of advertising that Lotus put its way, Colin was really subsidising us.' True, but there was no magazine for Jaguar, Ferrari, Austin-Healey or Triumph, it was only Lotus which had the twinkle-dust factor.

Lotus also began to make itself felt on the Continent and scored its first major overseas success at Le Mans. There were six starters in the 1100cc class in 1956: three Lotus Elevens, a Cooper and two 750cc French cars given a re-bore to promote them to a higher class. In fact, the French cars were not serious contenders in the 1100cc class, they were concentrating on the Index of Performance, which was a parallel handicap event. The Index was given equal status to the main race by the organisers and the winner of each received the same prize money, £2,000. This fact was not lost on Colin.

Three works Elevens were built especially for Le Mans and they had wider cockpits to comply with new regulations (which demanded wider seats, of all things). Colin was nonplussed, since he washed around in the new seats. There were some weird rules at the time, but none as weird as the rule at Le Mans, 1956, which demanded that cars be modified to accommodate drivers with broad hips.

For the first time the Lotus contingent appeared in a team livery, a medium green, offset by yellow. There is no such colour as British Racing Green, any shade of green is permitted, and Colin chose a medium shade. On each side of the cars was a thin yellow coachline broken by the words 'TEAM LOTUS'. Until then it had been usual for British teams to call themselves Ecurie this, or Scuderia that, but before long there would be outfits all over Europe proud to call themselves Team Something. It's another small point, but it illustrates just how wide ranging Colin's influence was.

One of the Team Lotus cars, driven by Reg Bicknell and Peter Jopp, finished seventh overall, was fourth in the Index, and won its class. The leading Lotus was only a lap ahead of the Cooper after 24 hours, but few remember Cooper's fine effort. Eighth overall with an 1100cc car is a considerable achievement, but it was Lotus which had the halo of glamour. However, it was not showcase events such as Le Mans which spread the word about Lotus, it was consistent success in club racing in Britain and America where nothing could touch them. It was soon apparent that power claims from Continental makers for their engines were wildly optimistic: pony power rather than horse power. One owner of an Eleven fitted a Stanguellini engine to his car and, if the power claims had been accurate, he would have buried the opposition. As it was, he struggled.

Late in the year, an 1100cc Eleven fitted with a bubble canopy went to Monza and Stirling Moss took three international records before a chassis failure brought a halt to the attempts. The car returned home, was repaired, returned to Monza and Herbert Mackay Fraser, a gifted young American driver who had money, came away with six international records. Record breaking was a big deal in the 1950s and the fact that the Lotus, with an engine of only 1100cc, put in a lap at 143mph had a resonance not known today.

The Chapman/Costin Vanwall debuted at the International Trophy at Silverstone in May 1956, and, against Lancias entered by Scuderia Ferrari for Fangio and Collins, Stirling Moss scored a memorable win after setting pole and sharing the fastest lap. The race was even televised and Raymond Baxter, the usually suave commentator, could hardly contain himself as a green car took the chequered flag in a Formula 1 race.

Vanwall did not repeat that performance during the rest of 1956, but then Moss only drove for the team the once and those were the days when a driver could tip the scales. The Vanwall did show enormous promise, however, even when Moss was not at the wheel, and everyone knew that Chapman and Costin were responsible.

That year the French Grand Prix was held on the ultra-fast Reims circuit, which could have been designed to favour Vanwall. Furthermore, Reims offered exceptionally good starting and prize money so Vandervell entered three cars. When one of his drivers had to drop out, the Guv'nor called on Colin. The history books record that Colin put his car fifth on the grid, behind three Lancias and his teammate Harry Schell, and ahead of the Vanwall number one, Mike Hawthorn. Unfortunately, we do not know how quick Colin was in an F1 car. The time ascribed to Colin was actually set by Schell – in the days before helmet liveries and electronic timing, time-keepers could easily get confused. Colin had been experiencing problems with his brakes during practice and, as he braked for the tight right-hander, Thillois, at the end of the main straight, Colin rammed Hawthorn's car – hard. Only one Vanwall could be repaired in time for the race and that had to be Hawthorn's. That, then, was the end of Colin's career as a Grand Prix driver, and we do not even have a reliable qualifying time for him.

Vandervell did not repeat his invitation. In fact, he had had reservations about running Colin at all. It was nothing to do with his assessment of Colin as a driver, it was because the Guv'nor was worried about the future of Lotus. Colin had transformed the Vanwall project and Vandervell wanted to keep him in one piece. Colin had not been hurt when he crashed at Reims, but he had crashed because of a failure on a Vanwall. Mac Macintosh recalls:

> At the end of the season we all went to a showing of motor racing films and I sat next to Colin and Hazel. One of the films showed Colin's accident at Reims and Hazel said, 'That's it. You're not going to drive other people's cars.' Hazel put her foot down and Colin complied.

There were two other reasons. One was that Colin could not become a serious racing driver while running Lotus, and the other was the recent birth of the Chapmans' first child, Jane. Many top drivers of the time either refused to marry while they were racing, or else put off parenthood.

At the beginning of 1956 *Autosport* not only commented on the steady rise of Lotus, and of Colin as both a constructer and a driver, but also suggested that the Eleven would make an ideal base for a car designed to compete in the new international Formula 2 (for 1500cc cars), which was due to come into force in 1957. Some Formula 2 races were run in Britain in 1956, before the new formula officially came into force, and many people had entered stripped-down Elevens in Formula 2 races, some with the 1500cc Coventry Climax FWB engine. We speak here not of major revisions, but of tweaks like leaving the spare wheel behind. Cooper, however, had taken its mid-engined, mid-seater sports car and narrowed it to make it an open-wheeled single-seater. The Cooper won first time out and, with Cooper's reputation in single-seater racing, orders flooded in.

Colin had not been idle, and work had proceeded though 1956 on the first Lotus open-wheeler, the Mk 12. Colin decided to make a front-engined Formula 2 car despite problems inherent in such a layout. For one thing, optimum weight distribution was difficult to achieve, for another there was the problem of the prop-shaft. If the prop-shaft went straight down the centreline of the car then the driver had to be above it, and that meant aerodynamic drag since the driver had to sit high. If the prop-shaft ran alongside the driver then all the transfer gears added weight and caused power-loss through increased friction.

At the time when Colin designed the 12, Cooper had not yet made a cast-iron case for a mid-engined layout and Grands Prix were being won by front-engined cars. Colin and his lieutenants chewed over the problems and hit on what appeared to be the solution. The 12 would have to have a five-speed transaxle mounted at the rear, to spread the weight, and it would have to incorporate step-down gears to lower the driver's height.

Colin had been introduced to an Australian engineer called Richard Ansdale by Harry Munday, then Technical Editor of *The Autocar*, who had worked alongside Ansdale at BRM. Ansdale's brief was to design a five-speed sequential transaxle based on motorcycle principles. Munday and Chapman each had an input to the design and, following usual Lotus practice, it was a very compact unit which weighed just 49lb in its original form. It was fine in theory, but didn't quite work in practice and the reason appears to be that the casing was too tight. Not for the first time Colin was caught out by his instance on lightness.

Once Colin had committed to the design, however, there was no going back. A new gearbox was a major investment for a little company. It soon became known as the Lotus 'queerbox' and was the first of several Lotus queerboxes. Colin often tended to be on the right track, but he never did get one of his queerboxes right. Cliff Allison says:

> There were some design problems which were sorted out. In the early days, the crown wheel and pinion was not being lubricated properly, so they used to go. I thought the gearbox was a super idea in principle, but then I adapted to it better than most because I had raced motorcycles and my Cooper-Norton had a positive-stop change. I think some of the queerbox's reputation comes from people without my background. I also think that the same basic design could work today with the improved metals we have now.

In charge of the building of all Lotus gearboxes was Graham Hill, a man about whom opinions differ. Peter Ross and Mac Macintosh were both allowed, as was Graham, to build Elevens 'at cost'. Peter says:

> Graham was a great guy. At the end of the year, people would send their Austin A30 gearboxes back to be rebuilt with bespoke Lotus innards. Graham would go through the ratios and chuck out the worst stuff. When I was building my gearbox, Graham let me have ratios which he had rejected, but were actually okay.

Into the story here comes Keith Duckworth, who would co-found Cosworth. Keith was up at London University where, despite his brilliance, he would barely scrape a degree. Keith says:

> I didn't learn a thing by heart, I was interested only in things I could understand, which is why, even today, I can approach problems from first principles. Though I got only a 'Pass', one of my lecturers actually suggested I stayed on to do postgraduate research. I don't know what is the more unusual, someone with a 'Pass' being urged to do research, or an academic who can recognise an analytical mind.

Keith had bought a Lotus Mk 6 and a Coventry Climax FWA engine and he set off to conquer the world of motor racing. After three races he had shown no particular gift as a driver and he had decided that he couldn't afford motor racing anyway, so he sold his car. Having been a regular visitor to Hornsey to obtain parts, it was not long before Keith found himself a member of the band of volunteers. Since he was clearly brighter than the average person, he found himself looking after gearboxes under Graham Hill. It did not take Keith long to work out that the job was easy and that Graham knew very little, but had talked up the importance of his contribution. Keith never did learn how to appreciate Graham's charm.

Mac Macintosh's memory of Graham is at odds with Peter Ross's. He recalls: Graham could be charm itself, but I thought him a miserable bastard. I had two enemies at Lotus, one was Fred Bushell, who I thought was a crook of the first order, as was later proven, and the other was Graham Hill. Graham was in charge of building things like gearboxes and steering racks. I was building my own Eleven which had a Ford Ten engine and hardtop. My aim was to make a weatherproof car and that turned out to be harder than it may seem.

I soon found that bits were missing from my car. I'd work late into the night, do my day at de Havilland, and when I returned I'd find that, say, my steering rack was missing. After this happened a couple of times, Mike Costin, Keith Duckworth and I held a council of war. We knew that Graham was taking my stuff because it was easier than assembling the components himself, so we marked my components. One night we went into the works and finished my car using all the marked parts, which we found elsewhere. We then sat back and waited for Graham to complain. He couldn't.

Graham had Colin's ear and he reckoned that my input was all theoretical airy-fairy. One thing you have to know about Colin is that he thrived on intrigue. I always reckoned that one of Colin's grannies must have been a Borgia. Like Graham Hill, Colin had many faces.

When it came to the chassis of the 12, there was a kink in the frame just behind the driver's shoulder. I had stressed the frame and suggested a fabricated piece to strengthen it.

For some reason, this did not go down well with Graham and he persuaded Colin that I was only adding weight, I was only a theoretician from outside. I have to confess a certain amount of pleasure in knowing that were occasions Graham did not dare to put his foot down in the 12 because it would have distorted the frame and, with the gearshift attached to it, thrown the car out of gear.

The 12 was a tiny car, with an all-up weight of around 700lb. Colin drew on his knowledge of Frank Costin's work to design a tight torpedo body, which few thought was a thing of beauty, but it had minimal frontal area and a tiny radiator duct. Actually, most of the work was done by Charlie Williams. The 12 was light, but the lightness came at a price, and the car was also fragile. Coopers may have been crude, but they were solid. One rule in motor racing is that it doesn't matter if a car falls to pieces once it has won the race, because it can be rebuilt for the next race. That was the line that Colin took, but his obsession with saving weight went against another rule: 'To finish first, you've first to finish.'

The 12 was also the first Lotus to feature the famous 'wobbly web' cast alloy wheel, which became a Lotus trademark for several years. Apart from anything else, it was 'bolt-on' which meant that wheel changes in a race would be slow. Wire wheels with 'knock-off' wheel nuts were usual in racing because people in racing thought back to the days when tyre changes had been frequent. In fact, tyre changes had not been a part of formula racing, except in the odd emergency, since 1951, and in 1952 Cooper had demonstrated that it was possible for a light car to go a full Grand Prix distance (about 300 miles) without changing tyres.

Ferrari used wire wheels, but then Enzo Ferrari was a man without an original idea in his head. Colin knew that a car which weighed only about 700lb (320kg) would not make excessive demands on the rubber. Whisper it softly, but the blacksmiths down in Surbiton had never fitted a wire wheel to any of their cars. There have been articles written about how Colin's genius was demonstrated by his invention of this wheel, but although he was involved in its planning, it was actually the work of Mac Macintosh. Mac says:

> The wheel was my baby, start to finish. I didn't mind that Colin got the credit because Colin needed the credibility, he was the front man for us all.
>
> The way we worked was to look at things which had failed and work back from there. We had an idea for a magnesium alloy wheel, but we were working in the dark so Colin went to Stone's, who made the wheels for Cooper.
>
> The man at Stone's who met Colin knew that he was Cooper's main rival and he wasn't prepared to do business with him in case Stone's lost the work from Cooper. Colin must have done the charm bit because the man did suggest that Colin could take the odd thing from the stores, in other words, the wheels which had failed.
>
> That was gold-dust. That is what we wanted more than anything else. Colin, a very happy man indeed, loaded his car with Cooper's rejects. We had everything that had gone wrong with their wheels and that is precisely what we needed. We operated from the basis that you looked at the failures and worked back, and Stone's gave us all of Cooper's failures that Colin could load in his car.

Before the end of 1956 Colin took on Len Terry, his first full-time draughtsman. Len turned into a fine designer in his own right, but had no engineering qualifications at all. He had once designed theatre programmes for a West End producer and had also done cutaway drawings for *Autosport*, but he had built his own special, and a special on your CV swung things with Colin. Len says:

> I was a down-to-earth practical sort of bloke and so I was exactly the sort of person Colin needed. He needed someone to filter some of his wilder flights of fancy and I could usually do that. The only problem came when the bee in his bonnet was buzzing so loudly that he would not listen to reason.

The bee in the bonnet would cause Colin to make some of his biggest errors.

In October 1956, Lotus had a stand at the London Motor Show. The Society of Motor Manufacturers and Traders encouraged small makers who had made a mark to exhibit, and Lotus had won its class at Le Mans. On the Lotus stand was the new

12, fitted with a dummy engine and gearbox, and two Elevens. One Eleven was a conventional sports racing model, the other was a 'show car' with lots of chrome, special upholstery, and a stove enamel paint job. It is said that the 'show car' was bought by King Hussein of Jordan, who was a great motor racing enthusiast. Royalty bought a Lotus? That was heady stuff indeed. The appearance of Lotus at the Motor Show was both a boast and a statement of intent, and the following year Lotus would steal the show with its first GT car, the Elite.

A year of solid achievement was crowned by the award of the Ferodo Gold Trophy. The Trophy is awarded annually to the person from Britain or the Commonwealth judged to have made the greatest contribution to motor racing. Officially, it was awarded to Colin for his contribution to the design of the Vanwall (Tony Vandervell would receive the trophy the next two years when his cars won Grands Prix) but, of course, the award was also for his achievements with Lotus. Colin would receive the Ferodo Gold Trophy again in 1965 and 1978.

Within 10 years Lotus had gone from a special built from an Austin Seven, too clapped-out to find a buyer, to being the most exciting young motor racing outfit in the world. Colin could feel contentment except for one thing: there was always next year.

CHAPTER 8

TWO FOR THE ROAD

COLIN had been been toying with the idea of building a GT car because he realised that a road car was the way to keep the money rolling in on a regular basis. Chapman was like Enzo Ferrari, who built road cars to fund his racing.

A pal of Colin's, Peter Kirwan-Taylor, had suggested a GT car based on the Eleven, but that presented serious technical problems. Kirwan-Taylor was an accountant and financier who also fancied himself as a car stylist. He had created a fastback coupé on a Swallow Doretti and an entire body on a Frazer Nash Continental, and both had their admirers though neither was unanimously acclaimed. Even earlier than the Swallow and the Frazer Nash, Peter had bought a Mk 6 and had designed an enveloping body for it which he had made by Williams & Pritchard. That had taught him lessons which would come in handy when Kirwan-Taylor produced the basis of what would become the Lotus Elite. Len Pritchard recalls:

> Charlie and I told him that he'd find it difficult to get in and out of this thing. He said, airily, that he'd done all the design and it would be fine. He took delivery and set off to fill up the car at Tudor Garage, owned by Percy Teychenne. I needed to fill up as well and when I arrived on the forecourt, Kirwan-Taylor was literally crawling out of his car.

Mac Macintosh remembers:

> At the Motor Show, Colin saw the little Berkeley sports car, designed by Lawrie Bond, which had a 332cc two-stroke engine and, of all things, a fibreglass monocoque. He came back fired up by the Berkeley and had two questions: what would we have to do to beat Porsche – that was important – and would fibreglass take the stresses of a larger, much more powerful car. I had worked with fibreglass, we used it in aircraft, so I went away, did my sums, and concluded that fibreglass could do the job.

Colin set to work and learned everything he could about fibreglass. He read everything he could lay his hands on and even attended lectures. It was Chapman at his best: there was a problem and, as usual, he sank his teeth into it.

On the same preview day of the 1956 London Motor Show that Colin had been inspired by the Berkeley there occurred a chance encounter which was to change the history of Lotus – the introduction of Ron Hickman. Ron had come to Britain from South Africa where he'd undergone legal training. He was gifted in other ways, however, and when he arrived in Britain he had gone to Ford and pestered people, week in, week out, until he he was taken on as a model maker in the styling department. Before long, Ron was promoted to being a stylist. In order to support himself when he first arrived in Britain, Ron had taken to writing articles for a South African newspaper after being inventive with his CV. It was as a motoring journalist that Ron was at Earls Court for the Motor Show, having slipped off from work at Ford for the day. He asked for press releases on Lotus and that caught the attention of Alfred Woolf. Ron says:

> Alfred said that he hoped that I was going to give Lotus a good write-up. I told him that I was actually a bit of a fraud and my main job was as a stylist at Ford. He pricked his ears up at this and said that Colin was thinking of building a GT car based on the Eleven, but he wanted a professional stylist and all he had was Peter Kirwan-Taylor.
>
> I agreed to meet Colin, but since I knew how difficult it was to style the initial model, I thought I should bring along a couple of pals from Ford: John Frayling, the best clay modeller Ford has ever had, and Peter Cambridge, whose speciality was interiors and who was dying to bring sports car interiors into the modern age.
>
> We agreed to meet in the Railway Hotel. Colin was late for the meeting and he announced his arrival by the screech of brakes from his souped-up Ford Consul. As soon as he got out of his car, he was mobbed by half a dozen Lotus people who wanted answers or decisions. It was most impressive, the way he snapped out answers and decisions.
>
> He then told us that he planned to build a car made almost entirely from fibreglass and were we up for it? Of course we were and that was more or less it, we were each told to play to our strengths. There was never anything in writing because Colin put things in writing only when it suited him.

Until then nobody at Lotus had come from mainstream automotive engineering. Lotus had grown through Colin's charismatic ability to attract gifted amateurs.

In essence, the style of the Elite was suggested by Peter Kirwan-Taylor and was modified by John Frayling with Frank Costin working on the aerodynamics, while Peter Cambridge looked after the interior. Hickman played relatively little part in the formative days of the enterprise because he had to return to South Africa before the end of 1956. He had served his National Service there, but he was still of an age when he could be called to the colours in Britain, and he had no wish to spend two more years in uniform. He would return when he was too old to be eligible.

Ron did, however, assist the group by smuggling out the American modelling clay Ford used which then cost £1 per pound and was not commercially available in Britain. Had he been caught, it would have meant instant dismissal. When Ron returned to South Africa, Peter Kirwan-Taylor obtained clay for a second model on one of his business trips to the States.

Frank Costin has said that the group worked harmoniously, but that Frayling had the largest input of anyone. He not only made radical alterations to Kirwan-Taylor's original outline, but his skill as a modeller, as an artist, determined the final shape. It was put out at the time that Kirwan-Taylor styled the Elite and Frank Costin always reckoned that this was because he was a City financier and Colin over-emphasised his role because he could be useful to Lotus, as, indeed, he would be. In fact, Kirwan-Taylor's original presentation had a completely different roof-line, no separate boot and the front and rear wheels were semi-enclosed, which not only gave the car a bloated look, but made it virtually impossible to park in a tight space.

It was only after Colin's death that John Frayling's huge input into the Elite became widely known. The shape was largely Frayling's work, with Frank Costin suggesting the 'Kamm' tail treatment – which, mercifully, looked nothing liked Frank's sketch by the time that John finalised the style. Frank also suggested the general aerodynamic principles which gave the Elite a drag coefficient of 0.29, the lowest in history for a production car to that time and a figure which would not be bettered for many years to come.

Frank got that figure even lower on four cars he modified for racing which had perspex bubbles over the headlights, a smaller air intake, a flush windscreen and a slightly raised wing-line. These four were more aerodynamically efficient, but they were nowhere near as pretty as the standard car. In fact, most of the cars Frank designed were ugly and his response was always, 'I agree, but they are correct. You cannot argue with the laws of physics.' At the time, John Frayling was still working for Ford and he completed his models in his flat. Then one was baked in Hazel's oven. Mac Macintosh says, 'The smell was appalling and it even permeated the taste of everything she cooked for some time afterwards.'

One problem with the Elite was the engine. Being a small, light car, intended for racing as well as road use, a 1300cc or 1600cc engine was desirable to suit the appropriate GT classes. There was no suitable British proprietary engine, but Colin persuaded Coventry Climax to enlarge the 1098cc FWA engine to become the 1220cc FWE, and it drove through a Lotus-modified BMC gearbox. Even more pressing was the problem in finding a contractor to make the bodies. Fibreglass bodies for the special builder were coming onto the market, but their quality was indifferent. On the other hand, Maximar Mouldings in Pulborough, Sussex, produced a superb dinghy, the Maximar 505, designed by John Westall, who would play a key role, with John Frayling, in making a production Elite from the proto-type. The prototype itself was made in a workshop in Edmonton, North Londo

Colin wooed Maximar's owner, Max Johnson, who fell for the Chapman charm and was delighted to be part of Team Lotus at race meetings. It was agreed that, if response to the prototype justified production, Maximar would get the contract to build the body shells. This sounded good to Johnson, though he might not have been so enthusiastic had he known that every shell Maximar would make would lose the company several hundred pounds.

Since the Elite was to be a road/race car, little attention was paid to niceties that major manufacturers accepted as a matter of course. Frank Costin suggested curved windows, which meant they could not be wound down. Ventilation came only through leading quarter-lights, though it was possible to remove the windows entirely. Deadening of vibration and interior noise was not a high priority and when the prototype was exhibited at the 1957 London Motor Show, it had not even turned a wheel under its own power: the show car had yet to have an engine fitted.

Also making its debut at the 1957 London Motor Show was the Seven, which has become an automotive icon. Mac Macintosh recalls the genesis of the Seven:

I parted company from Lotus before the end of 1957 because, as Hazel put it, I committed matrimony.

Earlier in the year I was at the Chapman house one Sunday, as usual, when Hazel said, 'I think we need a more basic car, a successor to the Mk 6. The Eleven is fine, but it's expensive to buy and even a slight dent in the bodywork is expensive to repair.'

Colin looked dubious, but I said, 'I think Hazel's right, that's a very good idea.' Colin thought a moment and then said to Hazel, 'You do the washing up and Mac and I'll get on with it.'

We based it on the Eleven and we'd done all the stressing by 10 o'clock that night. Colin took the drawings into work the next day and a week or so later, we had built the first Seven!

Early Sevens had tight cycle mudguards, but when Lotus attempted to sell examples in America, the car was rejected because the authorities thought there was insufficient cover for the front wheels. Colin was worried because the American market was large. Charlie Williams and Len Pritchard said, 'Leave it to us.' It was Charlie and Len who created the sweeping wing-line which could become a major styling cue of the Seven and its many imitators.

The Seven was relatively easy to conceive and put into production, as it was done in much the same way as all previous models. The layout was agreed, Colin did the small-scale drawings, Peter Ross drew the detail drawings, Mac did the stressing, Progress built the frame, Williams & Pritchard built the body and any problems were sorted out relatively easily. The Elite was a different proposition entirely. For a start, it was to be sold fully assembled, not as a kit, and its method of construction meant that once the design had been signed off, it could not easily be altered.

While one team in North London was busily making Lotus into a manufacturer, quite a lot else went on during 1957. Early in the year, BRM went testing at

Goodwood and present was a local publican, John Brierley. John had been a racing mechanic before he pulled pints for a living and his pub, 'The Fleece', was popular with racing drivers based in nearby Chichester. John's working day meant that he could visit Goodwood to watch testing and to indulge his passion for photography. At the time, photographers rarely attended test days and few of them ventured to the back of Goodwood on race days because it was a long hike. John Brierley's photograph of Ron Flockhart's BRM lifting a front wheel as it went through St Mary's made the cover of *Autosport*. The BRM had a dreadful reputation for handling and the photograph proved that something was badly amiss. It showed that not only was the suspension faulty, but the front of the frame was also twisting.

BRM was humiliated, especially since *Autosport* followed up with a sharp cartoon, but bit the bullet and asked Colin for his help. Colin went testing at Goodwood with BRM and, as a result, redesigned the BRM's suspension, sorted out a few other problems, and turned a dangerous machine into one which many regard as the sweetest of all front-engined cars. Before the end of 1957, BRM had won two non-championship Formula 1 races and the team was turned around.

Since BRM was under pressure to deliver results, Colin may actually have saved them from extinction, an act which was to rebound on him in the early 1960s. It was, however, simply a small interlude in an extraordinary year. Vanwall won its first world championship races, BRM had a safe car, the Lotus Eleven was unbeatable and there were exciting projects in the pipe-line.

In 1957, Colin more or less hung up his helmet, though not before he first won his class in the Sebring 12-Hours. As it happens, his absence from the cockpit proved to be not a great loss, because just about every gifted young driver in Britain was beating a path to his door. Even though Graham Hill had precious little racing experience, and that mainly in the 1172 Championship, he was promoted to the works Lotus team. Colin updated the Eleven for 1957 and the Series 2 version featured coil spring and double wishbone front suspension, similar to that on the 12, and the Eleven swept all before it. Keith Hall says, 'The new front suspension was a great improvement. With the old swing axle arrangement, the car used to dive all over the place when you hit a bump.'

Before long, it could be claimed that the Eleven had won more races than any competition car made up to that point. That is an easy sentence to write, but think of it. Lotus was not winning Grands Prix, true, but the 1100cc class was fiercely fought – remember Ermini, OSCA and Stanguellini? – and there were plenty of makers that used the Coventry Climax engine and yet failed to make a mark.

The highlight of the season was undoubtedly Le Mans.

France had given up any hope of winning Le Mans outright, but it had a wealth of specialist makers which used Renault and Panhard engines and one or another of these makers had made the Index of Performance a French affair. Colin went to Coventry Climax and persuaded the company to make a 748cc engine by shortening the stoke of an FWA. Colin also got Jabby Crombac to negotiate with the organisers at Le Mans. Jabby was able to slip the 750cc entry by them. They had no idea what would hit them.

New rules called for a high windscreen so Frank Costin revised the body of the Eleven and raised the tail section while adding a tonneau cover over the passenger seat which puffed up at speed. The effect was to create a coupé type of body, except that the driver still had the top of his head poking over the screen.

One headline of the 1957 Le Mans was that five Jaguar D-types started and they finished 1-2-3-4-6. There has never been a better result, especially since the Jaguars were all private entries. The other headline was that Lotus took two classes, and 1-2 in the Index of Performance. Many thought that the Lotus achievement was at least as great as Jaguar's. Four Lotus Elevens were entered and all four finished. Lotus took the top two places in the 1100cc class and simply walked the 750cc class. Lotus actually didn't simply walk the 750cc class, Lotus took it by 30 laps: that's 250 miles. That was a massive achievement, but the way that Lotus walked the Index of Performance was even more amazing. The 750cc car won and the leading 1100cc Eleven, driven by by the American duo, Herbert Mackay Fraser and Jay Chamberlain, was second in the Index. Lotus had arrived on the international scene.

The car which won the Index of Performance was driven by Cliff Allison and Keith Hall. Keith says:

> I had to leave for home before anyone else and Colin asked me if I would
> take some spare parts with me and drop them off at the factory. I was happy
> to. It was only later that I discovered that I had been used to smuggle all
> the prize money out of France.

There were very tight controls on the movement of currency at the time and had Keith been caught, he would have been in very deep water indeed. It was not the kindest thing to do and one wonders what Colin's response would have been had Keith been stopped – he generally expected other people to cover for him.

The performance at Le Mans was spectacular and it seemed as though it was a case of Lotus going ever onward, ever upward, except that the Lotus 12 was a flop. The 12 had its moments of promise, but Cooper had signed some of the best drivers and sold a lot of cars. Cooper dominated Formula 2 by sheer weight of numbers and, besides, Cooper made the better car. There is a subtle art in matching an engine to a chassis and the 12 had a remarkable number of engine failures. Since Cooper and Lotus used the same Coventry Climax FPE unit, it is possible, one puts it no stronger than that, that the chassis of the 12 was putting undue stress on the engine.

No fewer than 24 different Coopers started in a Formula 2 race in 1957 against five Lotus 12s and the early part of the season was marked by Lotus entries which were scratched because the cars were not ready to race. Only one 12 was sold to a private customer, Dennis Taylor, and since he laid down money, he got priority over the Team Lotus cars. Taylor was racing his 12 when Team Lotus was scratching entries because its cars weren't ready. In some of the early races of the year, Team Lotus nominated Colin as a driver, but his car was never fit to run and, by the time it was, he had retired from serious driving. Cliff Allison was the first to race a Lotus 12, at Goodwood in late April, but the transmission gave up after three laps. A number of drivers were nominated to race, but only Allison had anything near a full season. The young American, Herbert Mackay Fraser, was next in the pecking order because he brought money.

Three weeks after Le Mans was the Reims weekend, which featured a Formula 1 race run to full Grand Prix length, a Formula 2 race and a 12-hour sports car race, which started at midnight on Saturday and went through to noon on the Sunday. Very high speeds were achieved at Reims and, over the years, many teams built streamlined bodywork especially for the circuit. They were all flops except for the Mercedes-Benz streamliner of 1954, but then that didn't work except on very quick circuits. On medium-fast circuits the flawed aerodynamics of the Mercedes-Benz W196 made the car understeer and then snap into oversteer.

Several entrants figured that a stripped-out Lotus Eleven with a 1500cc engine was the way to go and that is what Team Lotus provided for Mackay Fraser. Mackay Fraser was duly quicker than Allison in his 12. Cliff says, 'Mac was worried because the front end of the car was lifting on the straights. I told him to do a couple of laps to qualify for starting money, and then pull off.' Mackay Fraser ignored the advice and, on lap 27, he crashed and was killed. Cliff Allison believes that it was the car which killed him – the car ended upside-down – but no reliable eye-witness account exists. Keith Hall was in the same race and he is none the wiser.

During the rest of the season, the Lotus 12 appeared only occasionally and made little impact when it did so. Early in the season, however, the de Dion rear axle gave way to an independent layout using a variation of the MacPherson strut, which Colin immediately called the 'Chapman strut', and the name stuck. One wonders what Mr MacPherson would have made of the hijacking of his design.

For a time, Colin was no longer selling cars in order to fund his own racing. He'd stopped racing personally, but for the rest of his life would race through Team Lotus. In 1957, however, riding high on the success of the Eleven, the customer took precedence. The single-seaters, which were largely intended for Team Lotus, or became so through lack of interest elsewhere, took a back seat. Colin had to make money to finance the Elite, which was to be the cash earner which would provide the funds for Team Lotus. One by one, the first generation of key people, the men who had put Lotus on the map, left or were about to leave, and Lotus began to feel their absence. Mac Macintosh left in 1957 when he married. Frank Costin resigned from de Havilland to become a freelance designer, which meant that he expected to be paid. Keith Duckworth had joined Lotus full-time on leaving university, but his time at Hornsey would be short, only about ten months. Keith says:

> Colin was a brilliant conceptual engineer, but he had no idea of limits and fit, the details. He would get up extremely early in the morning and soon had all his ideas marshalled. He was very good in an argument but, if he thought he was losing one, he would throw out red herrings to see who

would chase them. I did. Often. Eventually I would say, 'Okay, I'll think about it overnight and talk to you in the morning.

One thing which fascinated me was the way he would tell the press different stories when they asked him why such-and-such had gone wrong. With a perfectly straight face he would tell them all a different tale. It was fascinating to watch.

The people who Colin had brought in to Lotus were up to all sorts of stunts. The men at Cooper had devised their own mortar bombs: the turnip was the favoured projectile. The men at Lotus bought lots of fireworks prior to 5 November and made rockets out of aluminium tubing. They had hardwood noses. The range was about 3,000ft. The rest does not bear thinking of. But, hey, they were bright young chaps and they were having fun. When Lotus re-invented itself, such high jinks had no place.

It has become a cliché to claim that such-and-such a car was a 'sensation' when it was launched. In the post-war years that can properly be said of fewer than half a dozen cars, but the Elite ranks among that select company. For a start, it emerged amid all the excitement generated by the international success of the Eleven. Then it came along with the Seven which proved that 'Good Old Colin' had not lost touch with the grassroots. The Seven was overshadowed, true, but it was there like the loyal henchman to a good prince.

These days, 'scoop!' pictures, or artists' impressions, of new designs often appear in the media long before a new model appears and, often, these scoops are arranged by manufacturers to pre-empt the opposition. In 1957, however, the PR industry, such as it was, did not work like that and cars really could cause a sensation when the dust sheets were removed at a motor show.

When the dust sheets were removed from the Elite, it caused gasps because it was so beautiful. It still is. It was lovely in a delicate way, like Audrey Hepburn in her prime. It was finished in two shades of grey which spoke of a very expensive bill at the paint shop – Audrey Hepburn in one of Dior's masterworks, perhaps – the production models had to do with High Street chic. Despite the fact that the Elite had not turned a wheel, the press lapped up the very skilful press pack which Alfred Woolf had assembled. There were diagrams of the construction of the car, which were widely printed, and the fibreglass monocoque was, of course, 'revolutionary'. Forget the fact that, a year before, Colin had been inspired by the Berkeley's fibreglass monocoque (and the Berkeley was to out-sell the Elite, two-to-one), Alfred Woolf won the PR battle. Even today one reads that the Elite was the first.

Many of the photographs published in the press showed Colin, handsome and immaculate as ever, in a suit of complementary grey, a typical touch, standing by his car. Not yet turned 30, Colin was the 'boy wonder' of car design and given the success of the Eleven, the Vanwall and BRM, that is no wonder. Not even when Lotus won world championships did Colin's stock stand higher than at the 1957 London Motor Show. He dominated it in a way in which no individual, or manufacturer come to that, can even dream of repeating.

CHAPTER 9

AN ELITE IS FEW INDEED

LOTUS was soon besieged by orders for the Elite, it simply had to go into production, and a contract was drawn up with Maximar Mouldings. The theory was that Maximar would deliver fully trimmed shells to Hornsey, where the mechanical components would be added. At the time Lotus had about 30 full-time employees and since it was anticipated that there would soon be a need for more space, Colin and Fred began to cast around for a new factory.

In the meantime, the stable block sprouted a shallow two-storey extension; it had a showroom at the bottom and the drawing office above. Pilgrims could see an Elite in the showroom and glimpse Len Terry and other draughtsmen at their drawing boards. The people who went there were pilgrims because Tottenham Lane, Hornsey, was, and is, off the beaten track. Who can blame them? It was the only place on earth where you could see an Elite and every enthusiast wanted to see one. The showroom was a PR stunt to give the illusion that Lotus was going from strength to strength. Photographs of the extension were published in magazines round the world and that is what mattered. Nobody dropped in at Lotus to buy an Austin and drove off in an Elite, the showroom was an illusion, but it was a magnificent illusion.

Of more substance in Colin's life was the birth, in January, of a second child, Sarah. This happy event necessitated moving to a larger house. John Frayling also moved, but down to Sussex to be close to the Maximar works. Since Pulborough is a good two-hour drive from Hornsey, and the motor racing season was under way, he and John Westall worked more or less independently of Colin and it is probably as well that they did. Chapman was used to making changes on the hoof, while Frayling understood production engineering and it was best that he was left alone to get on with his work.

The late Denis Jenkinson once concluded that early road-going Ferraris were actually glorified specials. Ferrari supplied a simple, though rather good, chassis, an engine and a gearbox and the rest was down to the customer who, in the traditional way, chose a coachbuilder. There was no such thing as a standard Ferrari for more than 12 years. Ferrari could change chassis details, unit to unit, and Bertone, Ghia, Boano, Pinin Farina (and Pininfarina), simply worked to the chassis that they were given.

Colin, though, had decided on a single chassis/body design and there was no possibility for change. It was a fundamental mistake. When Ford, or BMW, or Toyota, puts a car on the market, it has at least been tested. The Elite was put into production before the prototype had even been finished. With hindsight, it was madness, but Colin was arrogant enough to believe he could do anything and he had adoring acolytes who were caught by his vision.

One of the problems with fibreglass is that while the surface of a panel can be mirror-smooth, the underside is crazed. Colin thought that this could be disguised by lightweight trim panels, but John Frayling, a perfectionist, decided on 'double skinning' so that a second fibreglass panel, shiny side out, acted in lieu of Colin's trim panels. This was a feature which has often been been admired on the Elite, because for the addition of a very little extra weight, the double-skinning greatly increased the car's rigidity. It has often been cited as an example of Colin's cleverness, and he was not quick to disabuse anyone, but in fact he was absolutely furious when he found out what John had done because double skinning pushed up the cost of production.

Colin had not quite grasped that if he was to truly compete with Porsche and Alfa Romeo, he had better make a car that looked the part in detail. In Britain, in 1960, an Elite cost £1,949 while a Jaguar XK150 cost £1,665 and the Jaguar came with an engine which had won Le Mans five times. You had to be dedicated to buy a Elite.

There were endless problems making the complicated design of the Elite into a viable proposition. Michael Christie, who had landed the concession to sell Elites in the UK, recalls driving the first complete Elite home from the Geneva Motor Show in March, 1958: 'I drove through heavy rain and the further I went, the more odd the handling became. I stopped and opened the boot and found my suitcase floating in what had become a water tank.'

Production may have proceeded more smoothly had Ron Hickman been on hand to help John sort out the problems. Ron said:

Ford had kept my job open for me and I rejoined them when I arrived back in England from my stay in South Africa.

Colin decided that development of the Elite was taking too long and John suggested that I should join him. Colin made me an offer, and I had to point out that he was offering a monthly salary, whereas I was clocking up a lot of overtime at Ford. Eventually he met my demands and I joined Lotus Developments on 1 September 1958.

As soon as Ron joined Lotus, he set to work at Maximar.

Meantime, a few Elites were assembled as 'pre-production' models. They were sold only to people who intended to race them and who would be more interested in the car's supple handling than its many shortcomings as a road car. In other words, customers were invited to pay for the privilege of being guinea pigs. Releasing a handful of 'pre-production' models was a deft way of accelerating data about the Elite's shortcomings while keeping it in the public eye.

Frayling and Hickman managed to simplify the Elite's construction, but they were feeling their way, there was no precedent for making a car of that size from fibreglass. Ron describes the car as being like 'a jigsaw where some of the pieces didn't fit.' Moreover, Maximar's contract with Lotus ran for pages and was incredibly tight – Frayling, Hickman and Westall had little room to manoeuvre. John Westall could see that it was impossible even to break even on a shell and eventually, after Maximar had made around 270 shells, the contract passed to the Bristol Aircraft Company, which had established a plastics division. Quality improved when Bristol took over production, but that was as a result of a typical Lotus scam. Ron Hickman and two assistants spent two months carefully preparing a 'bog standard' Elite and then told Bristol that was the standard that Lotus had come to expect – and Bristol fell for it.

From Colin ripping off the secrets of Derek Jolly's engine, and passing off the ideas as his own, to his final weeks as the net closed round him after John DeLorean's arrest by the FBI, the history of Lotus was littered with scams. The way that Bristol was fooled is a relatively innocuous one. Bristol could have done its homework, but an aircraft company is not used to a standard of ethics honed in Warren Street. Peter Ross recalls an occasion when Colin sold the same engine to two different people within 10 minutes.

The company's accounting was creative to say the least. One refers to 'Lotus' simply for convenience, but there were several companies. If you bought a Lotus Seven kit, you bought the parts for a rolling chassis from Lotus Components. If you wanted an engine and gearbox, you bought them from Lotus Developments at the same time – the only difference between the two companies was the letterhead on the receipt. There was even a phantom finance company called Randall, which existed only on paper, but which would 'buy' cars if that was needed to balance the books to Lotus's best advantage. No doubt other companies do similar things, and most people would do them as well if it meant paying less tax, but one thing can lead to another. Most people are happy to play the game, but most people draw a line somewhere.

Take this story, told by a senior designer at Lotus in the 1970s and corroborated by his wife:

When I took the job at Lotus, part of the package was a house in the grounds of Ketteringham Hall. It was a good size, with stables, I suppose it might have been where the Estate Manager once lived.

At about six o'clock one morning we were woken by the noise of cars. We looked out of the window and there were senior managers parking brand new cars in the stables, up a track, behind bushes, everywhere. It looked as though they were being hidden.

Then someone stuck signs on the windscreens saying 'Property of the Acme Finance Company', something like that.

I went to work as usual and everything seemed normal until about 10 o'clock when a team from Customs & Excise arrived.

When I got home that evening, the cars were gone.

If the two events were connected, then it means that someone had received a tip-off from someone within Customs & Excise. It could have been something as simple as the wife of someone at Lotus working as an office temp and picking up the information. One would not like to consider the possibility that someone who worked for Customs & Excise was rewarded for such information.

Also in the 1970s, Colin was involved in making the 'Moonraker' line of motor cruisers. One of the Team Lotus Formula 1 mechanics tells this tale:

During the winter there were often slack times. There was no more work for me to do on the F1 side, we'd built the cars and there wasn't much testing back then so, to find me something to do, to justify my existence, I was sent to do a few odd jobs at Moonraker.

I arrived on the Monday and the place was bustling, making boats. By Wednesday, the shop was almost dead. On the Thursday morning there was just one shell of a hull left in the unit. It was on the Thursday that the Receiver arrived to make an inventory of the company's assets.

Team Lotus was always a separate company, and it was the flagship of the Lotus fleet, but not many people know about Team Lotus Overseas, which Fred set up to take care of the money that came flooding in when Lotus entered Indy car racing. According to Ron Hickman, who had a share of Team Lotus Overseas, the only physical manifestation of TLO was a brass plaque, among many others, on a building in the Bahamas. Moreover, in the early 1960s TLO was generating more cash than all other Lotus operations combined. Ron also says that though the Indianapolis cars were actually built in England, the paperwork had them built in a fictitious factory in America. It would take a team of accountants a long time to unravel the entire complicated network of deceit. Indeed, such a team, led by Sir Kenneth Cork, did manage to discover where most of the British government's 'missing millions' went in the wake of the DeLorean affair, but Cork's investigation, which was complicated in itself, had a narrow brief.

In his early days in motor racing, Colin was known to be a sharp dealer, but so many people in racing were car dealers, or similar sorts of traders, so he was admired. He was 'one of the boys', a spiv among spivs. There were, there are, some shady characters in motor racing because it is a sport which is fuelled not by petrol, but by money. Another part of Colin's personality, however, was his impetuousness, and nowhere better is that illustrated than by the way he took Lotus into Formula 1 in 1958 when, rationally, it was a mistake.

Coventry Climax had made a 2-litre version of its FPF engine. Rob Walker put one in the back of a Formula 2 Cooper and transformed it into a Formula 1 car. Moreover, Stirling Moss drove it in the 1958 Argentine Grand Prix and won. The win was Stirling's rather than Cooper's, he had driven with unmatched brilliance, but he had won in a Cooper. The blacksmiths had a world championship win.

Colin had not wanted to be involved in Formula 1 just yet – he knew what a drain it could be. When Cooper won in Argentina, however, that was it. Colin was fired up and all reason went to the wind. He had to be involved. It was not the wisest move of his life, the timing was wrong, but he had to be in Formula 1.

Team Lotus had fielded Graham Hill and Cliff Allison in early season Formula 2 races and they were on the pace. They hadn't battled for the lead, but their performances were respectable. Come the Monaco Grand Prix the same cars, fitted with either a 2-litre or 2.2-litre engine, became Grand Prix cars. In 1958, there were only three factory teams (BRM, Ferrari and Vanwall) in the world championship, so Cooper and Lotus were welcomed with open arms.

At Monaco, Team Lotus struggled and, to make matters worse, the race was won by a Cooper. That was two in a row and Cooper headed the standings in the new Constructors' Cup. Throughout the season, the two Coventry Climax teams could do reasonably well on tight tracks, but they struggled on the speed circuits. The difference is that Lotus struggled more than Cooper. At Reims, for example, the leading Cooper was a good 10 seconds off the pace, but was it still more than 10 seconds quicker than the leading Lotus, which was Graham Hill in the new Lotus 16.

There were only two bright moments in the entire year of Grand Prix racing. One came in the Belgian GP where Allison brought his car home fourth. Moreover, the three cars in front of the Lotus were in no condition to complete another lap, while Cliff reckons that his car was going like a train. One could say that Allison was unlucky that the race did not last one more lap, but one could also say that the three cars in front had complied with Colin's philosophy: they had stayed in one piece long enough to take the flag. The other highlight was Cliff qualifying his Lotus 12 fifth on the grid at Silverstone with the same time as Mike Hawthorn in the quickest Ferrari, but in the race, Allison did not run above 11th and had retired before one third distance.

The Constructors' Cup was inaugurated in 1958 and Cooper, the blacksmiths, finished third overall with 32 points, beaten only by Vanwall and Ferrari, while Lotus was sixth, and last, on five points. Maserati, which was represented only by privately entered examples of the obsolete 250F, took fifth spot. Colin had yet to learn how to race against really tough opposition.

A team has to have the right mental attitude in order to win and Lotus had yet to learn it. It would take Colin about three more years to develop the approach that separates winners from the rest.

In 1960, the future superstar designer, Robin Herd, was up at Oxford, but secured three months of work experience at Lotus during the summer holiday. Robin recalls: 'Team Lotus went testing at Goodwood. We were at the circuit when Colin asked, "Anyone think to bring a stop watch?"' Is it any wonder that Rob Walker's excellently prepared private team had won four world championship races using Lotus cars before Team Lotus scored its first win? A fortunate win at that. It was not just the fact that Walker had Moss driving for him, Colin was not ready to win until 1962. Cooper was ready to win, but then so much of the team's psychology emanated from Jack Brabham, backed by Bruce McLaren.

Against all appearances, motor racing is a psychological sport. There are teams which fall apart when they get a win because they don't know what to do with it: Jordan is a current example. Other teams, Williams is a prime case, take their first win and use it as a building block. When Colin did develop the right mind-set, nobody could get near him. Colin had to learn his craft, but learn he did. Colin soaked up information and his edge was that he knew that you can never stop learning. The downside was that he could be stubborn, very stubborn, and he resolutely refused to put the engine where it should go, which is behind the driver. He said, 'What would John (Cooper) think?' John Cooper was an easy-going man without an ounce of malice in his body. Colin's attitude was a point John was always puzzled by. Colin saw rivalry where there was none.

He faced another problem, which was the gearbox. There was only one manufacturer of a suitable gearbox for a car with the engine behind the driver, the French firm ERSA, and Cooper had an exclusive deal with them, which had been negotiated by Jack Brabham, one of the best operators motor racing has ever known. In 1958, partly because of the development of the Elite, Lotus was bleeding money and Colin was stuck with the queerbox. Keith Duckworth had made fundamental changes to the unit and had made it reliable, up to a point. There still needed to be more space between the ratios, we are speaking only of 1/10th inch, but that would mean a new gearbox casing and for Colin, that was a move too far – he would not, or could not, do it.

Keith became thoroughly cheesed off. He had become friends with Mike Costin and the pair of them began to talk about setting up business on their own. Perhaps Colin got wind of this because he signed Mike to a three-year service contract. Frank Costin recalled:

> It was while the Elite was going on that Geoff Murdoch, the Competition Manager of Esso, phoned me at Chester and said, 'Frank, there's hell of a mess. Mike is threatening to leave Lotus. If that happens, things will fall apart and we have a big investment in that company. I wondered whether you'd sort things out?'

I hopped on a ferry plane from Chester down to Hatfield and saw Mike. We had a long yarn and it turned out that though Mike was working anything up to 18 or 20 hours a day, he was being regarded only as the chief mechanic and his remuneration was comparatively small. The odd bonus came Colin's way and Mike reckoned he should have his share.

Mike said, 'I've mentioned it to Colin, but nothing has happened, so I'm off and that's final.'

I said, 'Do you mind if I see Colin?' He said, 'You can see who you like, but I'm leaving.'

I rang Colin and said, 'It's no skin off my nose either way, but in view of the fact that the arrangement has worked well so far, it would be a shame if it didn't carry on working.'

We met the next day and had a fair old chat. I'll give Colin his due, he took it very well considering that I pulled no punches. I told him that, in the motoring world, his reputation as an engineer was unsurpassed but, in other areas, his name did not exactly have the scent of a Lotus flower. I told him what people said about him, which was pretty stinging, but it had to be done.

Colin said, 'Why didn't Michael tell me all this?' I said, 'Because he's a Costin. Our father drilled certain ethics into us. If someone is not paying us what we are worth, that person is dishonest. So we walk away. We don't deal with dishonest people. If someone is paying us more than we are worth, then we're being dishonest so we should walk away and find something we can do honestly.' Colin simply couldn't understand this concept.

He said, 'Why didn't Mike tell me this?' I said that he didn't have to. We Costins are who we are. We don't ask for favours, we make statements. Colin then said, 'How much did I pay you?' I said, 'There you go. You know very well that you paid me nothing. I have never complained about that, I got an enormous amount of pleasure from working with Lotus. I got more fun than money can buy. But the fact that you ask the question is dishonest because the question implies that you did pay me something and you know that you didn't. You know bloody well that you're lying and that's what gets up Mike's nose.' He said, 'How about a Ford Anglia?' He must have had some deal going, and I said, 'Fine,' so I was paid with a Ford Anglia.

I told Mike to go and see Colin, which he did a couple of days later. Later I got a phone call from Colin who thanked me and said that everything had been settled amicably. Mike was made something like Technical Director and got a decent salary, so it all worked out in the end.

Mike signed a three-year service contract, but he and Keith went ahead and established Cosworth Engineering – Keith left to run the new company, while Mike helped when he could, mainly with ideas. The new company's main business was tuning engines, mainly Coventry Climax units.

At the 1958 French GP, Lotus debuted the 16 F1/2 car which was immediately dubbed the 'Mini-Vanwall' and it has often been written that the body was the work of Frank Costin. It was not, it was the work of Charlie Williams, working from a chassis and a sketch, and it was stunning. The overall shape of the 16 was efficient, but it missed Frank's knowledge of airflow and ducting. Overheating was a constant problem and the drivers often finished a race grilled medium rare.

The 16's general layout followed that of the 12, but its frame was wider and stiffer and the engine was canted 62 degrees on its side to gain a low bonnet height. It was also slightly offset from the centre to take the driveline to the left hand side of the driver and then to the latest version of the queerbox, which was offset eight inches to the left of the differential. The arrangement allowed the driver to sit low in the car, but that came at the cost of power loss since the drive-train had to run round the houses. During the life of the 16, the position of the engine changed several times and, indeed, after initial testing it first raced with the engine canted over to a less radical 17 degrees. The engine was not designed to work at an angle, which helps to explain why Cooper had an edge.

Whatever else the 16 was or was not, it was the smallest, lightest, smoothest and altogether most advanced front-engined Formula 1 car ever. Unfortunately, that was a little like saying it was the most advanced biplane ever made. Even Ferrari was considering putting the engine behind the driver and Enzo Ferrari had said it would never happen. Whether Lotus ran the 12 or the 16, 2-litre or 2.2-litre engine, the result was the same. Neither Lotus nor Colin was ready for Formula 1. All of Colin's successes had come in sports car racing and, to be brutal, it was a case of Colin the special builder being ahead of other special builders.

Even in sports car racing, competing for class wins not outright victory, Colin was losing the plot. Early in 1958, Lotus introduced the Fifteen, an Eleven on steroids with the 12's rear suspension and the queerbox (export cars got a conventional four-speed gearbox). It was designed to take the 1.5-litre, or 2-litre, FPF engine and its body closely resembled the Eleven but, again, Frank Costin had no input. It was another instance of Charlie Williams using his craftsman's eye. Team Lotus could not give the Fifteen its full attention so it spent almost all of its competition life in national races in Britain and America. True, there was not much to touch the Fifteen in the 2-litre class in 1958, but the trouble was that by then there was not a great deal of interest in the 2-litre class.

Lotus returned to Le Mans in 1958, the scene of its triumph 12 months before, and it went mob-handed. No fewer than six Lotuses started the race, but only one was still running at the end. Even then it was so many laps in arrears that it was not even classified as a finisher. Hardly anyone wanted to buy a Lotus single-seater – the only advantage of buying one was that adding variety to a grid meant that an owner could negotiate good starting money. Few wanted a Fifteen and there was little demand for the Eleven. There were already so many Elevens on the scene that the market was saturated. There was no doubting the excellence of the Eleven, it was winning all over the world, but it was the victim of its own success.

Cooper had given up on small-capacity sports cars to concentrate on the lucrative Formula 2 market and none of the cars made by rivals such as Elva and Tojeiro were up to knocking the Eleven off its perch. While the Eleven reigned supreme, there appeared to be no reason to introduce a new model. This was Colin thinking purely as a racer, not as a businessman. Had he been thinking as a businessman, he would have introduced a car to make the Eleven obsolete.

Lotus was going through a patch so rocky that it might have folded except for the money brought in through sales of the Seven. There were periods when Lotus was kept going only through the deposits paid on Sevens, just as Colin had once been kept in business by deposits laid down for the Mk 6. Before long there was a 'Super Seven' which, in top specification, had a Coventry Climax engine, wire wheels, and a de Dion rear axle. It was virtually a full-spec Eleven with a slipper body.

Lotus's international reputation had been built on the Eleven and the Eleven would receive a mortal blow in August 1958. Among those who attended the 750 Motor Club's meetings at The Red Cow was a quiet, unassuming, quantity surveyor called Eric Broadley. Eric and his cousin, Graham, had designed and built an 1172 special they called 'Lola'. The cousins shared the driving of Lola during 1957 and Eric won the 1172 Championship, beating, among others, a number of Lotus Mk 6 drivers, and so became the recipient of the Colin Chapman Trophy.

Eric Broadley fancied himself as a racing driver and the next step up the ladder was the 1100cc class. Eric says that the sensible thing to have done would have been to buy an Eleven, but since he could not afford that, he and Graham set about building a second special, also called 'Lola'. Mo Gomm, who rivalled Williams & Pritchard, had some spare body panels, originally intended for a Tojeiro, and Eric was able to arrange a deal. Eric applied some sound thinking to the chassis and layout of his car, but the bodywork was used because it was cheap. Broadley did not have someone like Frank Costin at his elbow. The second Lola became the Mk 1 in retrospect, while the original car was re-named 'Lolita'. Lolita's new owner won the 750 Motor Club's Colin Chapman Trophy in 1961, this time beating many a Lotus Seven.

The Lola Mk 1 was a tiny car, much smaller and lighter than an Eleven. It was also beautifully constructed and detailed, and the design showed an original mind at work. It was a breakthrough, whereas the Eleven had evolved. Eric was no great driver but, during practice for a fairly important national meeting at Brands Hatch at the end of August, the Lola became the first sports car, regardless of size, to lap the circuit in under a minute. That alone was enough to raise eyebrows, but then Broadley won his heat by no fewer than 24 seconds, and the cars that he beat were mostly made by Lotus. Eric stamped his authority on the 1100cc class in a single afternoon.

Colin was rocked and Len Terry recalls:

He was so completely fired up that he simply would not listen to reason. The new 1100cc sports car, the Seventeen, began with the demand that it had to be smaller than the Lola Mk 1. That was the main design parameter.

I tried to tell him that cars can be too small because you have to allow for things like suspension movement. There was no reasoning with him, so I had to go along with it.

Unlike the Eleven, the Seventeen was a pure sports racer. There was no dual-purpose Seventeen, there was no Ford-engined Seventeen. From 1958, sports racers no longer had to comply to road rules, they could be what they had been for a long time: two-seat formula cars.

At the 1958 Boxing Day meeting at Brands Hatch, Colin turned up as a driver. He had a new Lotus Elite and so did Mike Costin. Mike did not race often, but when he did he was blindingly quick. One of the pre-production Elites had been sold to a Scottish team, Border Reivers, and the team's driver was a young sheep farmer, Jim Clark. During the meeting Clark went to take a leak and he overheard Colin and Mike discussing the forthcoming race. Colin suggested that they should toss a coin to decide the winner. Jimmy was not impressed.

The race itself was fierce, neither Chapman nor Costin took prisoners, but Jimmy managed to open a small gap and might have won had not a car he was lapping spun in front of him. Jimmy did well to avoid an accident, Chapman seized his chance and scored a win from Clark. Having raced wheel to wheel with him, Chapman recognised Jimmy's talent and he stored his name.

Colin knew that Clark had not even seen his car until the morning of the race, when it had been handed over, but he did not know that Jimmy had never before driven at Brands Hatch. When he made further enquiries, Colin discovered that Clark had only just completed his first full season. Colin had encountered the man who would become the centre of his life for the greatest period of Lotus's history.

CHAPTER 10

WHATEVER LOLA WANTS, LOLA GETS

URING the winter, 1958/9, Eric Broadley built two more cars and, at their first important race meeting, at Goodwood on Easter Monday 1959, the three Lolas simply ran away and hid from the rest of the field. The race was one of the few to be featured on British television that year, so the humiliation of Lotus was a public affair. Lotus had not been able to prepare the Seventeen in time for the race at Goodwood, but when the Seventeen did appear it disappointed. Again, it was Charlie Williams and Len Pritchard who were left to do the body, which was like an Eleven after months at a particularly rigorous health farm.

The Seventeen marked an important departure, it had a fibreglass body. Williams & Pritchard made the prototype body from aluminium and the moulds were taken from that. Len Pritchard says:

> It was clear that fibreglass was going to become important, we were losing business to it, but there were some horrible examples of it around at the time. While Charlie concentrated on metal prototypes I read up everything I could find on fibreglass and started that side of the business. All the prototypes were built up in aluminium because we were able to get them exactly as we wanted, and to a high standard, so we could take moulds off them.

This arrangement with Williams & Pritchard continued up to the introduction of the Elan.

There was another important departure, which was the way the Seventeen was entered in races. During 1958 Team Lotus had entered two pukka works cars and had provided an umbrella for four of the better privateers. Though privateers would occasionally run under the Team Lotus umbrella, the operation was slimmed because it did not pay for itself. Fred Bushell was the guy picking up the pieces: it was he who laid the financial foundation on which Colin could perform as a star turn. Colin realised this at heart, but he was often so arrogant that he took out his frustrations on Fred. Several witnesses recall times when Chapman, whose temper could be poisonous, turned on Bushell and spat venom. Ron Hickman, for one, finds it hard to understand how Bushell could take Chapman's exceptionally unpleasant explosions and live with himself. However, after any explosion, Colin still had a bucket of charm into which he could dip a ladle.

As for the Seventeen, the car which damaged Colin's reputation more than any other, Len Terry says:

> Colin insisted that everything had to fit into this tiny package and so to make everything fit, we had to adapt the 'Chapman strut' to make the front suspension. There was so little space to move that when a car went into a corner, the front seized up, causing massive oversteer. Coming out of the corner, the suspension was released so the car went into massive understeer.

For the non-technical, that means that the damned thing wouldn't go where you wanted it to go, which is a shortcoming in a competition car.

If you had bought a Seventeen Colin eventually had some good news for you. He was prepared to go back on his design and he was prepared to give you, free of charge, a unique event in Colin's life, an updated front suspension system. The update dispensed with the 'Chapman strut' front suspension and replaced it with double wishbones, which Len Terry had wanted all along. It made the Seventeen a reasonable proposition, but it came too late. Lotus lost the market for the small sports racing car and it was mainly due to Colin's complacency and, when riled, his cussedness. For the first time, Lotus was soundly whipped in a class which once it had ruled. There were only three Lolas at the start of 1959, but they swept everything before them. Even the welding on the chassis of the Lola was superior to anything John Teychenne was allowed to make for Lotus – he was tied to a price – and John's team included men who were artists with a welding torch.

The Fifteen had been cock o' the walk in the 2-litre sports car class for a few months but, for 1959, Cooper introduced the 'Monaco', which was virtually a two-seat Grand Prix car. That was the end of the Fifteen's brief reign. The Monaco also marked the beginning of a new era in sports car racing as ever larger engines were fitted.

During 1959, Lotus was being beaten off the tracks: it was failing to make an impression in formula racing. The Elite was bleeding money, though the pre-production cars performed well in racing, and Colin also had the problem of moving the entire business. Restrictions on building in inner London prevented further expansion of the stable block in Hornsey and Colin was not satisfied with the vacant factory units within easy reach. He didn't wish to move too far because he might lose employees, but he found a site at Cheshunt. Cheshunt is just outside

London and its building regulations, but is only about 10 miles from Hornsey. Peter Kirwan-Taylor helped Colin buy the plot of land and half the site was soon sold at a healthy profit.

The new factory was fresh from the ground up and Colin was finally able put his training as a civil engineer to practical use. Colin had a considerable input to the new factory's design and it remains the only evidence of his academic training – he never did get round to building the skyscrapers and bridges of his father's dreams. The factory was not a grand affair, but it suited Lotus's requirements, because Lotus was still making only a few hundred cars a year.

There was even Nigel Allen on hand at Cheshunt to look after everyone's teeth.

Some years later there was a cleansing product advertised as 'The White Tornado' which would whisk through your house, whoosh! and leave it spotless without, apparently, any need for a little elbow grease. By the time the slogan was used, Colin's hair was white and people at Lotus nicknamed him 'The White Tornado' because he was here, he was there, he was everywhere. That was certainly true of the time between the 1957 Motor Show and moving into the new factory.

In the meantime, there was still the business of Formula 1, where Lotus had been so comprehensively upstaged by Cooper. For 1959 Coventry Climax had its new 2495cc FPF engine which gave around 240bhp, less than the best opposition but enough to be exploited by lightweight Formula 1 cars such as the Cooper and Lotus. The Lotus 16 had a number of detail improvements for 1959, but they were were nowhere near enough. The chassis frame still flexed, so the bodyshell of the 16 often cracked and crazed, while the record for the number of fractures in a frame after a race appears to have been 14. Mac Macintosh says:

When I was connected with Lotus, I used to stress the structures according to normal aviation principles. After I married, Colin and I remained friends, but I severed the working relationship. I think that Lotus went through a period of imitating the type of stressing I had done, but without using the methods we used in the aviation industry. I think, also, that Colin was trying to juggle too many balls in the air at once.

Works or privateer, Formula 1 or Formula 2, the season was a disaster. More often than not the cars retired or, if they survived, they finished way down the rankings. There were flashes of promise during practice for races, but frames would crack, the suspension would break or the transmission would fail. In world championship terms, the team's best and only points-scoring result was Innes Ireland's fourth place in the Dutch Grand Prix. Worse, Coopers dominated F2, most non-championship F1 races, and carried Jack Brabham to his first world championship title.

At the end of the season, Cliff Allison was on the Lotus stand at the London Motor Show. He recalls:

A smartly dressed gentleman invited me to the Ferrari stand and before long I was a Ferrari driver. I was great mates with Mike Hawthorn who had just

won the world championship and had immediately retired. I believe that
Mike had recommended both Graham Hill and myself. BRM was also
looking for drivers and Graham went there.

Thus Colin lost both his principal drivers.

BRM had won its first Grand Prix in 1959 and Graham also had an offer to drive
works Porsches in Formula 2 and the World Sports Car Championship. Either Cliff
or Graham would have had to have been barking mad to have stayed with Lotus
with offers like that on the table. They were both being offered sensible pay-days
and, more importantly, a chance to win races.

Lotus was not only on the ropes in single-seater racing, its sports cars were being
beaten in every category and production of the Elite was progressing painfully.
There was even worse to come. Len Terry was not Colin's chief designer, there was
no chief designer except for Colin, but he had become Colin's pen. In 1959,
however, Len teamed up with a young engineer called Brian Hart. Len designed an
1172 special, the Terrier Mk 2, and Brian tuned the engine and drove the car. During
1959, Lotus had been kept going largely through sales of the Seven. Driving his
Terrier, Brian Hart swept all before him in the 1172 Championship, beating all the
drivers who had bought Sevens, and Brian collected the Colin Chapman Trophy.

It was another humiliation and Len had to be fired. He went on to a career in his
own right, in fact, he became the first British designer to start with a racing car
company and become a freelance. He would be the first of many and that is
something for which Colin has not received credit. There had been other factors at
work, however, before Len's final dismissal. He had encouraged the staff of the
drawing office and development shop at Lotus to rebel against rules that Colin
wanted to apply when they moved to Cheshunt. The rules included one which said
you could not hang your jacket over the back of your chair, you had to hang it on
a rack, and one that said that you could not take a Thermos flask of tea or coffee
into work. Len got the workers to pull together and they stood up to Colin. He had
to back down, and he felt that he had to sack Len Terry. When the Terrier won the
1172 Championship, it provided a handy excuse.

In 1957, Colin and Lotus were on top of the world, but just two years on Lotus
was struggling. 1959 was the nadir of Colin's fortunes and on top of everything
else, he had a major problem in America as he tried to service Lotus's first dedicated
export drive.

In 1956, Colin had raced at Sebring and there he met the personable
driver/mechanic, the late Jay Chamberlain, who had been racing a Lotus Mk 9 with
considerable success on the West Coast. The two men became instant friends and
Colin persuaded Jay to visit England in 1956, which was a long haul then. Jay
returned home as the official Lotus importer to California and, with his friend, Herbert
Mackay Fraser, would win the 1100cc class for Team Lotus at Le Mans in 1957.

One of the things which Chamberlain did was to fit an Eleven with a Nardi-
modified 750cc Fiat engine for Class H racing, and he offered this as a distinct

model. When Chamberlain first saw the Elite, he fell in love with it and thought it was ideal for the American market. He therefore sought, and won, the sole concession to sell the Elite, and other Lotuses, in America. Jay found a wealthy backer who arranged a line of credit, which also helped to underwrite the new factory at Cheshunt, he established a dealer network and spent a considerable amount on advertising. Jay then sat back and waited for the cars to arrive, as you would when your best friend in the world is telling you that everything is about to happen.

Colin sent over a couple of Elites for the 1959 Sebring 12-Hour race, but they were near-standard cars, which means they were not really suitable for an international race, and they did not set the world alight. They remained in the States, however, to drum up business. Jay reasoned that Elite did not have to sell itself, the Elite had to do no more than be itself. However, Jay Chamberlain, honest mechanic, good racing driver and Colin Chapman's bosom buddy, would be nearly destroyed by Colin in the name of friendship.

By July 1959, just four Elites had been sent to America, in addition to Seventeens and Fifteens which Jay had had difficulty shifting, and the four Elites needed serous rectification due to their poor quality. Chamberlain was advertising the Elite at $6,000 and for that you could buy a top-of-line Chevrolet Corvette, plus a Chevrolet sedan, and you did not have to have them in right hand drive. By April 1960, 50 Elites had been sent from England, but most were still at sea making the long trip via the Panama Canal and Chamberlain had almost run out of money. He had certainly run out of patience and Colin had definitely become a former friend. Not only were many of the cars not up to an acceptable standard of quality, some even had to be cannibalised. Ron Hickman says, 'Some cars were even being sent incomplete with a note saying "engine to follow later."'

Furthermore, some Americans were bringing in Elites as personal imports. Jay and his backers had the sole concession, so they thought, but they had no option but to live with 'grey market' imports. And Colin smiled and smiled, but one can smile and smile and be a villain. It is not only a woman scorned that hell has no fury like. According to Robin Read, who was the Lotus sales manager at the time, Chamberlain and Chapman had similar personalities. Both could be relaxed and charming and, equally, could be fearsome when crossed. Jay believed, not without reason, that Colin had stitched him up. When Colin arrived in Florida to take part in the 1960 Sebring 12-Hour race, Jay stayed away.

What made it worse for Jay, who was staring bankruptcy in the face, was that he had regarded Colin as a close and trusted friend. Jay had been taken in by Colin's charm, he had been a member of Team Lotus, but he lived a long way from England and had not heard the stories of Colin's darker side. He had believed every word that Colin had uttered without knowing what an accomplished liar Colin could be.

Perhaps that is too stark an assessment. There can be no doubt that Colin wanted the Elite to do well. California was the world's most lucrative market for sports cars and Chamberlain, Chapman and Chamberlain's backers all thought they could make a killing. Colin did not deliberately set out to wreck Jay, he wanted to be earning dollars as well.

The problems encountered when putting the Elite into production have been touched on, but they come down to the fact that Colin had bitten off more than he could chew. He was in over his head, and then some. The trouble was that, when Jay had made his commitment, everything that Colin had touched had turned to gold and he had seemed unassailable. His only failure had been the 12, but that could be put down to 'teething troubles' with the radical gearbox. Colin was a man to whom a phrase like 'teething troubles' came easily. When Chapman promised this and that to Chamberlain, he probably believed almost every word that he uttered. He was more dangerous in that mode than he was when he was simply lying. Colin had every reason to want the Elite to succeed in America.

Porsche had gone from being a maker of Beetle-based specials to becoming a considerable company thanks to America's insatiable appetite for sports cars. The same went for Ferrari. At the time, more than 80 percent of Jaguars, Triumphs and MGs went Stateside, most to the West Coast. It was America which turned the VW Beetle from a quirky machine into a cult. There is no way that Chapman did not want Chamberlain to succeed, but Colin had, in his usual impetuous way, taken several steps further than common sense would have permitted. This impetuousness was at the heart of both Colin's brightest achievements and his nastiest moments. Jay did not see it that way, and there is no reason why he should have done. He had no reason to suspect that his friend was capable both of outright lying, while looking him in the eye, and of self-delusion. Colin seemed to think that if he willed something to happen, then it would happen.

Robin Read tells a very revealing story in a caption to one of the photographs in his book, *Colin Chapman's Lotus*. Colin had personally designed the strut which held up the boot lid on the Elite. Everyone told him that it was not up to the job, but he had designed it so it had to be correct. It wasn't. Owners of Elites soon learned to pack a length of broom handle to prop open the boot lid. Colin never considered a redesign which might actually have worked. He was completely indifferent to the fact that the strut did not do its job.

The Elite was actually little more than an interesting special with stunning looks, and the stunning looks were none of Colin's work. Colin's main contributions to the design of the Elite were the problems. Even in 1957 a mainstream manufacturer ran cars in deserts and beyond the Arctic Circle before attempting to sell them, while Lotus accepted orders for the Elite when the prototype had yet to turn a wheel.

The Elite's target market was centred on that part of California where there is a great deal of sunshine and, therefore, a generous supply of ultra-violet rays. The paintwork on early Elites, applied in a temperate climate, simply could not cope with Californian sunshine. Colin had not thought about that. Colin wanted to sell cars in California and had not realised that the sun shines brighter there than in Hornsey. Robin Read and Ron Hickman soon realised that this was a disaster waiting to happen and they found a paintshop in California which could do a respray to suit local conditions. Robin and Ron negotiated a keen deal, but it still added $150 to every Elite sold and that had to be passed on to the customer. It added to Jay Chamberlain's problems.

Jay was in a desperate position. According to Robin Read, he became so desperate that he began to cook his invoices to Lotus when claiming compensation for rectification. He was so desperate that he had taken to adding a zero to all claims. Ron Hickman, acting on the instructions of Fred Bushell, was sent to investigate.

One of Chamberlain's complaints was that if you accelerated and braked hard in an Elite, and there was no reason for buying one unless you wanted to drive like that, there was a severe difference of opinion between the final drive and the fibreglass shell and the difference was resolved with them parting company. You finished up in a shell in the middle of a freeway. This, in fact, was due to Bristol not building the differential box to the correct specification. Jay was forced to modify the cars he sold to reduce the chances of this happening, and he registered his complaint. Colin, in self-delusional mode, rejected Jay's comments until he was goaded into action. Colin took an Elite off the production line, installed Mike Costin in the passenger seat, and blasted it up and down Delamare Road, Cheshunt. After 20 minutes there was a parting of the ways.

After no more than 20 minutes, Colin sat in the shell of an Elite with its transmission elsewhere. He had to have a major rethink and some poor sucker (a.k.a. valued Lotus client) presumably bought a repair job sold, at best, as a 'works demo' car.

During 1960, poor Jay Chamberlain faded from the Lotus scene in America. His mistake had been to believe his friend. It is unlikely that Chapman had many sleepless nights about what he did to Chamberlain because people like Chapman do not have sleepless nights. The rest of the story of the Elite in America makes sad reading indeed. Lotus imports were taken over by Peter Hessler, who was wanted for fraud to the tune of $500,000 by the Canadian police. Not long after the Mounties arrived on the scene, and before he could appear in court, Hessler died in an accident while demonstrating a Lotus 20 Formula Junior car at Riverside.

The episode was a sorry mess from beginning to end, yet had Chapman been more straight with Chamberlain, it need not have been so.

CHAPTER 11

A SHOEBOX WITH DUSTBIN LIDS FOR WHEELS

ITALY had once produced the world's greatest drivers, but death and age had taken away most of them. Some people blamed the structure of Italian racing at a junior level and, in 1957, the Italian authorities announced a new single-seater category, Formula Junior.

Formula Junior used production car engines and was initially arranged on a capacity/weight ratio so there was a class for 750cc cars, to bring in the French, and there were classes for 1000cc and 1100cc engines. The Americans added more even classes but, mercifully, they did not catch on.

The first maker to build a car for Formula Junior was Stanguellini in 1957 and it resembled a scaled-down Maserati 250F. It was a Grand Prix car for the young driver and the fact that it looked every inch the part was enough to stir the blood. A couple of races were held in Italy in 1957 and then Formula Junior became an Italian national series in 1958. It was a runaway success and Formula Junior went international in 1959 and officially replaced the old 500cc Formula 3 which was well beyond its sell-by date. The first international season was a great success as well, helped in no small measure by the fact that the organisers of the Monaco Grand Prix revived the idea of a support race. The chance to race through the streets of Monte Carlo secured the success of Formula Junior.

Present at Monaco in 1959 were Colin Chapman and John Cooper and both looked at the cars in the Formula Junior race and knew that they could do better. They weren't the only ones, and soon Formula Junior cars were being made all over Britain. The first of the established specialists to complete a car was Elva. Elva's front-engined car won a couple of minor races in Britain in late 1959 (the only bespoke FJ cars in these races were Elvas) but that was enough to secure Elva a full order book.

At the 1959 Boxing Day Meeting at Brands Hatch most attention was focused on the first British Formula Junior race with a representative entry and there were new cars from Lola, Gemini, Cooper and Lotus. Any new Lotus was an event but reaction to this one was sceptical: 'a shoebox with dustbin lids for wheels' was how one correspondent described it. It was the Lotus 18, Colin's first mid-engined car, and it appeared that he had made a major blunder for, even with Alan Stacey behind the wheel, it was slow and its progress was not helped by a couple of spins. An Elva, driven by Peter Arundell, won and a Lola, with Peter Ashdown on board, was second and both were front-engined cars, just like the successful European FJ cars. Another Elva was third. Cooper was nowhere and neither was Lotus.

In fact, the Lotus's designated race engine, tuned by Cosworth, had blown up, and Stacey had to use a makeshift unit which was not to full racing specification. The crucial point about the engine was that it was the new 105E unit which Ford had just launched in its new Anglia. It was Ford's first small-capacity engine with overhead valves and it was notably 'over-square', which meant it had the potential for high revs. Colin had heard about the 105E engine through Ron Hickman and he was able to prise some units from Ford for Cosworth to tune. The Ford 105E engine, tuned by Cosworth, would make Lotus virtually unbeatable in Formula Junior and establish Cosworth Engineering as a company out of the usual run of tuning outfits.

It would also give Ford priceless publicity, which helped to bring the company into motor racing, a move that it had previously resisted. Ford's image had been that of a stolid, worthy maker, but before long Ford, Cosworth and Lotus had become more or less synonymous.

Alan Stacey had handling problems with his Lotus 18 at Brands Hatch because its springs were too soft. The car had been assembled in a rush and the springs had been chosen by guesswork. Its race debut was also its first test session, but Colin and his team soon put the car right.

Stacey was thought to be an exceptional driver, with the ability to drive at 100 percent from the moment he dropped the clutch. He was a farmer from Essex and, being a wild young thing, he had crashed his motorcycle and had lost a leg, so had learned to walk with an artificial one. Alan used to impress girls by picking up a fork and driving it into his tin leg. He had mastered the artificial leg so well that few noticed, even though his racing cars had to be fitted with a hand throttle.

When it came to international races, drivers had to pass a medical test. With only one naturally working leg, Alan was at a disadvantage. He would present his good leg and the doctor would tap him on the knee to prove that he had a reflex. Then another driver, it was usually Innes Ireland, would do something outrageous to distract the doctor. Alan would then present his one good leg again. Innes Ireland was a colourful character who worked hard and played hard. Innes had an enormous appetite for women and whiskey and all of the most outrageous stories told about him came from his own lips. With Hill and Allison going to other teams, Stacey and Ireland were chosen to lead Team Lotus.

The second appearance of the new Lotus 18 came in the Argentine Grand Prix on 7 February where (sensation!) Innes Ireland put it in second place on the grid and led the race until all sorts of troubles intervened. He eventually finished sixth with one brake not working and the steering deranged but suddenly everybody had to take notice of Lotus.

On the long flight back to England, John Cooper put his head together with Jack Brabham and they sketched the T53 'Lowline'. Jack had been in touch with an old friend, Ron Tauranac, and Ron had airmailed him the parameters for the suspension. Between them, Brabham and Tauranac would go on to give Chapman a very hard time in the production racing car market. As soon as they arrived home in England, Jack Brabham, his teammate Bruce McLaren, John Cooper and Cooper's draughtsman, Owen Maddock, set to work on the new car. It was ready to race within three months and, against all predictions for the Lotus 18, the new Cooper would take Jack Brabham to his second world championship title.

The spaceframe of the Lotus 18 was a properly triangulated affair. There was a heavy duty chassis for Formula 1 and Formula 2, and a lighter chassis for Formula Junior. In a sense, Colin had made a 'scientific' Cooper and, according to Stirling Moss, who is the last word on the subject, the 18 was a less forgiving car than contemporary Coopers but, within a more narrow envelope, it had better road holding and traction. Where Colin really made his advance, however, and turned the fortunes of Lotus at a stroke, was by making a single model into a range, as he had done with the Eleven. Moreover, Lotus had the cream of new talent for its works teams in the lesser formulae.

Thus, at Goodwood on 19 March 1960, in the first British meeting of the year, the Lotus 18 FJ car had its first win in the hands of Jim Clark, who had been drafted into Team Lotus. Colin had not forgotten his brush with Clark at the Boxing Day Brands Hatch meeting in 1958. Colin had followed Clark's career but not even he had latched on to how good Clark would become. In that race at Goodwood the real headline was John Surtees, who was making his debut on four wheels. John had five motorcycle world championships under his belt at the time, but he had not so much as seen a car race until he lined up on the grid in his new Cooper, entered by Ken Tyrrell. Surtees would be the last motorcycle racer to make the transition to cars, although previously it had been a well-worn path.

Clark won from Surtees and in third place was Trevor Taylor in his own car, but running under the Team Lotus umbrella. That race at Goodwood set the pattern for the year and by the end of the season the works Lotus team of Clark, Taylor and

Peter Arundell, who had defected from Elva, using Cosworth-Ford engines, had won virtually everything in sight. Clark and Taylor actually tied for first place in the British Formula Junior Championship. The only rival which gave Lotus any trouble was Cooper, but Cooper's BMC engines did not have the measure of the Ford.

There had been more than 50 makers of Formula Junior cars at the beginning of 1960 and since they used 12 different types of engine, there were about 150 chassis/engine combinations to choose from, but by the end of the season Lotus, Ford and Cosworth had wiped most of them out as both America and Europe turned to England for their FJ cars. That one season destroyed the embryo racing car industries in every other country and changed the balance of power in the sport.

National headlines followed the 18's second Formula 1 race, the Glover Trophy at Goodwood, when Ireland beat Moss's Cooper by nearly three seconds and, in the Formula 2 Lavant Cup, Innes beat Moss's Porsche by six seconds. In a burst of media frenzy Ireland was hailed as a new star. The two wins made the front pages of most newspapers and the Lotus 18 was dubbed a 'wonder' car.

Moss's entrant, Rob Walker, ordered a Lotus. Colin was delighted because Moss stood head and shoulders above any other driver of the time. Only Cooper works drivers got their hands on a 'Lowline', but Colin had no problem in selling his latest car to Walker. It was better to have Moss in a Lotus than a Cooper and Stirling would win four Grands Prix in a Lotus before Team Lotus took its first world championship win.

Innes Ireland also won the International Trophy, beating Brabham in the new 'Lowline' Cooper by a couple of seconds with Graham Hill, in the new mid-engined BRM P48, in third. At Monaco, however, Moss had his new Lotus 18 and those were the days when a driver could make a difference. In fact, Stirling had both his old Cooper and his new Lotus and after trying both in practice, Moss elected to drive the Lotus, which he had put on pole. He won even though he had to pit to have a plug lead replaced. Towards the end, he had felt severe vibration behind him – the engine mounts had broken – which did not reflect well on the strength of the design.

Moss and Walker gave Lotus its first world championship win just as they had opened the score for Cooper two years before. It shouldn't have mattered to Colin that it wasn't a works car, Lotus had scored its first Grand Prix win. Peter Ross, who was with the team for the race recalls, however, that Colin was furious that it had been Rob Walker's Lotus and not a works car which had won.

Mike Cooper, son of John Cooper, recalls that his father felt the same when Rob Walker stole a march on him by winning first the 1958 Argentine Grand Prix (courtesy of Stirling Moss) and then the Monaco Grand Prix with Maurice Trintignant driving.

Moss and Ireland sat on the front row for the Dutch Grand Prix with Brabham in between. Brabham led from Moss and Ireland but, on lap 17, one of Jack's rear wheels dislodged part of the concrete kerbing and propelled some of it at Moss's car close behind. Since the kerbstone weighed about 25lb, it is lucky that it only hit one of Stirling's front wheels, not his head, but that was enough to shatter the wheel and Moss lost two laps replacing it. Brabham won comfortably from Ireland but Moss, as usual, was the star as he drove back to fourth place.

Almost unnoticed was Jim Clark making his Grand Prix debut. He was not particularly quick in practice and he retired in the race, but it was less than six months since he had first driven a single-seater. Colin had an incredible knack for choosing drivers, but Jim had not been his first choice: that had been John Surtees. John had not fully committed to car racing and, during 1960, he took his sixth and seventh motorcycle world championships. In 1960, he flitted between two wheels and four. In retrospect, all sorts of claims have been made for Clark, but in 1960 the hot news was Surtees. Clark is supposed to have had natural talent oozing from every pore, but this was not the case. Jimmy did not burst on the scene as Michael Schumacher did, or as John Surtees did. Clark was no better than a promising youngster in Colin's eyes, Colin wanted Surtees. John, however, reckoned that he had a lot to learn and the place to learn was not in a works team where the spotlight would be on him.

The season was settling down to a straight Cooper vs Lotus affair, with the BRMs looking stronger all the time, and Ferrari struggling, when calamity struck at the Belgian Grand Prix. Mike Taylor had bought the prototype Formula 1 Lotus 18 and was making his bid for the big time. Belgium was to be his first Grand Prix. Then, during practice, a weld in his steering column broke and he crashed heavily, breaking his ribs, clavicle and neck. Taylor survived, and later sued Lotus successfully, but he never raced again. Not many people have successfully sued the maker of a racing car, but Mike Taylor did. The evidence against the maker has to be overwhelming for an action to succeed.

Also in practice, Moss had a rear stub axle fail on his Lotus 18 and lost a wheel at 135mph in the Burnenville curve. Only his superb reactions saved Stirling from being killed, because he managed to spin his three-wheeler round, which rubbed off speed, and he hit the bank backwards so that the engine took the impact – no car of the time could withstand a 135mph front impact. Even so, among the injuries he sustained were a broken nose, cracked vertebrae, broken ribs and broken legs. Colin immediately grounded all three works cars and discovered that the rear hubs on two of them were cracked because they had been machined wrongly. All the hubs were replaced by those from a different batch. The incident gave nobody much confidence, however. Colin had taken Lotus into Formula 1, but had not installed a quality control system to match his ambitions. Lotus was still operating as though it was churning out Elevens by the dozen. The Eleven was generally a safe car because in normal use its components were not unduly stressed.

Although Moss made a remarkable recovery, the incident changed the face of the season because his absence altered the balance of the competition. Two Lotus drivers were out, both seriously injured because of failures on the cars, and Lotus's

Colin Chapman and Hazel Williams (the future Mrs Chapman) mud-plugging in 1950 in 'Austin Seven Special'. It was only in retrospect that the car became the Lotus Mk 1. *(FF)*

Hazel Williams at the wheel of the prototype Lotus Mk 6, Silverstone, 1952. The car was fitted with a Ford Consul engine reduced in size to qualify for the 1500cc class. *(FF)*

Colin demonstrates the lightness of the spaceframe of the Lotus Eleven outside his father's pub. It weighed half a hundredweight and then a hundredweight was the standard measure for a sack of potatoes. *(LAT)*

The Eleven received that most rare of things at the time, a press launch. The car has not quite been finished (there are no covers over the headlights), but the launch was timed to hit a dead period for motoring magazines. *(LAT)*

John Cooper, 'that bloody blacksmith', and Colin. The two were friendly, but not close friends. They are possibly the two most important figures in British motor racing history. *(PN)*

Colin stops to chat having won in his Lotus Mk 9. No champagne, no razzmatazz, just a bleak, damp, wind-swept road. *(LAT)*

Colin again, this time seated in the first Lotus single-seater, the Formula 2 Mk 12. It was the first Lotus to feature the famous 'wobbly web' wheels which were designed by Gilbert 'Mac' MacIntosh, one of the unsung heroes of the early days of Lotus. *(FF)*

Colin with his former mechanic, Graham Hill. Graham's career as a racing driver took off thanks to Chapman allowing him the use of a car. They are at the 1959 Aintree 200, where Graham led the Team Lotus Formula 1 effort. *(DJ)*

Colin at the wheel of an Elite at press day at Goodwood in 1959. Not only was the Elite among the prettiest cars ever made, it won its class at Le Mans six years in a row. *(FF)*

Off to Le Mans in 1959 in a Ford Zodiac. Colin liked big saloons and would soon start a love affair with American cars. A style consultant would say, 'Lose the pens in the in the top pocket, Colin.' *(DJ)*

Colin and Hazel at Le Mans, 1959. To their left is Graham Hill, to their right is Bette Hill. *(DJ)*

Scrutineering at Le Mans, 1959, and Mike Costin holds the 'recalibrated' ruler which 'proved' that the cockpit width on the Lotus 15 was legal. It was a typical Lotus scam of the time. *(DJ)*

Stirling Moss soon had his hands on a Lotus 18, Chapman's first mid-engined car. Moss is seen at Monaco in 1960 on his way to scoring Lotus's first world championship race victory, the first of 79 Grand Prix wins for Lotus. *(FF)*

Peter Warr in his works Lotus Super Seven. Peter became a long-term fixture of Team Lotus. The Seven became an icon, copied on every continent. *(FF)*

Innes Ireland, Colin and Jim Clark all looking pretty serious, but 1961 was not a great year for Team Lotus. *(DJ)*

Colin with his first wholly-owned aeroplane, a Piper Comanche, in 1961. He is beginning to display the physical characteristics which would earn him the nickname 'Chunky'. Not every style adviser would recommend the combination of a flat hat and a waistcoat. *(DJ)*

Colin 'jets' the carburettors at Le Mans, 1959. When was the last time you saw a Formula 1 team owner, as Colin then was, actually working on a car? *(DJ)*

Jimmy Clark making victory look so easy in his Lotus 25 at the 1964 Easter Monday Goodwood meeting. Clark was the only driver to win a Grand Prix in a Lotus 25 or its successor, the 33. He also won 19 of the 23 Grands Prix victories achieved by the 1.5-litre Coventry Climax V8 series. *(FF)*

reputation took a nosedive. Many years later, Jackie Stewart would refuse to drive a Lotus because he believed them to be inherently unsafe and Ken Tyrrell once remarked, of Chapman, 'That man should have his own private graveyard.' It is inconceivable that Colin would have put a driver's life at risk, but the reputation for making dangerous cars hung around him for the rest of his life.

In the Belgian Grand Prix itself the brilliant young Chris Bristow crashed his Cooper and was killed. In fact his body was unrecognisable and, as he passed by the body, Jim Clark's Lotus was splattered with blood. Clark nearly threw up and he came close to quitting the sport. Then Alan Stacey was struck by a bird in the face, crashed and died. Many have questioned the reason for Stacey's accident, believing it to be a cover-up in the wake of the two serious crashes in practice, but Alan's best friend, John Whitmore, affirms that Alan died because a pheasant hit him in the face.

As they left Spa, both Clark and Ireland were pretty sombre. Jimmy admitted later that the weekend made him evaluate his commitment to motor racing while Ireland said later that he too had considered giving up and the multiple tragedies changed his attitude as a driver and his attitude to life in general. Innes certainly changed his attitude towards Colin who, on the surface at least, appeared not to have been too perturbed by the multiple disasters.

Nobody had picked up the fact that the rear hubs had been incorrectly machined and that shook Innes, who was a gifted engineer who had completed an apprenticeship at Rolls-Royce. Lotus was simply not fit to win Grands Prix when something as fundamental as not checking major components was allowed to happen. It was, perhaps, an indication that Lotus was missing having all the guys from the aircraft industry around.

Jack Brabham, and Cooper, won at Spa, and Brabham won at Reims as well, which is the only occasion when a Formula 1 team has fielded three Scotsmen: Innes Ireland, Jim Clark and Ron Flockhart. Jack Brabham, and his Cooper, ran rings round them.

For the British Grand Prix, Lotus gave Surtees a drive and he responded by finishing second to Brabham, with Ireland in third place. Without Moss Lotus was not looking as sharp as it had at the beginning of the year. The new Cooper 'Lowline' was a very good car and Brabham was an underrated driver. Jim Clark, who would become a star with Lotus, was still learning his craft: he was not quick straight out of the box.

Incredibly, given the extent of his injuries, Stirling Moss was back for the Portuguese Grand Prix with a new Lotus 18, this time with a Colotti gearbox which necessitated outboard rear brakes. He was not on the pace, however, and had a troubled race even before a brake snatched and caused him to spin. Trying to get the car started again by going downhill on the pavement led to his disqualification. John Surtees, however, added to his growing reputation by leading in his Lotus 18 until leaking fuel covered his brake pedal and his foot slipped at a crucial time.

Clark had crashed his car in practice, it had been repaired and the body held together by masking tape, but he took things easy and came in third behind the works Coopers of Brabham and McLaren.

With the Portuguese win Brabham secured his second world championship and then the British teams boycotted the Italian Grand Prix because the organisers insisted on using the bankings at Monza. The British teams insisted that the bankings were unsafe, though they had all raced on them in 1959 without incident. Indeed, Moss had won in a Cooper. The subtext was that the use of the bankings favoured Ferrari and the Italian organisers wanted a red car to win. Ferrari hadn't won a Grand Prix all year: its cars were powerful, but still had the engine in front of the driver. Colin was involved in the boycott. The pounding that the cars received on the concrete Monza bankings would have shown up any weakness in his cars. That was something which Colin could not face – the previous year the spaceframe of the 16 had developed cracks at Monza. They were not terminal fractures, but quite enough to give pause for thought, especially after Spa when five drivers had been entered in Lotus cars and only two ended the weekend out of hospital or a coffin. The Italian Grand Prix was therefore a Ferrari benefit and it would be the last time that a front-engined car would win a world championship race.

There was only one other round of the championship, the United States Grand Prix at Riverside. At Riverside Moss and Ireland rounded off Lotus's late season revival by taking first and second. Stirling says:

> I didn't know that Mike Taylor sued Lotus, after his crash at Spa, that sort of thing never crossed my mind. I thought Colin was a brilliant man, but with no sense of humour. After I won the United States Grand Prix I was presented with cake which was decorated with a little Lotus 18 made from sugar. I took a knife and cut off the right rear wheel. Everyone thought that was hilarious, but Colin was furious.

'That doesn't surprise me,' says Ron Hickman. 'Colin could never take a joke against himself. You could tell a joke about a vicar and a show girl, and he'd laugh out loud, but subtle stuff, like word play, was lost on him.'

Cooper swept the Constructors' Cup, but in second place, in a spectacular reversal of fortune, was Lotus. Most of Lotus's points had been earned by Stirling Moss, however – Team Lotus had yet to score a win. Team Lotus had yet to learn how to win. The Lotus 18 had proved itself to be the cream of the field in every class it entered and nobody accused Colin of copying Cooper. Almost everyone had latched on to the fact that the engine should go behind the driver. Even Ferrari had built a mid-engined car. The one exception was Aston Martin, whose car moved at a snail's pace.

During 1960 Lotus made a sports car version of the all-purpose 18 and laid down a small batch of them for 1961. It was officially known as the 19 but since it was pitched against the Cooper Monaco it was nicknamed the 'Monte Carlo', but the name did not stick. Though people admired and respected Lotus, they did not have much affection for it and you need affection before a car is given a nickname. The 19 was very quick, and superior to the Cooper Monaco, but then having Moss and Gurney among regular drivers did not harm it. It did not, however, appear in classic races, largely because such racing did not figure in the plans of those who were allowed to buy the cars. The 19 featured only in sprint races, which were often the ones with the largest prize funds.

One significant move which Colin made during 1960 was to persuade Lotus to buy a second-hand Miles Messenger, an elderly single-prop four-seater aeroplane. Colin not only had a private pilot's licence, but also his RAF wings, and, by all accounts, he was a very skilled pilot even if (typical Chapman) he did not fly according to the instruction manual. In buying the aircraft, Lotus became the first team from the European motor racing community to go airborne. Before long the Miles Messenger would be replaced by a Piper Comanche, a much more advanced design. As in many things, where Colin led, others followed and before long other motor racing people were arriving at circuits in their own aircraft. Motor racing took off in a big way in more than one sense in the 1960s.

During 1961, Lotus underwent a subtle change. Peter Ross had gone to work in Belgium. Mike Costin's three-year service contract had come to an end and he had decamped to Cosworth. All of the old volunteers, the men from aviation who saw Lotus as a bright challenge, had gone. And there was still an acute problem, the Elite, Lotus's flagship car. It has often been written that Lotus lost money on every Elite sold and that may have been true about the cars which went through the books.

With Jay Chamberlain having difficulty in moving the Elite in America, and Bristol still making them, there was a stack of body/chassis units outside the factory, quietly rotting. Before the end of the year, Bristol would be owed £100,000 by Lotus. During 1961 Colin had to bite the bullet. He did something he never wanted to do: he offered the Elite for sale as a kit. He wanted to be a proper motor manufacturer, but he had failed. Selling the Elite as a kit reduced his status, but it also brought the Elite to under £1,300 in Britain because, as a kit, it escaped purchase tax.

During 1961 Lotus completed its job of wiping out almost every other aspiring car maker both in Europe and America with the Mk 20 Formula Junior car, which was low, clean and as stunning as the 18 had been functional. Nothing could touch it either on the track or in the paddock. It made everything else, even the Cooper T56, look swollen.

Colin instigated a policy of inviting potential customers to test days where they would not only drive the cars, but be subjected to the Chapman charm. The works drivers would be on hand and the youngsters would be made to feel pretty important. It was partly flannel, of course, but it was also a case of Colin having an empathy with drivers and a wish to get the very best into his cars. Derek Bell and Peter Gethin are just two drivers who admit to buying a Lotus because of the special treatment they received on one of these customer days.

Cooper and Lotus had tied up Formula 1 in 1960, but neither looked in good shape for 1961. The FIA had decided that Formula 1 would have a capacity limit of 1500cc. This meant that every Formula 2 car became a Formula 1 car on 1 January 1961 and every race had as many starters as the organisers wanted. The new formula worked in that it brought close racing and full grids. Apart from the eight races which counted for the world championship there were a further 21 non-championship events, many of which were promoted as Grands Prix. From the point of view of spreading the popularity of the sport, the 1500cc formula was a success, but the British constructors had kicked against the proposal.

The Brits, with Colin to the fore, had thought that they could use force of numbers to keep the 2.5-litre formula, but they were wrong. The FIA dug in its heels and the British constructors, who had been confident of winning, were left without a competitive engine. Ferrari, of course, had one, and Enzo Ferrari had been active in promoting the new formula since it played into his hands. BRM and Coventry Climax set to work, but they were behind. Cooper, Lotus and BRM all began 1961 with the four-cylinder Coventry Climax FPF engine and that was no match for Ferrari's new V6 units. There seemed no way that Lotus could maintain its new position as a leading Formula 1 team, except that Stirling Moss drove a Lotus and he pulled off two of the most remarkable Grand Prix wins even in his remarkable career.

In retaliation to the new formula, the British devised a 3-litre category called the Inter-Continental Formula, though most entries were actually 1960-style F1 cars. Five races were staged and each was won by a Cooper with the final score being Moss 3, Brabham 2. The significant thing is that Stirling had a choice of both Lotus and Cooper chassis and he chose Cooper. This rather spoils the story, told by some, that the Lotus 18 was superior to the Cooper T53 'Lowline'.

Ferrari sewed up the championship at the Italian Grand Prix where two things happened which had an effect on Lotus history. Coventry Climax had begun delivering its V8 engine. Cooper, being world champions, had the first, and the next two went to Lotus and to Rob Walker since he was the entrant of Stirling Moss. Walker's chief mechanic, Alf Francis, hacked about at the back of the modified Lotus 18/21 Stirling had been driving and installed the new engine. Stirling tried the car at Monza and decided that he didn't really like it. Innes Ireland realised that if a Lotus won at Monza then Lotus still had a chance of clinching the Constructors' Championship and if anyone could win with a Lotus, it was Moss.

Innes therefore persuaded Colin to allow Stirling to drive the works Lotus with the V8 engine, the car that Innes himself was to have driven. Colin agreed and the car was handed over to Rob Walker, who merely replaced the bodywork so that it raced in his colours. This was an act of supreme sportsmanship, but while Innes could be a scamp, he held gentlemanly ideals.

On lap two of the race, the Ferrari of Wolfgang 'Taffy' von Trips and the Lotus of Jim Clark touched, sending them both into lurid spins. Clark was attempting to pass von Trips, but Taffy had moved over to make his own move on the man in front of him. One of Taffy's rear wheels and one of Jimmy's front wheels occupied the same space for a fraction of a second. It was a racing accident, neither driver was at fault. Two cars touched and while Jimmy's car spun out of the race to the infield in one direction, in the other direction the Ferrari spun violently on rougher ground. The upshot was that von Trips and 14 spectators were killed.

The Italians are crazy about motor racing, but the Italians also have some of the strictest laws when it comes to examining the cause of any fatality in the sport. There loomed over Jimmy and Team Lotus possible charges of manslaughter.

The next race, and the final round of the 1961 world championship, was the United States Grand Prix. Ferrari gave it a miss despite the fact that their new world champion, Phil Hill, was American. Innes Ireland won in America and so gave Team Lotus its first world championship win. Innes was a very honest man and he knew that on this occasion he had been lucky to inherit a win. There was no pretence about Innes, but a debut win for a team is a debut win and it was Innes who pulled it off. His car had stayed together when it mattered, though he had notched up a couple of wins in non-championship races during 1961.

BRM offered Innes a drive for 1962 and he turned them down because he was a Lotus man. A couple of weeks after Innes gave Team Lotus its first world championship win, he turned up for the preview of the London Motor Show. As Innes told the story, Colin was presiding over the Lotus stand and Innes greeted him and lightly referred to plans for the following year. Innes recalled: 'Colin looked furtive and started to look at his feet. He then said, "There is no place for you next year."' It was a joke, of course, except that with his stomach rolling into a small clenched ball, Innes knew that it was not. For once, Colin averted his gaze. It was an act of betrayal of the most cowardly sort, according to Innes, who always said that Colin could not give him a reason, rather than would not give him one.

Innes had turned down an offer from BRM because he could not conceive that he would have to negotiate a contract with Colin for 1962. Worse, he assumed that he had been forced out of his seat by machinations set in motion by Jim Clark though, many years later, with Jimmy in his grave, he learned that this was not the case. To his dying day, Innes grieved that he did not make his peace with Clark. Also to his dying day, Innes never knew why he been sacked. As he saw it, he had just given Team Lotus its first Grand Prix win. He felt a deep hurt.

Innes was liked by all who knew him, but everyone knew that had the breathalyser been around there were many times when he could have been hauled off the grid for failing the test. Peter Arundell believes that this was the reason for Innes's sacking. A lot of alcohol sloshed around in motor racing at the time, but Innes's fondness for Scotch was remarkable. Unfortunately, when he had taken of liquor he was liable to pick fights.

At the time when Innes found out that he had been sacked, Ron Hickman was having lunch with Fred Bushell and Colin. Ron says:

Innes had gone to the Motor Show and someone on the Dunlop stand said that he was sorry that he wouldn't be with Lotus the following year. Innes found out where we were eating and phoned and asked for Colin, who told the maitre d' to tell Innes he wasn't there. The maitre d' said that he had told Innes that he was there. Colin absolutely refused to take the call and eventually turned to me and said, 'Now you are a director, you have to learn to take the rough with the smooth, you deal with it.'

I took the phone, Innes swore at me and slammed down the phone. He was right to say that Colin was cowardly, Colin hadn't had the guts to tell him, but Innes wasn't sacked. He'd had a three-year contract with Lotus and it had expired. Innes merely assumed that he could negotiate another contract, but he had no right to assume that.

Colin had Ireland and Clark, and they did not get on. Jimmy was quiet, introspective, and Innes was an extrovert who could be quite nasty. Colin simply saw Jimmy as the future and, besides, he was sure Innes would find another drive.

Cedric Selzer, who was a Team Lotus mechanic, 1961–4, says:

> The fact is that Colin and Innes did not get on, they were poles apart. Colin tolerated Innes because he was a good driver. I know for a fact that it was a joint decision between Colin and Geoff Murdoch of Esso because they felt that Jimmy could win the world championship and Innes couldn't. The big problem was that everyone, except Innes, knew that he wasn't going to be retained.

Clark was a shy man who chewed his finger nails to the quick. In a racing car, however, he was transformed. He bonded with his car and made it flow. According to many of those around them, Colin and Jimmy could communicate on almost a telepathic level. It was a rare case of a driver and a designer being completely in tune with each other. According to Cedric Selzer, 'That was only true from 1963 on, when Jimmy started he had very little idea. He could tell you that his car was oversteering, or whatever, but he had no idea why. It took him time to learn.'

Jimmy would be with Lotus for his entire career as a professional driver and, when he died, he had entered his ninth year with the team. Such a relationship was unique in motor racing at the time, and it has not happened often since. Clark and Chapman worked as a team, each putting total trust in the other, unlike the typical team which simply employed drivers. With Innes gone, Colin promoted Trevor Taylor from the Formula Junior team to being Jimmy's partner, while Peter Arundell, who now led the Formula Junior team, and did so brilliantly, received the odd drive in Formula 1. Colin had established a policy of nurturing and promoting young talent and this he did more often and more consistently than any other team owner in history.

CHAPTER 12

A BATH TUB ON WHEELS

OR 1962 Colin designed the the Lotus 24 to accommodate the new Coventry Climax engine, though when BRM made its V8 available, some 24s were fitted with that. The 24 had a conventional spaceframe but the front springs were mounted inside the body, which harked back to the Mk 7 'Clairmonte'. Meanwhile Colin was at work on the 25, the first Formula 1 car with monocoque construction, if most writers are to be believed. The structure on the 25 was not a true monocoque and the front suspension and the engine and rear suspension were carried on tubular subframes.

Colin knew that the 25 did not have a true monocoque and he never used the term: it was the press that used it and Colin did not disabuse them. In fact, Colin hit the nail on the head when he called it a 'bath tub' monocoque since the central structure of the 25 resembled a bath tub. Colin was aware of his legend and if people wanted to tell a story about him, which reflected well on him, he wasn't going to go out of his way to deny it.

From early in his career as a constructor, Colin had known how to work the press. The launch of the Eleven had been an object lesson in PR, as had the launch of the Elite. Considering the flow of exciting new models from Lotus, and the fact that Colin was the most charismatic figure in world motor racing, there were not that many formal interviews with him. He was always approachable but motor racing journalists in the 1960s tended to treat him with reverence. This is a shame because a sharp writer could have pointed out that the Lotus 25 had a configuration, down to the inboard suspension, similar to the Trimax Formula 3 car made by Irwin

'Spike' Rhiando in 1949. As it was, the press seized on the the word 'monocoque' and so, for ever after, a false story was spread.

According to legend, Colin had a sudden flash of inspiration over lunch at the Maple Leaf Café in Waltham Abbey High Street in 1960–1. He reached for a paper napkin and sketched the outline. It was a defining moment, says the legend, but Frank Costin and Mac Macintosh had drawn the outline for a monocoque design in 1954 and they passed over the drawings. Also in 1954 Connaught was at work on a semi-monocoque, mid-engined design, the Type J. This was to have the Coventry Climax FPF V8 'Godiva' engine, which was not released, in a stressed geodetic structure. Connaught had even designed, and built, a five-speed transaxle and cutaway drawings of the car appeared in *Autosport* in 1955. Like everyone else in the British motor racing community, Colin devoured *Autosport* every week. It is inconceivable that he missed the Connaught Type J.

In his four-part series for *Motor Racing*, Colin wrote:

Among the many special features of the Mk VIII Lotus was a semi-monococque-type of body panelling. Whilst this has been quite a worthwhile advantage in weight saving I can now say that the snags which arise during routine servicing, repairs to accident damage and so on are such as to render it inadvisable for sports/racing cars. This year's car and all the production Mk VIIIs have much more easily accessible components and more easily removable body panelling.

The year 1954 seems to have been the time when Colin first contemplated the advantages and disadvantages of monocoque construction, which supports what Frank Costin and Mac Macintosh have said. Frank Costin recalled being at a Racing Car Show with his Marcos GT car, which was constructed from plywood. 'Colin came up and was intrigued by the car and he asked all the questions a man like Colin would ask. I sketched out the design which had two large stressed tubes and tubular subframes, just like the Lotus 25.' Ron Hickman reckons that this was the Racing Car Show of 1961–2, in which case the Lotus 25 was already being developed. Frank told the story to the author several times over the years and always gave the impression that it was when the Marcos first appeared at a Racing Car Show, which was January 1960.

During 1961, Cooper worked on a monocoque which was rather more advanced than that on the Lotus 25, featuring as it did aluminium honeycomb stiffening. Its development took a long time and the Coopers, probably correctly, worried about being able to repair it after a crash. When the Coopers decided to scrap their monocoque they found that it was so strong that it was extraordinarily difficult to break up.

Just to add further confusion, Ron Hickman, the principle designer of the Elan, claims:

It has never been any secret that the twin-tube inspiration for the Lotus 25 was the (single) steel backbone of the Elan.

Though I was Lotus's Chief Projects Engineer, which meant I was in charge of the road cars, I had little to do with the competition cars, but I was up to speed about them. I know that it was John Standen who was the Chief Buyer for Lotus who made the suggestion for the Lotus 25.

All the above make the story about sudden inspiration at the Maple Leaf Café and the sketch on the paper napkin appear, at best, extremely dubious.

The 25 would not appear until the Dutch Grand Prix at the end of May and before that there was not only the Monaco Grand Prix, but a host of non-championship events. In one of them, the Glover Trophy at Goodwood, Stirling Moss would suffer a crash which ended his glittering career.

Rob Walker had been allowed to buy Coventry Climax V8 engines which were on restricted supply. Rob and Stirling had a secret agreement with Enzo Ferrari to use a Ferrari in 1962, and Walker also had a Lotus 24 on order. Neither new car was ready by the 1962 Goodwood Easter Monday Meeting, but Walker loaned the British Racing Partnership (BRP) his Lotus 18/21, modified to accept the Climax V8 engine. The work was undertaken by Walker's chief mechanic, Alf Francis, a motor-racing legend who had even published a ghosted autobiography. Alf was a superb mechanic who had ambitions to be an engineer, but he was no engineer. Stirling says, 'Alf was like an excellent secretary who thinks that she can run her own business. More often than not she comes a cropper.'

When Colin saw the Francis conversion, he laughed. He reckoned that the rear of the Lotus had the torsional rigidity of a sponge cake. Alf Francis's conversion robbed the rear of the car of about 75 percent of its torsional rigidity, as Stirling later discovered. This flexibility at the back would go a long way to explaining why the car had a sticking throttle in the Lombank Trophy at Snetterton and why, at Goodwood, Stirling had gear selection problems which cost him considerable time in the pits.

There is no definitive explanation for Stirling's crash, though Robert Edwards's authorised biography has unearthed previously unpublished letters between Stirling's father and an eye witness who maintained that Stirling was closing on Graham Hill's BRM at such a prodigious rate that Graham had not realised that Stirling was about to overtake and chose a line that squeezed Moss. To avoid a collision, Stirling took to the grass and hit a concealed concrete slab, probably left over from the war when Goodwood had been RAF Westhampnett. The impact nearly threw him out of the car and also took his feet off the pedals so he had no control. He could not spin the car as he had done at Spa in 1960. For fractions of a second, he was a passenger and that was long enough for him to hit an earth bank head on.

Another eye witness to the accident was a young engineer, afterwards an amateur racing driver, Tony Christie. Tony is adamant that Stirling's car was out of gear when he entered the corner. When, 35 years later, Tony was introduced to Stirling, Moss conceded that his car being out of gear was possible because he had previously had gear selection problems.

The two accounts are not mutually exclusive.

Whatever the reason, Moss nearly lost his life and it was most unfortunate that it was in a Lotus. It did not add lustre to Colin's reputation, but the car was a hybrid modified by someone without Colin's scientific training. Moss's crash could have been fatal had either of the aluminium fuel tanks on either side of the driver been ruptured, but though the car's spaceframe was severely buckled at the front, the sides retained their integrity. That would not have been true of many another car of the period. The part of the car for which Colin was responsible actually held up rather well considering the force of the impact. The race in which Stirling crashed was won by Graham Hill, his first Formula 1 win (he was six months older than Moss) and the first for the new V8 BRM.

Jimmy was absent from Goodwood since he was running in the Pau Grand Prix. Then, in the International Trophy at Silverstone, a few weeks later, Jimmy was cruising to a win when Graham caught and passed him in the last corner. Moss had stood head and shoulders above any driver, but when Graham caught Jimmy on the last corner at Silverstone, and won by a few feet, Stirling was in a coma with his left side paralysed. Few thought that he would ever race again and even when he came out of his coma, his traumatised brain meant that his speech was unintelligible. Stirling was in a state but every time a top driver is lost to motor racing people look for the next star.

British enthusiasts split into two camps, those behind the ebullient Hill and BRM and those behind Lotus and the introspective Clark. Hill came across as a Battle of Britain pilot born out of his time and, though few of his supporters would ever credit him with the natural ability evident in Clark, they admired him for the way he had made himself into a top-line driver through sheer grit. Hill's widow, Bette, says: 'Graham was not a great natural talent, but he always reckoned that there was only one limit, and he could learn that limit.'

The Hill/Clark battle would go down to the wire at the South African Grand Prix, and in addition to the world championship events the two frequently met in lesser F1 races. Enthusiasts had plenty of opportunity to see the pair in action, each man clearly superior to any teammate, and with the added edge that after more than a decade of failure, BRM had finally got things right. The chief designer at BRM was Tony Rudd, who some years later would join Lotus.

The Dutch Grand Prix was held on 20 May and there was a sensation in the paddock when Lotus arrived with a Lotus 24 for Trevor Taylor and a 25 for Clark. Innes Ireland had been snapped up by the British Racing Partnership which was run by Stirling Moss's manager, Ken Gregory, together with Stirling's father, Alfred, and Stirling himself was on the board of directors. BRP had bought Lotus 24s and when Innes saw the new car he asked Colin, 'When are we going be able to get one?' 'You're not,' came the bland reply. 'This is next year's car.'

In *Sports Car and Lotus Owner*, October 1961, Colin had told John Blunsden, 'We have in mind a pretty radical departure for the new works Formula 1 cars for the

1962 season.' Given usual lead times, it means that Blunsden had spoken to Colin in late August/early September. Colin's words were clear, they were public and they were ignored. In particular, Colin had emphasised the word, 'works'.

The 24 had the same suspension as the 25, the difference was that the chassis of the 25 was about twice as rigid as that of the 24. This allowed Chapman and Clark to set up the suspension to a level of subtlety previously unknown in motor racing. The 25 also had a slightly different nose-cone. Nobody at the time understood how much apparently trivial differences in shape could affect a car's aerodynamics. Jack Brabham knew because he was able to use motor industry contacts to test his own cars in the MIRA (Motor Industry Research Association) wind tunnel. Jack, who bought a Lotus 24, reckons that its relatively high nose meant that the front end of the car lifted at high speed. His own Brabham BT3, which appeared at the German Grand Prix, had a nose which dipped down.

Colin had produced the 24 as Lotus's 1962 car, and Team Lotus had raced it. It appeared first because John Teychenne could get the spaceframe done quickly. Mac Macintosh, who maintained a close friendship with Colin, said, 'Lotus made the 24 as insurance in case the 25 did not work.' Once Colin found that the 25 did work, Clark led the Dutch Grand Prix until, encountering clutch problems, he decided to retain the advantage. Eventually he would sell ex-works cars but the 25 would never go on general sale. In fact, from the 25 on, all Formula 1 cars were made by Team Lotus, while Lotus Components built the customer cars.

It has often been reported that Colin's customers felt that they had been conned, but chief among his customers was Ken Gregory, who says:

I thought that Colin had every right to do that, and I'd probably bought more cars from him than anyone else. I had no problems at all in any of my dealings with Colin, and I'd like that made absolutely clear. I even once came close to buying his Piper Comanche from him, but we couldn't agree about the price.

A week after the Dutch Grand Prix, Colin produced another surprise, this time at the Nürburgring 1,000km. At the very end of 1961, Lotus had unveiled the 23, a tiny, mid-engined sports racer. It was, in essence, a two-seat version of the Lotus 22 Formula Junior car – many of the parts were interchangeable – and it weighed in at just 880lb. Since a Lotus was the only car to have in Formula Junior that was recommendation enough, but just in case anyone had any doubts, Peter Arundell took the prototype, fitted with an FWA engine, round Silverstone well under the lap record for 1100cc sports cars and he reckoned it would go even better when it was fitted with a body.

With a half decent driver at the wheel, a Lotus 23 could beat any other small sports car of the time, a point which was proved time and again on both sides of the Atlantic. That much was expected from Lotus, the company was going through a period of astonishing success, but not even the most avid Lotus enthusiast would have dared to predict the events of 27 May 1962, just one week after the Dutch Grand Prix.

Jim Clark and Trevor Taylor were entered at the Nürburgring 1,000km in a works 23 fitted, for the first time, with the new 1498cc Ford-Lotus Twin Cam engine. For the very first time, an engine bore the name 'Lotus' on its cylinder head. This engine, which would play a significant part in Lotus history, used a Ford 109E block with a bespoke cylinder head with twin overhead camshafts. The cylinder head was the work of the late Harry Munday, who had been with Coventry Climax before accepting the post of technical editor of *The Autocar*. Colin offered Munday the choice between a flat fee or a royalty on each unit made and Munday opted for the flat fee. Long before the first 10,000 units had been made, Munday was kicking himself.

In qualifying at the Nürburgring, Clark was seventh quickest overall and easily fastest in class, but the race began in the wet and Clark completed the first lap *27 seconds* ahead of a field of Ferraris, Porsches and an Aston Martin DBR1. Clark pulled out another 20 seconds on his second lap and continued to pull away until the track started to dry. He still had a huge lead on lap 12 but a broken exhaust pipe filled the cockpit with fumes, Clark became groggy, the car slid, Jimmy was unable to respond with his usual lightning reactions and he was out of the race. Even although the business was unfinished, that performance remains one of the most outstanding in the history of sports car racing. It was an astonishing feat but one which tends to over-shadow the fact that a standard Lotus 23, fitted with a tuned 997cc Ford Anglia unit, finished eighth overall and won the one-litre class by more than 70 miles.

The twin feats did not go unnoticed by the organisers at Le Mans, however. Lotus arrived at Le Mans with a 23, fitted with an Anglia engine, while BRP had one with a 750cc Coventry Climax unit. At the time, the only success the French enjoyed in international motor racing, or had enjoyed for about 10 years, was in the Index of Performance at Le Mans, which generally fell to a car with a 750cc Panhard engine. The pair of Lotus 23s looked a formidable challenge to this last expression of French pride.

At Le Mans, the scrutineers went through the cars carefully, determined to find something which could disqualify them. They searched hard and they found it. The front wheels were held by four studs, the rear wheels by six studs, therefore there were two hubs which any spare wheel would not fit. The cars were thrown out. Ken Gregory, who was closely involved with the whole project, says:

> The previous year, some teams had been running with wire wheels with knock-off hubs at one end of the car, and bolt-on alloys at the other. The organisers introduced a new rule which said that the fitting of all wheels had to be the same. We had checked this with a linguist and we were sure that we complied with the rules, because ours were fitted in the same way, all four wheels were bolted on.
>
> Colin asked if we could modify the cars. The Stewards graciously said that we could, but gave us so little time, little more than 24 hours, that they thought the task would be impossible.

Colin was straight on the phone to the works which drew and made new stub axles, I flew home to collect them. We had them fitted with 20 minutes to spare.

The cars were presented again to the scrutineers who, with impeccable logic, pointed out that if the design specification called for six studs at the rear, then four studs were clearly unacceptable. In fact they were likely to be unsafe. The two cars were thrown out and Colin went ballistic. He swore that never again would Team Lotus run at Le Mans, and the team never did during his lifetime. It was not until 1997 that a works Lotus next ran there. Colin's was quite a stand at the time, as it had been at Le Mans where Lotus had confirmed its status. Nobody had ever before publicly boycotted the event – it was considered so important that no manufacturer would dare raise his voice against Le Mans – but Colin did. Ken Gregory says, 'I agreed with Colin, and I refused to enter cars for Le Mans again. We went to the RAC, who negotiated on our behalf, and I think I am right in remembering that we later each received £1,000 as compensation.' Neither BRP (which ran only top drivers in top cars) nor Team Lotus returned to Le Mans, at least while Colin was alive.

France did win the Index of Performance. Incidentally, it was with a 750cc DB-Panhard, and 1962 was the last time that 750cc cars ran at Le Mans. Still, a private Lotus Elite won its class, as an Elite had done every year since 1959. An Elite would win its class at Le Mans in 1963 and 1964 as well. Six successive class wins at Le Mans remains a record for any production car. The Elite was incredibly successful in GT racing at every level, but it was far too complicated to build ever to be a commercial success. Before the end of 1962, however, its successor, the Elan, would appear and give Lotus Cars a much needed boost. During its life, the two-seater Elan would sell 12,224 examples while the four-seat Elan Plus-2 would add another 5,200.

General Motors wouldn't think much of such a production run over 11 days, let alone 11 years, but it was enough to put Lotus on a secure footing. Moreover, the Elan made a profit and offered handling equal to the Elite. The Elan has become a legend and when Mazda wanted to build a sports car in the late 1980s (MX-5, Miata in some markets) Mazda made no secret of the fact that it used the Elan as the standard to which it aspired. Mazda also deliberately styled the MX-5 to recall the Elan – it was a homage.

Although the Elan was a very important car for Lotus, Colin had virtually nothing to do with its development. He made important suggestions, he tested it, and he approved the final design, but on the whole he let Ron Hickman and his team get on with it. Colin was anxious that the Elan reflected Lotus values, but he was heavily engaged in racing and the Elan was primarily intended to provide him with the means by which he went racing. Ron Hickman recalls:

Colin tested the Elan and made a suggestion about the adjustment of the suspension. I didn't think he was right so I did nothing, I simply told him that I had adjusted it to his suggestion.

Colin tried the 'modified' car and declared himself satisfied. Fine, it was a bit of kidology on my part and typical of the kidology he himself employ-ed. One member of my team, however, told the story about the ploy, that we had not actually changed anything, and word got back to Colin. Colin had his pride, he did not like being made a fool of, and he was hurt. He said nothing, but the contract of the person who spilled the beans was not renewed.

He was putting on a bit of weight in the early 1960s and we gave him the nickname, 'Chunky'. He was a bit like a teacher who knows that the kids have given him a nickname, but you don't call it him to his face. Hazel, in particular, did not like the nickname. Word leaked out and soon that was what the motor racing press was calling him in irreverent moments. Of course he was 'Chunky', but not to his face.

When I was at Ford, we got wind of the Austin-Healey Sprite and we had the Anglia in preparation. We knew that we had a better small engine, and gearbox, than the Austin units used in the Sprite and Colin Neale, Ford's Chief Stylist, set me to work on a sports car with a fibreglass body and Anglia running gear. When I joined Lotus in 1958, I told Colin about this project, which was dropped by Ford, and also told him what a hot little number the new Ford engine was. That is why he was able to secure it for his Formula Junior cars, but he was also interested in using it for a small Lotus sports car which would replace the Seven, which was not that profitable.

Colin explained to John Frayling and me his idea for a design which would consist of five torque boxes. There would be a box-shaped engine-bay up front, and another box would form the boot, joined by three longitudinal boxes: the transmission tunnel and the side sills. If those five elements could adequately resist bending and twisting loads then we would have a light, rigid, and quite cheap structure without the need for a separate metal chassis. Thus Lotus would have a Ford-engined rival for the Frogeye Sprite which, by then, was in production and proving popular.

John Frayling made a one-fifth scale model which was based on the idea of using the Frogeye's windscreen, side screens, hood and bumperettes. We would be able to buy these items because the tooling had been paid for by Weathershields Ltd, a subcontractor to Austin-Healey. Initially, we called the project the S2.

Although we designed the S2 according to Colin's brief, we never got the styling right. The lines of the S2 simply failed to generate excitement. Remember, we were trying to follow the Elite and when it came to style, that was an impossible act to follow.

At the time when we were playing with the S2 we still had problems with the Elite, as our customers at the time will affirm, so the S2 (which I renamed M2 – Major Project 2) was put on the back burner for while. When we revived it, it grew into a roaring bullfrog. The capacity went up from 997cc to 1598cc, with the Twin Cam engine, it was given all-independent suspension and disc brakes all round. I upgraded everything else to fit, so it got a curved windscreen, slide-down windows, retractable headlights, new bumpers and dash and bucket seats. The M2 grew into the Elan.

The Rootes Group had meanwhile introduced the Imp which had pioneered the use of Rotoflex rubber half-shaft couplings, a system with which Colin immediately fell in love. Around September 1960, an M2 project engineer, Brian Luff, was worried that, with the greater power and torque of the Twin Cam engine, that these half-shafts might have a life as little of 200 miles, and he wanted to give them a good thrashing before we adopted them.

We were groping our way forward, we did not even have a body. I bought a fibreglass body from Falcon Shells, which we cut and shut, simply so we could address Brian's concerns. Colin had suggested to me that we should cost a folded steel backbone chassis. I can be precise about the date, it was 10 June 1960.

We made a slave unit and learned that Colin's idea for inboard rear brakes did not work. When you applied the brakes there was tremendous juddering as the expected 'grip-slip' took place. The brakes were moved outboard.

At the centre of the Elan was a simple pressed steel backbone chassis and that was a long-established idea, though Chapman did try to claim it as his own. Each end was like a tuning fork, the front fork cradled the engine, the rear fork the final drive, and both carried the suspension, which was all-independent and similar to the Elite. On this very firm spine there was a fibreglass body. At first it was offered only as a rag top, though a hard top was soon available. The Elan featured pop-up headlights which were then something of a novelty and also, as those who bought early examples of the Elan will testify, a major pain.

The Elan had a a 1588cc version of Lotus's Twin Cam engine and this was offered at first in a mild form, just 105bhp, but that would rise. This was good for a top speed of 115mph and 0-60 in nine seconds, which were respectable figures for the day, but the real performance came from superb road holding and handling. These remain the standards by which all cars are measured. The Elan was mighty. The Elan was, pound for pound, the best sports car in the world. It wasn't the world's most reliable car, but it stole hearts. From point A to point B with winding roads between there was nothing to touch it and it had a Lotus badge. By 1962 a Lotus badge carried a lot of weight. Lotus had come of age.

In a single year Lotus produced the 22 Formula Junior car, which dominated the category, the 23, 24 and 25, the Elan and the Twin Cam engine. Since the Twin Cam was based on a Ford block and the Formula Junior cars used Ford engines, Colin was getting close to key people at Ford in Britain and that had led to the Lotus-

Cortina which was under development in 1962. For years Ford had eschewed motor racing, though Henry Ford had made his reputation by winning the only race he entered.

British schoolchildren had a playground rhyme:

My Old Man's got a Ford
Four square wheels and a board
A biscuit tin with an engine in
My Old Man's got a Ford.

Ford's image had been dreadful. Its one trump card in Europe was that it had perhaps the best after-sales spares service of any manufacturer, but being able to supply a new part when the original has broken is not the greatest recommendation. Suddenly the Ford Anglia was going well in saloon car racing and Lotus was wiping the floor with the entire world in Formula Junior with Anglia engines tuned by Cosworth. For the first time in its history, Ford was perceived to be exciting, and that was not lost on Ford's management.

Colin had already met key people at Ford in Dearborn. Dan Gurney, who was then leading the Porsche F1 team, had been greatly impressed by the 25 when he first saw it in Holland and he dangled the prospect of the Indianapolis 500 in front of Colin, especially the prize fund which was almost half a million dollars. Everyone who started Indianapolis received something, while the winner's share ran into six figures. Dan spoke to Colin about the race and even went so far as to send him a return plane ticket.

Cooper had run a modified 'Lowline' at Indianapolis in 1961 and, despite giving away 1500cc, Jack Brabham had finished ninth. A couple of American teams began to build mid-engined cars and in Dan's mind was a Lotus, based on the 25, but fitted with a tuned Ford V8 engine. It was the first sign that Dan was looking at his own long-term future, which would lead to him founding two teams which fielded cars under the name 'Eagle'.

Colin duly went to Indianapolis where he was bemused by the lumbering great front-engined roadsters with their crude chassis and suspension and two-speed gearboxes. It was like being in a time warp. The standard of engineering was laughable, yet the Indianapolis 500 was then, as now, the world's most successful one-day sporting event.

Gurney had excellent contacts at Ford and, after the race, Dan and Colin went to Dearborn to make their pitch. They were listened to, but left without a decision being made. Ford did agree, however, to undertake a full feasibility study. The study, it was agreed, would be thorough and would include the very first detailed survey of the Speedway.

Ford made no commitment to an Indianapolis programme, let alone one with Lotus, which anyway was not well-known in America, but the study it undertook was both thorough and expensive. Colin reckoned that you did not invest tens of thousands of dollars unless you were prepared to be convinced. One of the selling points of Gurney's proposal was that a Ford V8 could run on petrol and so be considerably more economical than the average roadster which ran on methanol. A Lotus-Ford would have to carry only a maximum of 400lbs of fuel compared to the typical 800lbs carried by a roadster with an Offenhauser or Novi engine. That fact alone was enough to make a Ford entry attractive. A difference of 400lbs in maximum fuel load translated into all kinds of advantages: you could build a much smaller and lighter car, tyre wear would be less, and re-fuelling stops would take half the time. A Ford 'stock block' engine would not have to approach the power output of the bespoke racing units which were otherwise used because it would be hauling a lighter load and therefore a Ford unit could be relatively unstressed. It was an attractive package.

Ford went away and did its research. It tuned engines, surveyed the Speedway, and sought advice from Indianapolis veterans. One thing it discovered was that few entries which competed at Indianapolis were run by real engineers. The crew chiefs, who had enormous influence, were merely mechanics. The most successful constructor, A.J. Watson, was only a mechanic working on hunches and experience, he had no vision. Though Colin's academic career had been a disappointment, it had provided him with a sound basis on which to build and Colin never stopped learning. Indy builders such as Watson looked back, while Colin looked forward.

For Dearborn to back Chapman against the Indianapolis establishment would require an act of supreme faith. Ford's last attempt at the 500, in 1937, had been an unmitigated disaster. Lotuses with Ford engines were winning races, however, and there was the matter of the Lotus-Cortina. The American and British branches of Ford were not in as easy communication as they now are, but the message seeped through from the British arm that Chapman was okay. He could be bumptious, arrogant even, but Lotus was making Ford look good in Europe. During the summer of 1962 the key men at Ford explored the matter of Indianapolis and the more they did so, the more Colin and Lotus caught their attention. There was no firm commitment, but Dan and Colin could see that while Ford did not say 'yes', it did not say 'no'.

After the United States Grand Prix, which Jimmy won, Lotus took Trevor Taylor's car to the Brickyard and Jimmy pounded around for about 100 laps, having first had to take a rookie test, which annoyed him. The Lotus 25 must have been the smallest car ever seen at Indianapolis yet Jimmy was lapping not much slower than Jack Brabham, whose Cooper had a 2.7-litre Coventry Climax engine. He was slower over a lap than the roadsters with their 4.2-litre Offenhauser engines, but much quicker than them in the corners, and that was without the off-set suspension everybody used.

The Ford engineers were impressed, but still the company did not commit itself. There was an understanding that Ford would be at Indianapolis, work was proceeding on the stock block V8, but there was no contract. Colin decided that work would go ahead in any case and that he would give the impression that it was a done deal: he wanted to wind up and inspire the people on the Indy car team. Going into the factory and saying, 'If we do this or that right we may get the go-ahead' was no way to inspire people. Besides, if he had a car under construction, it would be so much easier for the executives at Dearborn to sign the deal. Word was out about Ford's interest, it could hardly be otherwise after a major survey of the track, and many people, led by A.J. Watson, had knocked on Ford's door.

Len Terry, who had rejoined Lotus in the September of 1962, having served his term in exile, was put to work on the Mk 29 Indianapolis car. Drawings of the engine arrived in October, but there was still no firm commitment from Dearborn. In essence, the Lotus 29 Indianapolis car was a larger and stronger version of the 25, but with off-set suspension. Len designed the 29 but has never claimed credit for it, and insists that he did no more than to work to Colin's ideas.

As 1962 drew to a close, Lotus was buzzing. As the end of the year approached all minds were on South Africa and the final round of the world championship due to take place on 29 December. Graham Hill had won in Holland, Germany and Italy and had taken two seconds, both to Jimmy, and had scored points on three other occasions. Clark had won in Belgium, Britain and the United States and scored in one other race – the Climax V8 engine was not always reliable. There were nine races in the championship but only the five best finishes by any driver counted. As they went to South Africa, Hill had actually scored 43 points to Clark's 30, but had to shed five points, so was on an official 38 points. If Jimmy won, the title would be his, by a single point: any other result and Graham was champion. Graham was top kid in the class in the world championship, but take a look at the non-championship races, which were very important at the time. The score was Clark 4, Hill 1.

In South Africa, Jimmy did everything right. He set pole and led with Hill close behind. On lap 61 of 82 smoke was seen to be coming from Jimmy's car. A small bolt which located the jackshaft had worked loose due to a fitter at Coventry Climax neglecting to put on a locking washer. Three laps later and Jimmy was in the pits with fluctuating oil pressure. Jimmy took his disappointment like the gentleman he was as Graham reeled off the last few laps to take the race and the title. Clark and the Lotus had been the quickest combination of the year, but Hill and his BRM were not far off and Graham finished in eight of the nine rounds. BRM took the Constructors' Cup with 42 points to the 36 of Lotus, but BRM had actually scored in every race and had scored 56 points, but had to shed 14 of them.

Throughout 1962, Clark was backed by Trevor Taylor, who began the world championship season with a fine second place in the Dutch Grand Prix and thereafter failed to score a single point. Taylor's wretched season led to the legend that the Lotus number two seat was jinxed. It is true that most of the time Lotus was not capable of preparing two cars to an equal standard, but this was true of most teams. When he was with Vanwall, Stirling Moss would test all the team cars and chose what he thought was the best engine and best gearbox from the three and assemble the car that he thought was the best combination. There was enormous inconsistency in manufacturing standards.

Trevor Taylor had gone to South Africa with Clark in December 1961 and had qualified on the front row for the Rand, Natal and South African Grands Prix, all non-championship events, but the grids were good, and then, in January 1962, Trevor had actually beaten Clark to win the Cape Grand Prix. He was a young man going places. Taylor had led the Belgian GP, despite having inferior machinery to Clark, and he was battling with Willy Mairesse for second place when Mairesse's Ferrari nudged him from behind and knocked Taylor's car out of gear. Before Taylor could engage gear, Mairesse rammed him hard and Taylor's Lotus left the circuit, felled a telegraph pole, and landed in a ditch. An impact which can knock over a telegraph pole is a big shunt and the Lotus 24 was a write-off, but Taylor walked away from it. Trevor says:

> Most accounts have got it wrong. Willy Mairesse probably saved my life by nudging me from behind, because he touched the gearchange and knocked it into neutral. What really happened was that the rear suspension had not been tightened properly and it dropped on the floor, which is why Willie nudged me.
>
> I'm an engineer and I used to do a lot of the testing, particularly of the things that were breaking. Colin was obsessed with with paring things to the bone, where other people were using 18-gauge steel, he'd insist on 22-gauge. At the 1962 Pau Grand Prix, I had ended up welding repairs to my own chassis.
>
> We had a problem with the ZF gearbox which was that it was magnetising any odd swarf on to the shafts and after a while that locked the gear. I got used to the gearbox and knew when it was going to happen. We were testing one day and I called in at the pits and told Colin that the gearbox was about to seize.
>
> He was livid to think that a junior driver could tell him anything. He even threatened me with the sack. He put Jimmy in the car and, sure enough, the gear locked solid and Jimmy crashed. Colin at least had the grace to apologise.

At the finish of the French Grand Prix at Rouen the Lola of John Surtees was in a poor condition. John trickled across the line and tried to drive into the pits but found his way blocked by gendarmes. Maurice Trintignant, who was next up, had to jink to avoid Surtees and that put his car right in the path of Taylor. The result was a high speed impact of horrendous proportions, and it was a miracle that neither driver was killed. In fact it was a miracle that nobody was killed since the collision happened right in front of the pits. Even more unusual was that neither Taylor nor Trintignant (who was also in a Lotus) sustained physical injury. Such was the scale of the crash that Taylor's car, the prototype 25, was a write-off.

On the first lap of the German Grand Prix, poor Taylor had his engine cough and splutter then suddenly it fired on all eight pots and caught him out. He went through a hedge, down a bank and into a tree. Again he walked away with no apparent physical injury which speaks volumes for the strength of the Lotus 24 he was driving.

Taylor had had three major accidents in seven weeks and none of them had been his fault. Trevor said 'A certain amount of fear was beginning to set in. I began to wonder what on earth was going to happen next.' Cedric Selzer tells of the time he was sent home from a race meeting:

> We were due to go up to Oulton Park, and Dick Scammell and I were waiting for an engine from Coventry Climax to fit to Trevor Taylor's 24, and the engine didn't arrive until eight at night. Part of the job of installing an engine was to wash out the oil pipes, a process which took hours, so we blew out the pipes.
>
> Trevor went out and ran his bearings. Colin turned to me and said, 'Did you wash out the pipes?' I said, 'No'. He was furious and ordered me out of his sight. I returned home by train and Colin did not speak to me for six weeks. I was still employed, but not a word did he say even though it turned out that Coventry Climax had fitted the wrong bearings. I was wrongly blamed.
>
> Trevor went out in the T-car, which Jimmy was due to drive at Monza the following week, and a rear radius arm detached itself from the tub. Imagine that happening at Monza, it doesn't bear thinking of, and we would not have known about the radius arm had Trevor's race car at Oulton Park not had the bearing go. After six weeks, I said to Colin, 'That turned out to be a blessing in disguise.' He grinned and said, 'Don't I know it.' After that I could do no wrong.
>
> He had been in the wrong, but I never knew Colin to apologise to anyone.

In 1962, the Lotus Formula Junior team, led by Peter Arundell, was well nigh invincible. Its superiority was such that, following a race at the Nürburgring at the end of September, two drivers, a German and an Austrian, complained that Lotus was cheating by running over-size engines. The two drivers had both been running way over the 1100cc limit, one had a 1340cc unit, the other had 'only' a 1300cc unit so he was not cheating quite as much, or so he claimed in his defence. Since neither could keep up with the Team Lotus cars they assumed that Lotus must be running even larger engines. Rumours of cheating are not uncommon in motor racing but an article titled 'The Biggest Disgrace In International Racing' appeared in *Das Auto Motor und Sport* which claimed that Lotus was running with 1450cc engines. To make matters worse, the author was the noted driver and journalist, Richard von Frankenberg, who claimed that he had proof. Alan Rees, one of the Lotus drivers, had crashed at the Nürburgring and von Frankenberg had spoken to Alan in hospital where he lay badly hurt and sedated.

Von Frankenberg's 'proof' was that Alan had said that some of his competitors used over-size engines. Von Frankenberg, scenting a scoop, thought that Alan was referring to his teammates, whereas Alan was talking about the cheats who were sprinkled around Europe. Alan agreed that Lotus used special crankshafts (they did, they used steel, not iron, crankshafts which was within the rules) and this became a point for von Frankenberg, but not as major a point as the fact that Alan would not sell him the engine from the Lotus. Alan couldn't sell the engine because it was not his to sell, but this point was lost on the crusading journalist.

Colin heard of the article, but he decided to ignore it. There have been some litigious people in motor racing, but Colin was not among them. Then von Frankenberg repeated his allegation in the following month's issue. This could not go on, but Colin did not want to get embroiled in a libel case: in fact he hated the idea of involving lawyers in anything, as a point of principle. Besides, he could not prove that Team Lotus had not run over-size engines at a specific meeting where the engines had not been checked by scrutineers. He could only point to the fact that his engines had twice been checked and found to be legal. The water was further muddied by the fact that Lotus did sell a version of its Junior car with a 1500cc engine. The 1500cc Lotus 22B was popular with hill climbers and in Formula Libre racing.

It may have been Peter Arundell who suggested a challenge. Colin issued a public challenge to von Frankenberg with £1,000 at stake. A thousand pounds was very nearly the cost of a Lotus 22, ready to race, so it grabbed the attention of everyone in motor racing. Von Frankenberg was challenged to nominate a circuit where Lotus would replicate the times it had set at the same circuit during 1962. Peter says:

> We knew that von Frankenberg would have to choose Monza. He couldn't choose any of the temporary road circuits we had raced on and, with winter on us, it couldn't be a northern circuit. That left Monza and we were very happy with Monza especially since the temperature would be cooler then when we'd raced there so the car would be quicker and, anyway, I'd be on the track alone.

Von Frankenberg had no option but to accept the challenge and, sure enough, he nominated Monza. The Italian magazine, *Auto-Italiana* was roped in to hire the circuit and the scrutineers. Peter's task was to replicate the time he set while winning the 30-lap Lottery race, and at least equal his fastest lap. It was not a straightforward task because there was frost all over Monza, so Colin went out spreading salt. Despite the conditions, Peter turned in 30 laps at a speed significantly higher than when he'd won the Lottery and then he shaved 0.4 seconds from his fastest lap. Peter then continued for another three laps during which he could take a chance and he took a full second off the best lap time he set in the Lottery. As soon as Arundell came into the pits, scrutineers dismantled his engine, which was found to be 1,092.348cc, comfortably within limits. The car itself was three kilos above the minimum weight limit.

Colin accepted a cheque for £1,000 and von Frankenberg had to eat humble pie in the form of a grovelling apology and retraction in his magazine. Von Frankenberg also lost his job but, instead of being a sportsman, he lost no opportunity to knock Lotus ever after. The story of the challenge went round the world and received far more publicity than the original accusations. Motor racing enthusiasts everywhere were delighted by the story both because it would have been a blow had Lotus been found to be cheating and because it was Colin at his most stylish. It is small wonder that he had hero-worshippers.

All in all, 1962 had been a most satisfactory year for Colin and for Lotus. The cars were pace-setters in every category in which they competed and orders were flooding in for the new Elan. Colin was a very happy man and his happiness was sealed when Hazel presented him with a son, Clive, who completed the Chapman family. Like his sisters, Clive was to receive a first-class education which, in England, meant boarding school. School holidays, apart from the Christmas break, tended to coincide with the busiest periods of the racing season, so Colin did not play a daily part in the life of his children once they went to school. Clive would be only 20 years old when his father died.

CHAPTER 13

CHAMPIONS!

WHEN the Elan came on stream Lotus was special. Lotus had won eight world championship races, which is more than Maserati did, and was on the up and up, whereas Cooper was in decline, Ferrari was in one of its periodic troughs and Lola's deal with Reg Parnell (Racing) had come to an end. In 1962 Lotus had slugged it out with BRM, with Ferrari nowhere, but in 1963 Jim Clark and his Lotus 25 were in a different class to everyone else.

The previous year, 1962, had ended with Graham Hill and BRM on top of the world and, at first, it seemed that they would continue in 1963 where they had left off. Hill had the better of Clark in the Lombank Trophy at Snetterton, and Graham had started last on the grid because he had missed practice. The Lombank Trophy was an all-British affair, but in 1963 there were no other players. Porsche had attempted Formula 1 and had withdrawn. The entire grid which mattered was British. It was not just a matter of cars and engines, most of the leading drivers were British or from the Commonwealth. Ferrari had no ideas and so recruited John Surtees (who had won six world championships for MV Augusta and was a hero in Italy) and Mike Parkes because they were drivers who were also engineers. The Italians had created Formula Junior to nurture home-grown talent and all that had happened was that Italy's specialist racing car industry was all but wiped out.

Italy's last world champion had been Alberto Ascari in 1953 and no Italian since has even looked like a potential world champion. The reason has nothing to do with something as nebulous as 'Latin temperament' for some of the finest drivers in history were Italian. The reason has everything to do with motor racing culture of a nation and, in Britain, Colin Chapman was the founder of that culture.

In 1963, that influence was reflected by the British Racing Partnership, which built its own cars. In overall layout they resembled the Lotus 25, but they were designed and built by Tony Robinson and were stronger than the Lotus because they were skinned with thicker aluminium. Like the Lotus 25, the BRP cars had inboard front suspension and they used Lotus uprights but, as Innes Ireland once ruefully remarked, the car might have been better if they had made a direct copy of the suspension on their Lotus 24s. It has been written that Colin was so upset by what he saw as an infringement of his 'copyright' that he brought a legal action and BRP settled out of court, but this is not the case. Ken Gregory said, 'Far from that happening, Colin helped us. We bought bits from him, including the "wobbly web" wheels.'

The 1963 world championship was dominated by Clark and Lotus. Only 10 races counted for the championship although there were 20 Formula 1 events. Jimmy had gearbox problems at Monaco which saw him so far down the field at the end that he was unclassified. He scored points in every other race, in fact he won most of them. Clark won in Belgium, though he hated Spa. His first international race had been there and during it his great compatriot, Archie Scott Brown, had been killed. Then there had been all the accidents at Spa in 1961. Jimmy hated Spa but he won there every year 1962–5. You measured a driver by the way he went at Spa, which was the most fearsome circuit in the world.

Jimmy then won the Dutch Grand Prix, the French and the British. Colin had taken to wearing a Dutch sailor's cap, it may have been the first style statement in a Formula 1 pit lane, and at the end of every race that Lotus won, the cap got thrown in the air. Colin was guilty of headgear abuse on a major scale in 1963. Jimmy was only second in Germany, his engine was sick, but he won again in Italy, was third in America (fuel pump trouble) though he started from the front row and set fastest lap. Then he won in Mexico and South Africa.

There has never been, before or since, such dominance by a driver in Formula 1. Seven wins from 10 races? Jimmy also won the Pau Grand Prix, the Imola Grand Prix, the International Trophy, the Kanonloppet in Denmark and the International Gold Cup at Oulton Park. That is 12 Formula 1 wins from 16 starts and that with just four mechanics to look after three cars and also transport them to the races.

Jimmy's secret was that he never stressed a car. The V8 series of Coventry Climax engines won 19 world championship races, 1961–5, and Clark won 16 of them. Cooper and Brabham had the use of Coventry Climax V8 engines, and Brabham was quite often quicker than Lotus during practice, though his retirement rate was high. All the versions of the Climax V8 were relatively fragile, but Jimmy knew how to nurse them. There has probably never been a driver who has been so light on his cars.

In Jimmy, Colin had a driver who was capable of expressing his engineering. The closest analogy would be a dramatist who has a particular actor in mind when writing a play. Though Jimmy had a tendency to drive through problems on his cars, by 1963 he was superb at feedback. He was one of those drivers who knew exactly how many revs he was using, what each wheel was doing in a corner, and how the gear ratios should be altered. He was the quickest driver of his day and also among the most accomplished at testing. He was not in Jack Brabham's class when it came to diagnosing problems, but Jack shouldered the engineering of his cars himself. Jimmy didn't need to, he had Colin to interpret his every comment.

Jimmy was everything that Colin could wish for in a driver. On top of everything else, he was a very pleasant man. He did not have Colin's exuberant charm, but he charmed people none the less. Part of Jimmy's appeal was his natural modesty and the fact that he was a man with deep-rooted values. Between races he could be found on his farm, or at the market buying and selling sheep. He was a man who went home between races, at high speed in his Elite, to fit into his local community. It was only very late in his life that he moved from Scotland to a tax haven. Jimmy was a superstar before the term had been coined. He could drive anything and do so with an intelligence and delicacy of touch unmatched by any of his contemporaries. When he died, he and Colin had entered the ninth year of their partnership. In the entire history of Formula 1 only the partnership between Ron Dennis of McLaren and Mika Hakkinen has been longer.

Colin and Jimmy used to share the same hotel room so there was plenty of opportunity for quiet reflection away from the track. With such a close relationship, it is little wonder that other drivers felt that they were on the periphery. Scots are known for being canny when it comes to money. Jimmy accepted a shake of Colin's hand for his first season with Team Lotus. The two men negotiated personally for 1961 and it is likely that, in conversation with other drivers, Jimmy found that he had sold himself below his market value. He did not want to fall out with Colin who, after all, had plucked him from relative obscurity, and so, from 1962, he employed a couple of lawyers to go through his contracts and negotiate a proper pay structure. It was a sensible thing to do. It meant that there was a distance between Jimmy and Colin when money was discussed and the deep bond of friendship between them was not affected when contracts were negotiated.

Early in the year the Lotus-Cortina arrived. It had the Twin Cam engine, revised rear suspension with coil springs, uprated brakes, and, most importantly, it was offered only in white with a green flash down the flanks, and a black, not chromed, radiator grille. It was a livery which was suggested by Colin and was one of those apparently simple ideas of which Colin was a master. It was one of those ideas of which everyone said, 'But of course.'

BMC had a runaway success with the Mini Cooper when an economy car was transformed into one of the icons of the Sixties. The Lotus-Cortina would never rival the production figures achieved by the Mini Cooper which, ironically, became an even better and more popular car as Cooper went into decline, but every enthusiast wanted a Lotus-Cortina. Even in standard form it was good for 108mph and with acceleration (0-60mph in 9.9 seconds) which was ground-breaking for a medium-sized saloon. It was the ultimate Q car and, as week succeeded week during 1963, the Lotus badge on each of the rear flanks became even more desirable, but at £1,100 the Lotus-Cortina was too expensive to ever be a great seller. A Mini

Cooper could be bought for under £700 and what the Mini lacked in outright performance it more than made up in sheer fun.

The first Lotus-Cortina to race was driven by Doc Merfield, who took his car to Snetterton and lapped *10 seconds* below the 2-litre lap record. During the season Team Lotus joined the fray and then, as later, one of the sights of British racing was to see a 7-litre Ford Galaxie rumble round, with Lotus-Cortinas snapping at its heels like terriers chasing a bull. Driving a private Lotus-Cortina for John Willment's team, Jack Sears won the British Saloon Car Championship. Jim Clark and Trevor Taylor both turned out in Lotus-Cortinas when other commitments allowed and, once, they dead-heated for second place behind a Galaxie.

For many enthusiasts, their most vivid memories of Jim Clark were at the wheel of a Lotus-Cortina. When he was in his Lotus 25, Jimmy was laid back and made everything look effortless as he simply flowed. It was easy for an enthusiast to think that, given the same car, he too could win Grands Prix. In a Lotus-Cortina, however, Jimmy was seen to work, and work hard, as he cornered with the nearside front wheel lifting high above the track. People saw that and thought, 'There is no way I could drive a car like that.'

During that initial year of production, Lotus converted 567 Cortinas, which was a good source of income. Furthermore, it tied Lotus and Ford, which was quite a consideration bearing in mind Colin's intentions for Indianapolis. In March 1963, Jimmy ran the prototype Indy car at Snetterton but Ford still had not produced a contract. Colin was running on self-confidence, of which he had no shortage. The prototype 29 was shipped to America and run on the Kingman proving track that Ford owned. The chassis proved to be fine, but there were problems with engine breakages. The guys at Ford set about rectifying them with help from Team Lotus's David Lazenby and Jim Endruweit.

Towards the end of March, the prototype, with Jimmy and Colin in attendance, was ready to run at Indianapolis. Ford's first revised engine was sent but, when fitting it, it was discovered that some important ancillaries were missing. Colin remembered that they were standard Ford Fairlane parts so went to a car hire firm and hired a couple of Fairlanes. The parts were removed and smuggled into the garage so as not to cause Ford embarrassment.

Once the Ford engine was fettled, then came the steep learning curve. The Indianapolis Motor Speedway is deceptively simple, an oblong with four slightly banked left-hand corners, but it is extremely sensitive to weather conditions. Robin Herd, who engineered cars in the 1980s, describes setting up a car for the Speedway as like trying to do a moving crossword. It can get very hot in Indiana in May and there can be 80 percent humidity – you try not test in the early afternoon. If there is rain, the Speedway's character changes even when the surface has dried.

Old Indianapolis hands knew when the track would be quick and when it would be slow. They had all manner of tricks to set up a car to its optimum. The guys at Lotus had to feel their way with a prototype which needed development. Despite this,

Dan Gurney became only the second driver in history to lap at more than 150mph. With a performance like that, allied to reliable long-distance running, Ford was hooked and an executive was dispatched to England with a contract. Throughout the month of May, Jimmy and Colin flitted back and forth across the Atlantic, as did Dan Gurney, who, for once, was a member of Team Lotus. The trans-Atlantic run has since become a familiar part of many a driver's professional life, but in 1963 it was novel.

The 1963 Indianapolis 500 has become notorious because Jimmy worked his way up to second place, and at lap 177 of 200 laps, Clark was just five seconds behind the Watson-Offenhauser roadster driven by Rufus Parnell 'Parnelli' Jones and seemed ready to take the lead. Then Jones's car began to spew oil and Jimmy dropped back a little. The rules were clear, a car dropping oil had to be black-flagged, but this was a 'good ole' American roadster leading and it was entered by A.C. Agajanian, who apart from being an entrant, promoted events, owned a circuit and was a member of the governing board of the United States Automobile Club, which organised the Indianapolis 500. 'Aggie' was in for the long haul, Lotus was a newcomer and Lotus was foreign.

Agajanian was soon in animated conversation with the stewards and the marshal who held a black flag in his hand was never authorised to wave it. As Jones left oil on the track, other officials took a close look and reckoned it was water coming from the car. Colin went to the chief steward to remonstrate and was brushed aside on the grounds that Parnelli Jones was not driving a Lotus so it was no concern of his. At moments like this, Colin used to raise his eyes to heaven. He had been stitched up before but he kept his volatile temperament under control. Jones was losing oil at such a rate that it was possible that his engine would quit, and there was the matter of the relationship with Ford.

Agajanian fixed the result in the most blatant way and Jimmy settled for a secure second place. He expected that, any minute, Parnelli Jones would be hauled off the track, especially since, on top of shedding oil, he committed the cardinal sin of passing slower cars under the yellow flags. While Jimmy played safe, several drivers spun on the oil slick and crashed into the walls. They were not amused and later there were fisticuffs between Parnelli Jones and one of the drivers, Eddie Sachs. In fixing the result, the stewards had put the lives of other drivers on the line – the walls at Indianapolis are unyielding.

It was a disgraceful episode, but it was not the whole story. Clark and Team Lotus were still learning about racing at Indianapolis and one of the crucial things is strategy when there is an incident, when the yellow flags come out and the field bunches behind the pace car. The late Andrew Ferguson, who was team co-ordinator for Lotus at Indianapolis, reckoned that Jimmy lost 59 seconds to Parnelli Jones under the yellow flag, yet he trailed in only 34 seconds behind. With a better strategy, Clark could have won. So Jimmy could have been leading Parnelli Jones if he and the team were up to speed on Indianapolis's peculiar ways. Just as Lotus was never going to be allowed to compete at Le Mans in 1962, so a foreign team was not going to be allowed victory at Indianapolis if it meant black flagging one of America's own. Team Lotus received many letters of sympathy and support from Americans, who were ashamed of the shabby way the invaders had been treated.

Jimmy made his point later in the year when he won the Milwaukee 200 run over a one-mile banked oval, though he had less luck at Trenton where he set pole, but retired, and ironically the reason for his retirement was that he was shedding oil. When A.J. Foyt Jr came to authorise a biography, he had some snide things to say about many of his rivals, but was, by his lights, positively dewy-eyed when assessing Clark. Even Foyt had to concede that Clark was special. Second at Indianapolis, and Rookie of the Year, Jimmy then won his first short-oval race. That was special indeed.

The Elan began to appear on the circuits in 1963, and Lotus made a special competition version, the 26R. In 1963 the Elan appeared mostly in national and club events and Ian Walker, a former Lotus racer himself, ran what was more or less a works team. The great little Lotus 23 and the 1600cc 23B continued to win at every level. Lotus would make 131 23s and they would be the car to beat in their class for several seasons. The Seven was still winning races and, apart from production sports car racing, some owners fitted fibreglass hardtops and converted their Sevens into 'GT' cars. The Seven was there in the background, though had yet to become a cult, and it did so only when there were enough people who had a company car, had a second car, and had enough spare cash to indulge themselves with a 'big boy's toy'. In the early 1960s a Seven was more likely to be someone's only car and there are are not many people with waterproof heads and hydraulic dampers in their butts. Still, it turned a profit and took up slack at the factory when the racing car building season was over.

Since 1960, Lotus had built its grassroots reputation on its Formula Junior cars. For 1963, it built a monocoque car, the 27, using a great deal of fibreglass. Colin knew that everyone who bought a single-seater at the lower level dreamt of being in Formula 1 and the 27 was sold on the basis that it was a 25 in miniature. It was the only mid-engined monocoque single-seater anyone could buy and Colin had the up-coming one-litre Formula 2 in mind as well. It was an incredibly slim car, five inches narrower than the 22 it superseded, but the winter of 1962–3 was unusually hard and many test sessions were snowed off. The 27, a radical design, suffered as a result, and it was only during the season that a major flaw became apparent. The fibreglass outer skin was pop-riveted to the tub and the rivets worked loose, robbing the structure of its integrity. Before long, the 27 had to be re-skinned with aluminium panels made by the ever-reliable Williams & Pritchard.

What Colin had forgotten was that most drivers in Formula Junior had a single mechanic and he was often part-time. Drivers who undertook a season in Europe did not need sophistication, they needed simplicity. In the event of a shunt, such a driver needed to be able to go a welder who could replace a few tubes. The last thing that such a person wanted was to return to Cheshunt for a major rebuild.

Over at Brabham, Ron Tauranac knew what the non-works driver needed so he made cars with spaceframes. He also made cars with outboard suspension because that made it more easy to set up in the limited practice time drivers had. Thanks to Jack Brabham's connection with the motor industry, Ron had put his cars in the wind tunnel at MIRA and, unlike Colin, he knew precisely what the penalty in drag was when using outboard suspension. It was a difference of two percent additional drag, which was nothing when weighed against the amount of time to be gained through setting up a car to its optimum. Colin did not know that because no Lotus had seen the inside of a wind tunnel. On the other hand, Colin did know the torsional stiffness of his chassis. In the early 1960s hardly anyone conducted tests for torsional stiffness.

There were three outstanding young designers at the time: Colin Chapman, Ron Tauranac and Eric Broadley, all of whom had begun by building specials and all of whom were self-taught. Chapman was the man with the charisma and charm and it was he who received the lion's share of media coverage.

Tauranac was a difficult man, who did not suffer fools gladly. There was no question of a journalist pausing in the pitlane with Ron to pass the time of day. Ron worked incredible hours, but he remained a hands-on designer whereas Colin would develop into an overseer as Lotus grew ever larger. Ron lived only to make racing cars and his great strength was that he was much stronger on detail than Colin and he understood what customers wanted to a far greater depth. There were times when Colin seemed to be carried away by his own public image.

Eric Broadley, by profession a quantity surveyor, was a shy man who found it difficult to discuss his work. The Lola Mk 1 was a little jewel and the Mk2 was the best of the front-engined Formula Junior cars. Tony Southgate, Eric's first assistant, said: 'Eric had a wonderful eye for detail and he was very conscious about safety. In the early days at Lola, he would insist on welding every wishbone himself, it was some time before he'd trust me to do one. We used to spend half the year designing the cars, and half the year making them.' When Eric designed the Mk 6, a GT car with a Ford V8 engine mounted amidships, he found his range and most of the best cars he designed personally were on a large scale.

While Lotus covered itself in glory on so many fronts in 1963, it lost a lot of its most important market, the category which ambitious drivers competed in as an important step on the ladder of a professional career. The works Formula Junior team, run by Ron Harris, who otherwise put food on his table by distributing porn flicks, did reasonably well. That was of small comfort to the customers.

In 1963 there were 37 major Formula Junior races and Lotus won 12 of them. This was down on previous years and, to make matters worse, Brabham won 14 races and that without a works team, though Denny Hulme did receive factory support. Year on year, MRD (Brabham) ate into Lotus's market and, apart from the commercial implications which were actually marginal in Lotus's case, Colin could no longer rely on a stream of drivers knocking on his door to be included under the umbrella of Team Lotus.

A privateer running a Brabham who took a win received far more kudos than a driver in Team Lotus, even though the privateer probably had the easier run since he had the better car. As the 1960s wore on it became noticeable that constructors with no original ideas built copies of Tauranac designs, they did not copy Lotus. Tauranac understood what drivers, out on the road towing their car on a trailer behind a VW Caravanette, really needed, while Colin was carried away by his concepts. This was something which would play out over the next few years as Lotus struggled to maintain its traditional base. It was not perceived to be a problem by representatives of three major makers who all tried to move on Lotus in 1963. They were Honda, Jaguar and Ford (America). Colin had become someone to woo.

During 1963 Honda decided that it would enter motor racing as a way of preparing the world for its entry into the car market. In a very short time Honda had become the world's most prolific maker of motorcycles. By 1962, Honda had won its first motorcycle world championship and had made its first car. Nobody outside of Japan bought Japanese cars in 1963. Japanese cars were a poor joke, but anyone who had looked at the motorcycles had a different story to tell. The first Honda car, a micro sports car, was essentially a four-wheeled motorcycle. On the plus side were such features as double overhead camshafts and one carburettor per cylinder, which otherwise you got only on racing engines, but chain drive to the wheels? Honda's daily car production was in single figures when Mr Honda decided that he would go into Formula 1.

Honda's was an incredible move. There then was no major manufacturer in Formula 1, and there hadn't been since the brief appearance of Mercedes-Benz and Lancia in the mid-1950s. A party of engineers, under Yoshio Nakamura, Honda's director of motor sport, was sent to Europe under the guidance of Jabby Crombac. Jabby says, 'I had put together a field of cars and drivers for a major race in Japan so I was known there. That was the point of contact and when they came to Europe, I took them to see Lotus, Brabham, Cooper, Lola, all the main teams.'

Tadashi Kume, who would succeed the founder as President of Honda, had designed a transverse V12 Formula 1 engine to be mounted amidships. It was a bold move, but motorcycles had transverse engines so Kume responded to his cultural background. It was typical of Honda's naivety that the engine was designed in isolation. A Formula 1 chassis engineer would have pointed out that while a transverse layout would allow a shorter wheelbase, it would inevitably increase frontal area. Jabby said, 'In principle we agreed that Honda would ask Lotus to design a car for Formula 1 – they wanted Jim Clark in the car – and Brabham would be invited to undertake a Formula 2 programme.'

Colin encouraged the approach and Honda dispatched a mock-up engine to Lotus. Chapman sat on it for some time, sending Honda a string of excuses, and he used the Honda engine to wind up Coventry Climax, which had been threatening to withdraw from motor racing following a takeover by Jaguar. Chapman wanted to continue with Climax and he said that if Honda was coming into Formula 1 with a 12-cylinder engine, which he thought would make the Climax eight-cylinder engine obsolete, then he wanted a 16-cylinder engine. Coventry Climax took up the challenge and designed, and built, a flat-16 engine. Honda was a long distance away and knew not the ethics endemic in Formula 1. Colin sat on the engine as the clock ticked. Every day he had the mock-up was a day he could use against Coventry Climax and every day he did so delayed Honda's entry into Formula 1.

Eventually, Mr Honda realised that he was being messed about and the mock-up engine was sent to Ron Tauranac, who lodged it, in secret, in his garage at home. Ron soon told Honda that he could not possibly design a chassis to accommodate their engine to the time-scale they had set. The upshot was that Ron Tauranac and Sir Jack Brabham remain consultants to Honda to this day and Colin was removed from Mr Honda's Christmas card list.

Colin, the Warren Street trader, had done the spiv thing. He had used the fact that some funny foreigners were coming into Formula 1 to work his corner, but when he saw the mock-up he was shaken: the Honda engine was state-of-the-art. He was not honest with Honda and Honda would have nothing to do with Lotus for as long as Colin lived.

Coventry Climax built the flat-16 engine because it was anxious to accommodate Colin for a reason not widely known. Climax had been taken over by Jaguar and Jaguar's founder, Sir William Lyons, was quietly assembling a corporation. He had also bought Guy Motors, the maker of trucks, and Daimler. Colin became Sir William's target. The guys at Lotus reckoned that they would like to get their hands on the excellent 2.5-litre V8 engine Daimler had in its SP 250 sports car, which Lyons had inherited. The 250 SP had a dreadful chassis and styling, and Lyons wanted help. A replacement body which had been essayed was too bland to rouse any excitement – though the SP 250 was ugly, it had personality. Putting the Daimler engine into the 2+2 version of the Elan which Ron Hickman had on the drawing board would be a mutually beneficial exercise.

Colin and his lieutenants went to talk and Sir William Lyons was very interested. He knew all about Lotus and he liked what he saw. Lyons began to woo Chapman and Colin did not discourage the wooing. If Lotus was under the umbrella of Jaguar it would remove a weight from his shoulders. All Colin wanted to do was to go motor racing, but Lyons was interested in Lotus because he wanted Chapman to inject his talent into Guy Motors and make it a modern company. There was no way that Colin wanted to be involved with trucks. There was no way either that he wanted his beloved racing to be under the control of anyone else. There is a remarkable parallel between Chapman with Jaguar and Ferrari with Ford.

While Sir William Lyons wooed, Lotus was trying to get deeper into bed with Ford. Ford had decided to get more involved in motor racing and had attempted to buy Ferrari. Enzo Ferrari had been in negotiations with the wealthy Texan oil men, John Mecom Sr and his son, John Jr, who were both racing enthusiasts and whose family fortune at the time was estimated to be about $250 million.

A few days after the 1962 Indianapolis 500 Ford renounced the Automobile Manufacturers Association agreement not to participate in motorsport. Ford, like most other manufacturers, had actually been participating despite the agreement, but through the back door. Stock car teams got unofficial support, for example. Ford realised that there was a growing new car market among young people for whom image was important (the Mustang would play a key role).

In Britain, Ford successes in motor racing, mainly with Lotus, had brightened its image no end. The Dearborn arm moved in on Ferrari in April 1963 and even the fabulously wealthy Mecoms decided that here was someone with even more financial clout and dropped out of the running. Negotiations dragged on for weeks and while Ford would buy the Ferrari road car business outright, Enzo Ferrari would retain 90 percent of his racing team. Even when word got out and there was national outrage in Italy, the negotiations continued. When, however, Ferrari realised that he would not have complete autonomy over his racing programme, he broke off talks. The response of Henry Ford II was, 'Okay, then, we'll kick his ass'. That led to the Ford GT40 and the epic Ford versus Ferrari battles at Le Mans in the late 1960s.

Having been thwarted by Ferrari, Ford turned to Lotus. Colin encouraged Ford's overtures, not because he wanted to sell, though he had perhaps intimated that Lotus might be for sale, but he wanted the contract for Ford's proposed Le Mans car. The Ford executives listened politely, noted that Lotus had never made a big-engined sports or GT car, and continued their rounds of British makers. Cooper and Lola were on their list and Lola was running, when money allowed, the Mk 6, a mid-engined GT car powered by a Ford Fairlane engine.

The Lola Mk 6 was more like what Ford had in mind and the upshot was that Lola moved to new premises, paid for by Ford, and entered an exclusive one-year service contract with Ford to do the basic design and early development of the GT40. Lola had been struggling financially since its Formula Junior cars could rarely compete with Lotus, Brabham or Cooper, so the deal brought an injection of cash, a respite from the highly competitive production racing car market, and Ford picked up the tab on a seven-year lease of the factory in Slough.

The year's association with Ford was not the happiest time for Eric Broadley as he had to deal with suits using Lola as a ball in a game of politics they were playing in Dearborn. When it was all over, Eric built the Lola T70, which was actually the car he wanted to build for Ford. Colin felt he had been thwarted when the contract went to Lola and in typical fashion he wound himself up and decided to build a better car, the Lotus 30.

Len Terry, who was the main designer on the 30, says, 'It was the Lotus Seventeen all over again. Colin was up in the air and wouldn't listen to reason. On this occasion he decided that the car had to have a backbone chassis. I told him it wouldn't work with a 5-litre V8 engine, but the Elan had a backbone chassis so the Lotus 30 had to have a backbone chassis. There was nothing I could say to dissuade him.' The Lotus 30 was a pretty poor car since Len Terry was right all along. The backbone chassis flexed under the power and torque of the engine which led to handling which could be described as 'character building'. Jimmy managed to win a couple of minor races with it in 1964, but it was a pretty much a flop.

Apart from Jaguar, Ford and Honda, there was also a flirtation with Reliant in 1963. Reliant's staple business was its range of three-wheeled cars and vans so at first sight a cooperative alliance between Lotus and Reliant was about as bizarre as trying to cross-breed a hippo with a race horse. Reliant, however, had huge expertise in the series production of fibreglass bodies, it had begun to made its own engines and gearboxes and was marketing the Ford Zephyr-engined Sabre sports and GT cars. Less well-known was that Reliant designed fibreglass-bodied cars for countries without a steel industry. Israel was the first, and would be followed by Greece and Turkey. For a fee, Reliant designed the car and set up the factory. The company was long on the sort of expertise that would be useful if Lotus was to expand. Ron Hickman had suggested exchange visits with Reliant in early May 1963, and recalls:

> The idea was enthusiastically taken up by Colin, so I made contact with Ray Wiggin, who was being groomed to head Reliant, and we acted within a matter of days. I was to rue the day as the love affair with Reliant took off with a vengeance and lasted longer than any other that I can recall.
>
> The Reliant Robin had a very agricultural chassis made of angle-iron. Colin looked at it in a derisory manner and asked Ray Wiggin what the torsional stiffness was like. He was very impressed when Ray pointed out that if you had only one wheel at one end then, in effect, you could not transmit a torsion load into the chassis at all.
>
> For a while, we all wondered whether a three-wheeled Lotus was imminent.

Outlandish though cooperation between Reliant and Lotus may seem, it was a serious proposal and one with potential benefits to both sides. It seems to have fizzled out because, in his usual way, Colin would go for an idea with enthusiasm right up to the time when along came another idea he could pursue with enthusiasm.

At the end of 1963 Lotus had won 15 world championship races in six years. Only Ferrari had won more, but Ferrari had been competing for 14 years. A total of 1,195 Lotus cars of all types were made and on top of that there were 567 Lotus-Cortinas. The turnover for Group Lotus was £1,573,000 (multiply by 20 to get a value for the year 2002) and had generated a pre-tax profit of £113,000. The financial figures do not take into account the money generated by Team Lotus, which was paid into the account of Team Lotus Overseas. Colin was doing very well for himself, but then Lotus was doing that most difficult of things, it was winning races.

CHAPTER 14

BACK TO THE BRICKYARD

FOR LOTUS to repeat its brilliant 1963 season in Formula 1 was a tall order indeed. BRM was back on the pace again and the influence of John Surtees and Mike Parkes at Ferrari was being felt. The season would be a three-way battle between Clark/Lotus, Hill/BRM and Surtees/Ferrari. Though Dan Gurney would win two races in his Brabham-Climax, and while he was usually to be found on the front row of the grid, he suffered terrible luck. Gurney was the one driver whose pace Clark feared, yet Dan raced under a handicap. He was much taller than all the regular F1 drivers and so stuck further out of the car and created more drag. He was also much heavier than anyone else and with cars weighing 450 kilos fitted with engines producing around 180bhp, this was a factor. Above all else, 1964 saw tyres playing an ever more important part in racing. Developments in technology allowed Dunlop to produce 13in tyres which were significantly wider than before.

Under Colin's direction, Len Terry was put to work on the 33, which was to be a stiffer and stronger version of the 25. By going back to basics, it was also intended to make the 33 as light as the 25 had been on its debut – it had acquired weight with development. One thing to go on the new car was the trademark 'wobbly web' alloy wheel – the 33 had six-spoke cast alloy wheels. Colin was famous for his insistence on shedding weight and the 33 was initially fitted with lightweight suspension units. Colin, who was always smartly turned out himself, also wanted his cars to look good and was prepared to add a little weight by chrome-plating the suspension. What nobody realised was that the process of chrome-plating made the suspension extremely brittle. Jimmy tested the first 33 and a suspension component broke. He tried to spin the car to a halt but the forces generated by the manoeuvre caused the suspension to shatter. Jimmy finished up on the infield in a tub with all four wheels elsewhere. He said that never again would he drive a car with that suspension. It was back to the drawing board.

Team Lotus began the season with the 25 and two ex-works 25s also lined up on the grid at Snetterton for the first, non-championship, F1 race of the year. These had been bought by Reg Parnell (Racing) and were fitted with customer BRM V8 engines. Innes Ireland won in a BRP-BRM. He inherited the win, certainly, but it was nonetheless a win. Then Jimmy won the *News of the World* Trophy at Goodwood, with Peter Arundell second and the only driver on the same lap. By the time the championship races began, John Surtees had won an F1 race and Jack Brabham had won two.

The championship season swung back and forth. Graham Hill won in Monaco after Clark, who had led, encountered engine troubles. The season was a very tight one. Jimmy won three races, Surtees, Hill and Gurney each won two. As they lined up on the grid at the final round, in Mexico, Hill was on a net 39 points (he had scored 41, but only the six best results counted). If Graham finished third or higher, he had to shed three points for fourth in Holland. Jimmy had 30 points, but had no result to shed, while John Surtees was on 34 points, again with no results to shed.

Hill fluffed his start in the Mexican Grand Prix, he was still adjusting his goggles when the flag dropped, so he was down in ninth on lap one. Surtees made an even worse start, his engine was misfiring, and he completed the first lap in 13th place. Out in front, however, Jimmy was driving at his imperious best. Graham, who had worked his way up to third, then had a collision with Lorenzo Bandini as Bandini, in the second Ferrari, attempted a passing move. The impact folded over Hill's exhaust pipes and that eventually ended his race. Had Graham held third to the end of the race, he would have taken the championship. Then, towards the end, Jimmy realised he had an oil leak. He went into the last lap still in front, but his engine failed with the chequered flag less than a minute away. That put Gurney into the lead from Bandini, who moved over to let Surtees through to take second in the race and so clinch the world championship.

John Surtees became the only man to win world championships on two wheels and four, and Ferrari took the Constructors' Cup. Graham Hill had grossed one point more than Surtees and BRM had scored two more than Ferrari, but only the best six results counted.

In eighth place in the championship was Peter Arundell on 11 points. In the first four championship races, Peter had scored a third and two fourths. Then he arrived for the Grand Prix de Reims, a Formula 2 race which featured most of the top stars. The broad, long, straights of the Reims circuit meant a slipstreaming battle was inevitable. Towards the end, Alan Rees and Jack Brabham had pulled away a little, but behind them six cars were passing and repassing each other around the track.

On lap 31, Arundell put a wheel off the road at a very fast right-hand kink. Peter spun and was hit by Richie Ginther's Lola. Both cars left the road and Peter was flung out of his Lotus as it careered down a bank. Peter flew high into the air: some witnesses estimate that he went 60ft in the air. He was lucky to survive but, when he came round in hospital, Colin was there to tell him that a Formula 1 drive awaited him when he was ready. He gave Peter a goal to aim for even though he thought that Peter was so badly damaged that he would never have to keep his promise.

With Arundell out, Colin recruited Mike Spence. Colin had spotted Spence during the 1962 Monaco Formula Junior race. He said later:

> From where I watched I could see a driver's every movement in the cockpit – the way he turned into a corner, the way he slid the car, every minute correction he made. I was struck by the very natural style of a particular driver. Now Peter Arundell won that race, and Peter's a very fine driver, but I could see him fighting his car every inch of the way. The driver of whom I am speaking, on the other hand, was very smooth and completely relaxed. I knew that, with experience, he would develop into a really top driver. You might say that I decided to start grooming Mike Spence for stardom that day.

This is a very revealing statement. Colin actually watched a Formula Junior race and and picked out a driver to groom for stardom. When did that last happen? Earlier in 1964, Ken Tyrrell had given a test to Jackie Stewart and signed him as a result, but Ken had not spotted Jackie while racing, Ken had received a tip from the Goodwood circuit manager, Robin McKay.

There was a myth among drivers that to compete in the Formula 3 support race at the British Grand Prix was to showcase your talent in front of Formula 1 team owners. It was a myth encouraged by anyone with a car to hire. The fact is that no Formula 1 team manager watched the race, as they were too busy looking after their teams. They followed the progress of drivers like anyone else, by reading the magazines, but Colin not only spotted Spence's talent, he considered him for future stardom and, remember, Spence did not win the Monaco race.

Mike had a drive for Lotus in the 1963 Italian Grand Prix and was lying seventh with 13 laps to go when his engine called it a day. Though the Formula 2 Lotus effort was run by Ron Harris, and run very efficiently, Colin influenced the driver line-up and Mike was drafted into the Formula 2 team. In 1964 he won the championship organised by *The Autocar*. There was no European Championship in 1964, but *The Autocar* awarded a prize to the most successful driver in the six British Formula 2 races. By the end of the year Mike was running at the sharp end of world championship races.

Lotus had a mixed season in the new Formula 2. Clark could make a difference when he appeared, but Brabham made the better car. Formula 2 became very important in 1964. Race organisers switched from non-championship Formula 1 to running Formula 2 races because they could get stronger fields. The non-championship Formula 1 race was in sharp decline, but most Formula 1 drivers were happy to race in Formula 2 because it was another pay day. About the only top driver who did not turn out very often was Dan Gurney, but if he had a problem with his size in Formula 1, it was worse in Formula 2.

Brabham made a better car for Formula 3 as well. Formula 2 and Formula 3 were new for 1964; they were both one-litre formulas with the difference that F2 allowed bespoke racing engines while F3, which replaced Formula Junior, was restricted to production units. Many people converted existing Formula Junior cars to one or other of the new categories, but what remained of the market was something Lotus let slip through its fingers. Colin realised that a monocoque design was fine for the more professional Formula 2 and updated the 27 for that market, but the Lotus Formula 3 car was a half-hearted affair, more or less a warmed-over 1962 Lotus 22. Colin lost credibility, and customers, and Brabham took his market.

When the new sensation, Jackie Stewart, raced his Cooper, entered by Ken Tyrrell, he was the class of the field, but Jackie did not actually race that often. He drove in Formula 3 just 12 times (he won 10 races) but in Europe alone there were 107 Formula 3 races in 1964. Because of Jackie's later association with Tyrrell a legend has grown, but Jackie was snapped up by BRM for 1965 not because of his exploits in Formula 3 but because of his performances for Team Lotus. That year, Jackie made his Formula 2 and Formula 1 debuts with Lotus.

Jackie is not normally associated with Lotus but, on 19 July 1964, he had his first Formula 2 race in the Trophée d'Auvergne at Clermont-Ferrand. The race had a field of a high quality and Jackie came home a strong second to Denny Hulme's Brabham. Jackie turned out six times for Team Lotus in Formula 2 and took three wins (one win was a heat), a second and a third.

Jackie also made his Formula 1 debut in a Team Lotus car, in the non-championship Rand Grand Prix at Kyalami. Jim Clark had slipped a disc in a snowball fight so Jackie was called upon to sub for him. Stewart set pole from Spence for a race which was run in two heats. When the flag dropped for the first heat, Jackie was left stranded with one drive-shaft snapped and the other badly bent. He won the second heat easily though he had to start from the back of the field. It was not the greatest field ever assembled, but Jackie did have to dispose of Graham Hill who, unusually, was driving a Brabham.

Jackie decided that Chapman made unsafe cars and never again drove a Lotus. It was as simple as that, and nothing would dissuade him. He did not make a big issue of it, rather he would always say that Colin had been one of the people who had most helped his career. Stewart was always the diplomat and when he retired at the end of 1973 he became a trusted consultant to Ford, which retained strong links with Lotus. There was no public statement on record that could return to embarrass him.

Lotus returned to Indianapolis, where Ford underlined its commitment to motor racing by producing a large batch of 'quad cam' racing engines. Everyone was after the new engine, but it is noticeable that Ford released them only to teams that ran mid-engined cars: it did not want to be associated with the traditional roadster which was about to be consigned to history.

The cars that Lotus sent over were virtually identical to the 1963 Type 29s, the main difference being a change of gearbox, but in order to please Ford they were designated Type 34s. During testing at Indianapolis it became clear that Dunlop tyres produced the better lap times, but they did not have the life that Firestones had. The drivers, Clark and Gurney, naturally liked the lap times, but experts at Ford were sceptical about the tyres' ability to last. If Firestone, which was within comparatively easy reach, could make a compromise tyre, that would be the ideal. Colin ordered Andrew Ferguson to track down the top Firestone people, and eventually they were located in New York just before they were due to fly home. On hearing that Colin wanted to discuss matters, they told their pilot to fly to Indianapolis.

Everything was hush-hush. The meeting was due to take place in Andrew's motel room, where the Firestone executives could park their car immediately outside and not be seen. Firestone had been a Ford supplier for as long as there had been Fords: it was an exceptionally important relationship for Firestone and two top men were undertaking a three-hour flight just to speak to Colin. When they finally arrived, Ferguson rang Chapman, staying in the same motel, and Colin told him to make the decision because he wasn't going to be there. The Firestone executives turned on their heels and left.

Senior men from one of the world's great companies had gone out of their way to meet Colin and he treated them in the most appalling way. Why upset Firestone when all he had to do was to walk a short distance from his motel room to Ferguson's? It was Colin who had caused them to be there in the first place. Who knows why he did it? Colin was unpredictable. This meant that everyone was kept on his toes, which is an asset in a motor racing team, but it also meant that he made some dumb decisions. Snubbing senior executives of a company so close to Ford was not the brightest thing to do. Frank Costin once described Colin's charm as a limitless supply which he could turn on like a tap, but he could also be extremely unpleasant, as another episode shows.

At the end of the 1963 Indianapolis 500, Len Terry was looking forward to the post-race celebrations – after all, he was the man who had drawn Jimmy's car. Len has never claimed it as his own, but he had done an excellent job in creating a Lotus 25 for Indianapolis and that is rather more complicated than it may appear. When the 1963 Indy 500 ended, Colin turned to Len and, out of the blue, handed him an airline ticket and told him that he must rush back to Cheshunt to deal with problems at the works. A helicopter was ticking over close by to carry Len to the airport and when he arrived in England Len found there was nothing to sort out. For some reason Colin had decided that Len should not be part of any celebration. It was a cruel thing to do, but Colin could be very cruel.

In the event, Clark set pole at Indianapolis, but Ford's worst fears were confirmed when Gurney attempted laps with a full load of fuel and found that the Dunlop tyres began to shed their treads. Dunlop engineers back in England worked round the clock to revise their moulds and new tyres were flown out.

On lap 36, Jimmy led the race and then began to feel vibrations from the rear. The left hand tyre had begun to chunk and, so severe was the vibration, that it caused the suspension to collapse on the 48th lap. Only Jimmy's supreme skill prevented him from adding to the seven crashes which had already marred the race as a result of a first-lap mêlée. Some laps later, Dan Gurney's sister car was pulled in as a safety precaution and Ford was left with egg on its corporate face. Worse, the race was won by A.J. Foyt in a traditional, front-engined Watson-Offenhauser roadster. Ford had urged that the team's third car be given to Foyt, but Colin had insisted that it was necessary to be held in reserve – another strike against Chapman.

Next day, Chapman and Ferguson were ordered to a post mortem and, as Andrew Ferguson has recorded, Colin was looking forward the the lavish hospitality they would receive. Colin was so confident that he told Andrew Ferguson to bring along the file on the Lotus 30. He had an idea of turning the concept into a road car and the meeting seemed an ideal occasion to pitch the idea to senior Ford managers. On entering the conference room, however, neither man could help but notice there were two chairs in the middle and in a great semi-circle around were chairs for the Ford executives. There was to be no unstinted welcome, rather an Inquisition. The idea of selling Ford the Lotus 30 as a road car was not raised, and Colin had no choice but to eat humble pie and make a contrite apology for choosing Dunlop tyres.

The collective voice of Ford demanded to be sold the three cars Lotus had made, so they could supervise the running of the cars, and the management of their image, and Colin, worn out by all the drama at Indianapolis, said 'Yes'. Then shortly afterwards he said, 'No'. It was one of those instant, unfathomable decisions which Chapman often made. It was probably more of a gut reaction rather than a considered response. Colin liked to be in control of everything, all the time.

This sudden turnabout perplexed the men in suits, but Colin went into charm overdrive and said that he would rather that the cars were retired than he left his American business unresolved. By the time that Colin left the meeting, he had won round the executives and had negotiated a new contract to run the cars at Milwaukee and Trenton, and Jimmy did win at Milwaukee.

You can win at Milwaukee, a one-mile oval, from now to the crack of doom and it will never equal a single win at Indianapolis. It is astonishing how Colin was able to keep Ford with him after the humiliation at the Brickyard but, in a nutshell, that is what Colin did.

Bob Dance joined Lotus Components in 1960 and before long transferred to Lotus Developments. He says:

I kept on at Colin to take me on board Team Lotus and his response was, 'What to do you want to do that for? It's a dead-end job.'

Eventually, he relented and I suppose I must have got along well with him because I stayed with him until the end of 1969. Then after spells with March and Brabham, Colin invited me back to be Chief Mechanic in 1976 and I stayed with Team Lotus right to the time it folded in 1994.

Colin was charismatic, which meant that he could get the best out of people right to the time he wore them down. He would drain every last ounce from a person.

When he came round the workshop, everyone kept their heads down, there was no such thing in his book as a break for coffee or a sandwich, but he would turn a blind eye when we let off steam. We used to make acetylene bombs and swede guns. A swede gun was a length of heavy duty tubing which we sealed at one end where we inserted a spark plug. We'd then pack in our missiles, in the same way as you do a cannon, feed in a mixture of oxygen and acetylene and activate the spark plug with a magneto.

Colin was secretly pleased. If we had had problems in a race, he would fly straight home, ponder the problem and debrief us at the factory. If we won he'd take us out to a meal in a place where racing people gathered and he'd be the first to start throwing the bread rolls. And he made sure that you first dipped your rolls in wine.

After we won the world championship in 1963, Esso laid on a coach and drove us all down their refinery at Fawley on the Solent. They laid on this spread and Colin led the food throwing. I heard him say to someone, 'Our boys always manage to do this better than the others.'

Even when it came to throwing food around, Colin had to be best.

In Cheshunt, things were humming along when the mechanics were not laying down trails of surplus methanol along Delamare Road and setting fire to it. The Elan was making a name for itself both on the tracks and as a contemporary icon. Customers had to endure an indifferent level of quality, given the price, but some people will suffer for style. Lotus-Cortinas were successful in their class everywhere and there were wins galore from the Lotus back-catalogue: the 23 sports racer remained a formidable machine. It was still made as the 23B (1600cc engine), but would be Lotus's last successful sports racer.

Colin originally intended that the Elan would be strictly a road car but, naturally, people were soon tweaking them and racing them. He gave in to the inevitable and Lotus Components marketed the 26R, which was a lightly modified road car with a strengthened chassis and a Cosworth-tuned Twin Cam engine which gave 140bhp to the standard cars 105bhp – 160bhp was available from Stage III BRM version.

During 1964 a Lotus Elan won its class in a race in a round of the International Championship for Manufacturers for the first time and, at Le Mans, the Elite took its sixth, and last, class win. The Elite had been a heap of trouble for Lotus, but it had performed superbly in racing. Six consecutive class wins at Le Mans is pretty special. Lotus won 'only' seven Formula 2 races in 1964 and 'only' came within a minute of winning two world championships. That gives a measure of how much Colin had achieved and he was still only 36 years old.

To get a handle on just how young Colin was, he was only nine months older than Graham Hill and, in 1964, Graham had another world championship and more than 11 years in Formula 1 ahead of him. Colin was two years younger than Jack Brabham, another driver with another world championship ahead of him, yet Team Lotus had already won 18 world championship races, which was two more than Cooper would win and twice as many as Maserati had won, and Colin had 59 wins ahead of him.

CHAPTER 15

THE EUROPA ARRIVES

FROM the beginning of the 1966 season, Formula 1 would be for cars with three-litre engines. BRM was going ahead with two projects, a V12 and an H-16, but Coventry Climax indicated that it was to withdraw from motor racing and, after a long and successful partnership, which went back to the latter end of 1954, that left Colin high and dry. Existing V8 engines could be enlarged to 2-litres, and some were, but this was a stop-gap.

The team at Coventry Climax, headed by Wally Hassan, did consider turbo-charging existing 1.5-litre engines, but could not trace a suitable turbocharger, the technology then being in its infancy. Besides, Coventry Climax's involvement in motor racing was draining resources of both money and personnel and diverting it from the main aim of any company, which is to succeed in the market place.

The Coventry Climax had been under Leonard Lee, an unsung hero of British motor racing, but the company had been taken over by Jaguar. Sir William Lyons, Jaguar's founder, had used motor racing to promote his company, but had never been drawn into it. Jaguar had a chance of winning the 1953 World Sports Car Championship, but Lyons had considered the cost of sending even one car to Mexico to participate in the the final round, the Carrera Panamericana, and had decided he could do without the championship. Lyons was only interested in winning Le Mans.

By the end of 1965, Colin had given Coventry Climax two world championships, countless wins in sports car events and had used Climax engines in the Elite. It had been a mutually beneficial arrangement, but it made little financial sense from Coventry Climax's end. During 1965, Colin approached Keith Duckworth and asked how much he would need to build a bespoke 3-litre engine. Keith thought for a moment, decided he'd have to build a minimum of five engines, and plucked a figure out of the air, or so it is said. It was £100,000, considerably less than most car manufacturers spent on the tooling to give an existing model a light face-lift. Anyone who knows Keith will know that he had already thought about it and he had his position sorted. Keith Duckworth was as aware as anyone that a 3-litre engine would be needed and he had to be high on anyone's list of possible designers.

Colin then set about raising the money. He first went to the Society of Motor Manufacturers and Traders, of which Lotus was a member. His idea for an engine backed by the British motor industry received a sympathetic hearing, but that was all. David Brown, the industrialist who owned Aston Martin, was interested, but he wanted more control of the project than Duckworth was prepared to allow. Other people, including Esso, were approached, but not even the Chapman charm could persuade them.

Walter Hayes, the former editor of the *Sunday Dispatch*, a man who had employed Colin to write a column for the paper back in 1958, had remained a friend of Colin and Hazel's and often dined at the Chapman home. Hayes had left journalism and was rising within the ranks at Ford. He was not only a motor-racing enthusiast, he was a great admirer of both Chapman and Duckworth. Hayes was a modest man, but he did pride himself on his ability to spot talent and Keith had played a major part in putting Ford's name on the map in the junior single-seater categories. One evening, when Hayes was visiting the Chapmans, Colin had shown him the layout for a car which was to become the Lotus 49. Colin's idea was radical: the engine would form part of the chassis as a stressed member. Behind the cockpit there would be a fuel tank and the engine and transmission would bolt directly to the fuel tank and would carry much of the rear suspension.

It was not the first racing car to use the engine as a stressed member, that had been Vittorio Jano's fabulous Lancia D.50 of 1954, but Colin's idea was different to Jano's because, on the Lancia, the engine had been used to stiffen the frame whereas Colin proposed replacing much of the conventional chassis. Unknown to Colin, Tony Rudd, then working for BRM, was thinking along the same lines and his H-16 engine would also be a stressed member of the chassis. BRM produced its H-16 engine before the Cosworth DFV appeared, but it was a case of two engineers thinking independently along the same lines. The difference is that it is the Lotus that people have copied ever since.

Actually, it was not Colin's idea to have a stressed engine, it was Keith Duckworth's. Keith says:

There was never any question that the engine was going to be a stressed structure. If you are going to mate a 3-litre engine to a cigar-shaped monocoque, there is no way that you are going to be able to find room for a chassis. I will admit, though, to being a little worried when I realised how much Colin intended to attach to the engine and gearbox.

When I drew the engine, I realised that its plane profile was about the same size as a monocoque, so I went on to design the way it was mounted.

It was my idea to attach it from the sump and the cam-covers. I did the installation as well as the engine.

Hayes was interested, especially when he learned that Duckworth planned a V8 engine and proposed to begin by constructing a four-cylinder 1500cc unit. This engine, the FVA – Four-Valve Series A – would test Duckworth's ideas but, Hayes quickly realised, and Duckworth was not slow to mention, the FVA could be adapted for use in Ford road cars, and so it was. The 1969 Ford BDA unit used the layout of the FVA's cylinder head, but on a 'Kent' engine block.

Keith proposed an engine with four valves per cylinder. Such engines had been around for a long time but the odd thing was that the concept had more or less died with the end of World War Two, at least so far as automotive engines were concerned. The German company Borgward made a four-valve competition engine in the late 1950s and Coventry Climax made a handful of four-valve V8s. Four-valve engines have become so common in road cars that, these days, few manufacturers bother to put a badge on the back to boast to the driver behind. Cosworth Engineering would be the company which, more than any other, would popularise the concept.

Colin fired up Walter Hayes, who spoke to Keith, then to Colin again, and finally to Harley Copp, who had come to England from Detroit to be vice-president of engineering at Ford. Hayes said that £100,000 was a trifling amount to a company the size of Ford and that Ford could not go wrong. Hayes convinced Copp, then the matter was raised at a board meeting under 'any other business' and was passed on a nod. The board had just approved spending 10 times that amount on putting synchromesh on the bottom gear of Ford's small-car gearbox.

Cosworth Engineering had just moved to Northampton, halfway between London and Birmingham on the M1 motorway. Keith left his loyal lieutenants, notably Mike Costin and Benny Rood, in charge of the factory while he went home to draw his two engines. The FVA would use the cylinder block of the 120E engine, the DFV would need its own block.

There is a story that Keith was once shown the engine designs of a major manufacturer. He was asked what he thought. 'Crap,' came the reply, to the consternation of the suits. 'Put yourself in the position of the gas,' said Keith, 'You've a bloody great piston coming up your chuff and you're looking for the quickest way out. Have you provided the quickest way out?' The suits had to admit that Duckworth was right and it was typical of his thinking – blunt and straight to the point.

Only someone very, very, bright can put so complex an idea in so simple a way. Keith has never blanched from confronting problems head-on and admitting he was wrong when he was wrong. He made mistakes in designing his engines and said, 'Bloody less expensive to take an eraser to a pencil line on a drawing board than it is to build the thing and find you've got it wrong.' Keith said of Mike Costin: 'Mike has a brain like a computer. You throw him an idea, he runs it through his brain and then he tells you if you are right or wrong. He can't tell you why he's reached the decision, but 99 times out of 100, he's right.' The Cosworth DFV and Lotus would win five Formula 1 World Constructors' Championships together. The engine itself would win 155 Grands Prix, plus Le Mans, and would be adapted for Indy car racing, where it would rule for years.

Duckworth was up to speed about the latest developments in tooling. Computer-Assisted Machining (CAM) was then at an early stage, but though the computing was relatively crude, the results were superb. The essential point was that, by investing in tooling, Cosworth was able to make a consistent product.

Ford did not put all its eggs into one basket and also helped Dan Gurney to commission Harry Weslake, a noted gas-flow expert, to build a 3-litre V12 engine. Weslake's approach to engine building was traditional: each part was hand-crafted. Weslake's design had potential, but the components were often not interchangeable. Cosworth made an engine which, from the start, was meant for series production. Keith knew that if his engine worked, and he had no doubt that it would work, that he would be swamped with orders. He had an agreement with Ford when he began work on the DFV, but he had no contract. That was fine by him, he trusted Walter Hayes. Keith had no time for lawyers or paperwork.

One detail is that when the Cosworth FVA engine first ran in a car, it was in a Brabham. Despite the relationship between Chapman and Duckworth, Lotus had lost the plot so far as production racing cars were concerned. Jim Clark in a works-backed Formula 2 Lotus 35 run by Ron Harris won most races he entered, and took both the British and French championships, but not many customers wanted a Lotus 35. It came down to the simple question: if you have a shunt in Denmark and you're scheduled to be racing in France the next weekend, how do you get the car repaired in time? The Formula 3 version of the car won just a single important race, though that was the jewel in the crown, the Monaco Grand Prix support race. Peter Revson was the driver and he was in a car entered by Ron Harris.

Jim Clark won six of the first seven world championship races in 1965, then failed to score a point in the remaining three. In fact, Jimmy won his first six starts because he missed the Monaco Grand Prix in favour of the infinitely more lucrative Indianapolis 500 which, that year, was held the day after Monaco. Team Lotus entered a 33 for Mike Spence and a 25 for Pedro Rodriguez at Monaco, but when the organisers realised that Clark would not be gracing their event, they decided to restrict Lotus to one entry. Colin was not going to have any of that and the upshot of a robust exchange of views meant that Lotus missed Monaco altogether. It was the first time since 1958 that either Colin or Team Lotus had missed a Grand Prix. Colin was hands-on, he was always at the races and nothing escaped his eye. Bob Sparshott, who joined Team Lotus in 1965, recalls, 'At the end of practice Colin would start to draw up a job list which grew ever longer. Jimmy would see this and would gently steer Colin to his car and back to the hotel. He knew that everything would be done properly without Colin's prompting.'

Jimmy's sixth start was the German Grand Prix and when he won that, he took his second world title. The Constructors' Cup was still open, however, and BRM, with Graham Hill and Jackie Stewart, actually grossed more points than Lotus. However, since only so many results could count, BRM had to shed points. Under the modern points system, when both cars can score points in every round, BRM would have waltzed the Constructors' Cup.

In dominating the championship, Jimmy scored fourth successive wins in both the Belgian and British Grands Prix – and Clark hated driving at Spa. Bob Dance recalls the win at Silverstone:

> Jimmy was leading by a huge margin when we detected that his engine was cutting out through Woodcote and Graham's BRM was eating into his lead. It looked serious, but he held on to win by just over three seconds.
>
> It turned out that he had detected that his engine was using a lot of oil and Woodcote corner was then long and very fast, just the sort of corner promote oil surge. To prevent the engine being under load when that happened, he was slipping the car into neutral. No wonder we mechanics loved Jimmy.

To play the game of 'counterfact' so beloved of some modern academic historians, what if Clark had driven for BRM and Graham Hill had continued to drive for Lotus? How much depended on the singer, how much on the song? The works BRMs had a better finishing rate than any team which used the Coventry Climax range of V8s and only Jimmy ever won a race in a Lotus 25 or 33.

One small detail: the last race of the 1500cc formula was won by Richie Ginther in a Honda, and Ginther led every single lap. It is true that, in the rarefied air of Mexico City, having 12 cylinders gave Honda an edge, but this was the engine that Colin had sat on in 1963. Another exercise in 'counterfact': what if Colin had played fair with Honda? A third, Honda-powered car added to the team in 1964 would have only meant hiring a few more people and Honda would have met the bill. Colin would not have rushed around to secure the Cosworth DFV, he would have had a a supply of Honda engines into the 3-litre formula, no doubt with many another mutually agreeable technical and financial arrangement.

Jack Brabham and Ron Tauranac played fair with Honda and, in a letter dated 21 July 1966, Honda's Mr Nakamura offered the Brabham team a deal. They could either have free V12 engines and retain independent control of the team in terms of drivers and policy, or Honda would underwrite the whole operation and expect a say. The offer was politely declined, sensibly as it turned out, but imagine a long-term arrangement between Lotus and Honda without the DFV in the equation.

Jimmy won the World Formula 1 Championship, both major Formula 2 Championships and also the Indianapolis 500. The relationship with Ford was back on course and Len Terry designed a completely new car for Indianapolis, the Type 38, this time with a full monocoque. The point has been made that Colin never claimed that the Lotus 25 was a true monocoque. BRM had made a true monocoque with the P261 but in an interview published in *Motor Racing* (16 January 1966) Colin said:

BRM can get away with it because they have more mechanics and spend more on their racing team. In the Indianapolis car, we accepted it as it's only the one race, but to work on the car all the year with the very tight schedule we had for the European season, standing on your head every time you look inside the tanks and things, would become a real nightmare.

This has echoes of Colin's assessment of the prototype Mk 8, with its 'semi-monocoque-type' body, written for *Motor Racing* in 1954.

As a member of the SMMT, Lotus had access to the society's full-size wind tunnel at MIRA and Colin began to use this. Aerodynamic development of racing cars was still in its infancy and Colin used his limited time in the tunnel to design new windscreens for single-seaters. That may seem mundane, but a driver being buffeted by airflow at 200mph at Indianapolis is not going to perform at his best.

At Indianapolis, just over half the field was equipped with Ford V8 engines and there was only one traditional front-engined roadster, which sat in the last slot on the grid. The five Lotus-Fords filled the first five places with A.J. Foyt's Sheraton Thompson-Special (a lightly modified year-old Lotus 34) on pole and Clark alongside. Also at Indianapolis were two cars built by BRP. The team had given up the unequal struggle in Formula 1 at the end of 1964.

With only five world championship points to its name in 1964, BRP could not negotiate good starting money from race organisers and its sponsorship deal with UDT had come to an end. Furthermore, the other four British teams had organised themselves into a cartel which, in essence, was the forerunner of the Formula 1 Constructors' Association. By acting as a group, they could negotiate better deals, but they excluded BRP from their group on the grounds that it was not a proper manufacturer.

With the top teams forming a cartel, BRP was squeezed out. Race organisers had to pay the cartel more, which meant that privateers and BRP had to be paid less. BRP therefore obtained a deal to build cars for the Indy 500, and one ran as high as fifth, but it failed to finish. BRP tried to stitch together another attempt at Formula 1 for 1966, but it came to nothing and a fine outfit fizzled out. In its wide portfolio of racing, BRP had employed more than 30 Formula 1 drivers, including four world champions.

BRP had managed to secure such high levels of funding that it had frightened the other teams, and it has been suggested that the cartel was a punishment inflicted by Colin upon BRP for daring to make a near-copy of the Lotus 25. Ken Gregory says:

It is true that Cooper, Lotus, Brabham and BRM did sign what became known as the Paris Agreement, but I know of nothing which suggests that Colin was making a move against us – he supplied us with parts – I have no idea what part John Cooper or Jack Brabham played either.

I suppose that suspicions have been aroused because Andrew Ferguson, who had close ties to Lotus, acted as the cartel's secretary and, though invited, he never came to visit us. I can only repeat that I enjoyed nothing but excellent relations, on a personal and business level, with Colin.

Bob Dance and Bob Sparshott were in America looking after a Lotus-Cortina programme when Team Lotus found itself short of hands and they were called to Indiana. A problem was that Sparshott was only 19 years old, and there was an unofficial rule at Indianapolis that you had to be aged at least 21. Colin was going to have none of that. 'If he's good enough for Team Lotus, he's good enough for Gasoline Alley', he snapped, and that was that.

Foyt led the first couple of laps, but then it was Clark all the way, apart from when he called in for scheduled pit stops. Foyt held second until he retired on lap 110, by which time he was close to being lapped by Clark. Jimmy stroked home to a tumultuous reception from the crowd, ahead of Parnelli Jones in a Lotus 34, or Agajanian-Hurst Special as it was called.

Ford milked the win for all it was worth and it is possible that Jimmy's face became better known in America than it was in Europe. Ford even sponsored a strip cartoon featuring Jimmy and aimed at 'future buyers'. Naturally, Colin and Lotus did not feature strongly in the strip. On the other hand, a lot of money flowed into Team Lotus Overseas, the most successful Indy car racing team from the Bahamas.

It was Jimmy who received all the attention in Ford's advertising, but Lotus began to acquire another sort of glamour. In the popular TV series, *The Avengers*, a new character appeared: Emma Peel, played by Diana Rigg (now Dame Diana Rigg). Clothed in the trendiest 1960s gear (gentlemen admired the exquisite stitching on the black leather catsuit), Emma Peel righted wrongs and thwarted villainy at the wheel of a Lotus Elan.

Thanks to this type of exposure, Lotus began to permeate the general public's consciousness. Motor racing, even Formula 1, was not then a major sport. Of course, a world championship received patriotic attention, but it did not often feature on television and coverage of races, even in broadsheets, was rarely more extensive than a county cricket match. Colin had a massive reputation among the racing community, but he was never the sort of public celebrity that, say, Eddie Jordan would become a generation later. Television companies did not make documentaries about his lifestyle. Colin was not often interviewed, even by the specialist press.

When he was interviewed, he was brilliant. He had the capacity to express complex ideas in a simple way and a straight question got a straight answer. At a race track Colin spread misinformation like a farmer spreads muck, but in a formal interview he demonstrated his complete grasp of his business.

How Colin would have coped with the constant, intrusive, battering that so often now passes for media coverage is another matter. He did not suffer fools gladly and while he was happy to cooperate with the serious journalists of his day, one can imagine his impatience with today's media equivalent of the 'Wottle Club'. When Lotus was still in the stable block, some of the lads stamped out little badges from bottle tops. These were for the 'Wottle Club'. Kids would look in, see the cars and, wide-eyed, would say, 'Wottle she do, Mister?' Each kid who asked the 'Wottle Question' was presented with a badge.

There was an aspect of Colin's life which had no clear-cut start. Bob Dance tells this story:

> Colin and I had one thing in common in that we both suffered from hay fever, Colin suffered terribly. I had a gearbox to prepare overnight and I was suffering. Colin sympathised and brought me one of his special pills. I finished the gearbox all right but, later, I felt dreadful. All I know is that the pill was not intended for hay fever.

Amphetamines, barbiturates and the like were not tightly controlled prescriptions at the time. Ron Hickman says:

> Colin was completely open about his use of uppers and downers. His use was brought on not only by the incredibly long days he worked, and the broken sleep, but also by his often crossing 20 time zones in a few days. I recall his telling us how he went to his doctor to insist that that he needed these things to keep up with it all, and I'd say most of us were more understanding than horrified.

Stirling Moss is on record as saying that he was helped to win the 1955 Mille Miglia by Fangio, who gave Stirling one of his 'special' pills, which kept him wide awake for 48 hours. Neither Moss nor Fangio could be described as 'dope-crazed'. So far as many of these drugs were concerned, it was an age of innocence. There were over-the-counter cough medicines at the time which contained morphine, and if you planted in your garden the most popular brand of seed for pet birds, you could raise marijuana, and millet.

One cannot escape the feeling, however, that for for someone like Colin, predisposed to being overweight and with a frenetic lifestyle, popping uppers and downers might eventually put an unsustainable strain on the heart. Colin was a bundle of energy to begin with: Colin on speed was awesome.

During 1965, Len Terry left Lotus to design Indy car and Formula 1 machines for Dan Gurney. His replacement was Maurice Phillippe, who despite his name was a Londoner born and bred. Maurice had built his own 1172 special, the MPS, in 1955, and some of the work on it was carried out by Lotus, so he and Colin went back a long way. Maurice had trained at de Havilland and was working there when he built a Formula Junior car, the Delta, which he soon managed to write off. The experience with the Delta was enough for him to decide that his future lay with cars rather than aircraft and he joined Ford, working on its small passenger cars. The racing bug would not leave him and he contemplated buying a Lotus Seven. With a couple of specials and race driving in his background, plus de Havilland and Ford, Maurice was almost a photo-fit Lotus man. He joined Team Lotus as chief designer, with Colin, in effect, as technical director.

Against all evidence and common sense, Colin was determined to make to make the concept of the Lotus 30 work, so he ordered a revision. The result was the Lotus

40 and some wag was quick to say that the 40 was a 30 with 10 more mistakes. Ron Hickman tells a revealing story:

Jimmy was testing a 40 at Ingleston and Colin flew John Standen, Maurice Phillippe and I up to see the test. Jimmy reported that one or the other of the rear wheels was lifting when he accelerated out of a corner. He reckoned that the rear dampers were too small.

Colin looked at them and exploded at Maurice, who tried to tell him that he had been ordered to use those specific dampers. It turned out that we had some in stock and Colin wanted to use them up. We had a seriously bad car for the cost of a few pounds.

Colin was still livid when we flew back. He did none of the proper preflight safety checks and John, who had a pilot's licence, remonstrated. That was a mistake, Colin exploded again. None of us said a word until we landed at Luton Airport.

The Lotus 40 was made only for the works and the cars were sold on after competing, unsuccessfully, in the Can-Am series. The message finally got through to Colin that his concept was a non-starter and the 40 was the last sports-racer that Lotus made.

Ever onward, ever upward, was Colin's motto and he had plans for a second road car to be marketed alongside the Elan. A team under Colin had devised the Europa, which would become the world's first mid-engined GT car outside of hand-built, very expensive, exotica. There have been different versions of the story of the genesis of the Europa, but Ron Hickman is adamant about what happened. He says:

When Ford was trawling for a company to build what became the GT40, they visited Lola, Cooper and Lotus. They laughed at Cooper because Cooper didn't have much idea about design, but they were interested in Lotus, though I wasn't that keen because we had more than enough work.

Colin was away racing when Ford's people arrived in May 1963. Although I wasn't keen on getting involved with the programme, I did a concept drawing of a mid-engined GT car. I was quite pleased with it and hung it on my wall. One day Colin came in and said, 'What on earth is that?' He was greatly taken by it and said, 'We'll build that one day. It could replace the Seven.'

Colin was always looking for something to replace the Seven and usually it would be more expensive and (he hoped) would generate bigger profits. The Seven actually never did much more than cover the overheads of Lotus Components.

We sat on the idea for a time waiting for a suitable engine/gearbox and that arrived when Renault produced the 16. By putting the Renault 16's engine and transmission into a backbone chassis similar in concept to the Elan, and turning the engine and gearbox through 180 degrees, we had the basis of a car.

Colin said that he wanted me to be in charge of the project and he was prepared to earmark £11,000 to develop the car, which was code-named P5. I said there was no way I could do it for that money, the Elan had eventually cost £42,000 to develop. Colin said that he wanted the job done in 11 months so he was thinking of £1,000 per month. I wasn't going to fall for that so he increased the figure to £14,000 and I would still not bite the bait. Colin said that I had become so much more clever since doing the Elan so I would not need so much money. I retorted that I was now so clever that I would not fall for his line.

Colin then said that he would do the car himself, but I would have to second some of my staff to it. Derek Sleath, who had been lured to Lotus from the Rootes Group became project engineer and Peter Cambridge did the interior. John Frayling took my drawing and made a scale model from it and Peter Jackson at Specialised Mouldings did the full-scale body.

Despite the early idea that the Europa would replace the Seven, Colin decided that the Elan would be the high-performance road Lotus, the Europa would offer a lower top speed, but with a similar level of handling, while the Seven, by then in Mk 2 trim with a simplified spaceframe, would continue to be the basic entry-level car. The plan was to make 500 examples of the Europa in 1966 and these were to go to Lotus, not Renault, dealers in France. Production would then settle at a steady 50 cars a week, most intended for export. It was not expected that the Europa would be sold as a kit, but in the event it was.

Early Europas had a cramped cockpit, poor ventilation, the windows did not open and rearward visibility was, at best, marginal. Against that was brilliant handling with most mechanical spares from your nearest Renault dealer. Despite the Lotus badge, the Europa never did achieve its projected sales figures. It is hard to say why. Perhaps it was because by the time it was launched, customers were no longer prepared to put up with a cramped cockpit, poor ventilation and windows that did not open. Like most Lotus cars made while Colin was in charge, more thought was given to the concept than to the customer.

CHAPTER 16

MOVE TO NORFOLK

BEFORE the start of the 1966 season, Lotus held one of its test days at Goodwood. These were designed to encourage the most promising young drivers to buy a Lotus for their Formula 3 campaigns. The Lotus 41 was shown to such upcoming talents as Roy Pike, Derek Bell and Piers Courage. Colin had listened to the criticism of his most recent Formula 3 cars and had also noted the success of Ron Tauranac's deceptively simple designs for Brabham. The Lotus 41 followed Brabham in having a spaceframe and outboard suspension. It was perhaps the only time that Colin took his lead from a rival.

The Lotus 41 proved that it was not perfect on its first runs, and the drivers were critical of its handling. To Colin that was a red rag to a bull, so he borrowed a helmet and, dressed in his slacks and checked shirt, climbed into the car and promptly broke the Formula 3 lap record. That much has passed into legend, but less frequently recalled is that on his fifth or sixth lap he lost the car at Woodcote Corner and stuffed it into the banking. Colin came back to the pits and said, 'Yes, it is a little tricky, isn't it?' There is at least one other story of Colin climbing into a car and beating the professional drivers. It should be remembered, however, that laps were timed by stopwatch and, with a stopwatch, it is not that difficult to massage a time. Before electronic timing made that impossible, producing surprising times in winter testing was a minor art.

By the time it was ready to race, the 41 was a competitive car and a quasi-works team (Courage and Pike) run by Charles Lucas won half a dozen important races and was the only serious opposition to Brabham. As the 41B, it ran in Formula 2, but that was the year that the works Brabham team had Honda engines. Jack Brabham and Denny Hulme won all but the last race when Jochen Rindt, in a Brabham-Cosworth, pipped Jack by a 10th of a second.

Jack had run a Honda engine in 1965 and it had been embarrassing. He and Ron Tauranac, however, had worked with Honda to improve it and at the end of 1965 they had flown to Japan and had educated Honda about the subtle way in which an engine has to work in harmony with the chassis. The 1965 unit had been top heavy, for example, and the shape of the block was not ideal for stressing in a spaceframe. Honda was still designing engines in isolation from the car. Colin was content to accept an engine from Cosworth and build a car round it, and Keith Duckworth took full responsibility for the installation of the DFV, whereas Ron and Jack were less concerned with concept than with detail.

Team Lotus began the 1966 season with its 33s using Climax V8 engines enlarged to 2-litres. Regular drivers Jim Clark and Mike Spence were joined by Peter Arundell, who believed that he had recovered from the injuries he sustained in 1964. In later years, Peter would spit bile at the very name of Chapman, but the fact is that Colin made him a promise and he kept that promise at heaven knows what monetary cost. Peter never again hit the form that he had shown before his 1964 crash, but whatever else he may have done, Colin was pretty straight with his drivers. Despite what Innes Ireland later claimed, he was not sacked, his three-year contract had come to an end.

Peter's position was clear, he would drive the new 43 fitted with BRM's complex and heavy H-16 engine which was supposed to produce 420bhp but which, in 1966, never approached that figure. It was also a long time coming and it was not until the French Grand Prix in July that Peter started a world championship race, but that was from the back row of the grid and he was out after three laps with gear change problems. The rest of the season was equally wretched for Arundell, though he showed his class a couple of times when given a 33. Indeed, he scored a point in the United States Grand Prix. That race, however, was won by Clark in a 43-BRM, the only time that an H-16 engine finished a race in 1966. BRM spent most of the season running 1965 cars with the engines enlarged to 2-litres and, like Lotus, finished the season with 18 points in the Constructors' Cup.

Jack Brabham won his third world championship with a car powered by a Repco engine. Repco, an Australian company, made spare parts for the motor trade and had also taken on the old four-cylinder Coventry Climax FPF engine which was the mainstay of the Australia/New Zealand 2.5-litre 'Tasman' series. Jack obtained an Oldsmobile V8 cylinder block, took it to Repco and suggested that it might form the basis of a replacement for the old FPF unit. Repco took the bait. Jack worked his corner and soon had a lightweight 3-litre engine which was not particularly powerful (it peaked at 310bhp), but was reliable. Repco engines won the world championship in 1966 and 1967, but the 2.5-litre Tasman engine proved to be an embarrassing flop. Jack got what he wanted, however, it was not only Colin who could duck and dive. Jack was supposed to sell Repco engines, but as soon as he got his supply he forgot about that.

For Indianapolis BRM had built a 4.2-litre version of its H-16 engine and this was installed into a one-off Lotus, the 42. When Lotus took it testing at Snetterton, it was an occasion when the machine actually completed a lap. The team reverted to the 1965 38 for Jim Clark and Al Unser. The two cars were finished in fluorescent red and entered as STP Gasoline Treatment Specials. It was the first time that a Team Lotus car was entered under a sponsor's name and the experience would give Colin an edge when overt sponsorship was permitted in Formula 1. He could not have had a better mentor than Andy Granatelli, President of STP.

Granatelli had built an awesome reputation as a hot rodder before the war and he was a consummate salesman. At the time, a can of STP, it was claimed: 'Supercharges Engine Performance. Tunes Your Engine As You Drive. Cleans Your Engine As You Drive. Makes Engines Come Alive. Restores And Protects Engine Life.' These were just the headlines. It seemed that if you drank a can of STP you would be able to make yourself invisible, speak to animals, and fly.

Granatelli had tried year after year to win at Indianapolis with the fearsomely fast, though fragile, Novi roadsters with their supercharged V8 engines. A Novi first ran at the Brickyard in 1946 and made a final appearance in 1958, with its highest finish, third, coming in 1948. The fans loved the Novis, however, and that was enough to make STP a market leader. Granatelli made an impression on Colin, whose previous business dealings had been with executives and managers in the mainstream of the automotive business. Granatelli belonged there as well, but he was also a snake oil salesman and Colin took note.

Andrew Ferguson tells one story. One of the American mechanics attached to Team Lotus had been conducting a liaison with a married woman and her husband had sent the mechanic a note, composed from cut-out letters from newspapers, which said that he would be opposite the pits during practice and the race armed with a rifle fitted with a telescopic sight. Most of the Brits on the team thought this was a huge joke, but Colin was rattled. He abhorred anything connected to death and would call identical lap times 'evens' rather than 'dead heats'. Routine American newspaper reports of deaths by shooting left him lost for words.

Nobody who speaks of Colin suggests that he was a religious man, or even that he showed a spiritual side. Nobody says, 'Hey, remember when Colin came into the works waving a book or an LP and shouting, "You have to know this"'. Nobody recalls him enthusing him over the latest rock band. But he did favour checked shirts because they were 'lucky'.

Jimmy qualified on the middle of the front row at Indianapolis and it was a more remarkable achievement than it may appear. At Indianapolis, pole position can only be set on the first day of qualifying and Jimmy's harness had broken. It was late in the day and had he had the harness replaced, he would have had to run the following day, so he set his time without crotch straps, an alarming prospect at Indianapolis, though no driver in Formula 1 used any form of safety harness at the time.

Also on the grid were two rookies in Lolas, Jackie Stewart and Graham Hill – word had spread about the Speedway's prize fund. At the first turn on the first lap, a car either got out of shape or the driver accelerated too hard and rammed the car in front. There was a lot of bent metal, 10 cars were out, but the only injury was to A.J. Foyt, who cut his hand trying to scramble over the chicken wire fencing which surrounded the track. After 90 minutes the race restarted and Jimmy was leading on lap 65 when he spun and managed to bring the car under control without brushing the wall. Twenty laps later Jimmy was still in the lead when he spun again, and this time he did brush the wall. He called at the pits for a check, but while nothing seemed to be wrong, the car did not handle properly for the rest of the race.

There were two factors at work. One was that the track was still slippery following the first lap pile-up when oil was shed. The Lotus 38 was terrible to drive under such conditions and Jimmy, who spun so rarely, showed his skill by not hitting the wall and catching the car on two other occasions when it had started to spin. The other factor was that the company supplying the fuel was supposed to have added 10 percent nitromethane to it, and the engine was tuned for that fuel. When he came into the pits for refuelling, Clark complained that the engine was not pulling strongly and Andrew Ferguson suspects that the fuel company had forgotten to add the nitromethane and that error, more than the spins, cost Jimmy the race.

At the 150-lap mark, the race was led by Lloyd Ruby's Eagle and Jackie Stewart's Lola with Clark in third. Ruby's car was shedding oil, however, and he was black-flagged. As lap 180 approached, the order was Stewart, Hill and Clark, until Jackie's engine lost oil pressure with 10 laps to go. Hill then led from Clark, or did he? Both teams thought that their guy was in the lead. At the end of the race, Graham Hill was waved into the winner's circle and presented with the traditional bottle of milk, while Colin simply could not believe that he had made a mistake with a lap chart. It was a case of 'No more Mr Nice Guy' as Colin screamed at the organisers. When he had been calmed – Colin's furies rarely lasted long – an examination of his chart against the official charts proved him wrong, though Granatelli was never convinced.

The year 1966 was not the most glorious in the history of Team Lotus, though second place at Indianapolis did bring in $76,992. It was, however, the year that Lotus decamped from Cheshunt and relocated to Norfolk, where the company has remained ever since. If Lotus was to expand, to make the Europa as well as the Elan and Seven, it needed a new factory. It was no longer necessary to move to a site nearby so that key workers could drive from their digs or parents' houses in some old banger, as had been the case when Lotus moved from Hornsey to Cheshunt all of a dozen miles away. By 1965, economic and social conditions had changed, home ownership was increasing and the population as a whole was becoming more mobile.

According to Clive Chapman, Colin decided that a new site had to be within 100 miles of London and should also provide him with a runway for his aircraft. Norfolk, on the east coast of England, moved into the frame. Norfolk's main industry was and is agriculture, and at the time the introduction of modern farming methods meant that the number of jobs in agriculture was shrinking year on year. Anyone who established a factory in Norfolk and created jobs was in line for government grants and subsidies. Colin arranged meetings at the factory and sold the idea of moving to Norfolk, emphasising the the county's many positive points, especially the low price of property. Coaches were laid on to take workers and their families to look over the county and, indeed, most of the people at Cheshunt did make the move.

It also happens that East Anglia is rich in ex-World War Two military airfields, which are ideal for the testing of racing cars. Colin and Fred were able to obtain an airfield at Hethel, near Norwich. During the war the US Second Air Division had flown more than 95,000 sorties from Hethel, and it had a runway for Colin's aircraft and a perimeter track which was ideal for testing cars. Some local farmers owned parcels of land on the Hethel site, but Norfolk County Council brought pressure to bear, there were inducements, and the farmers signed on the dotted line. Colin and his accountants arranged a mortgage with a pension fund and, according to Ron Hickman, managed to get the valuation of the site increased three-fold so that the mortgage covered the cost of building the factory.

Colin was able to buy Ketteringham Hall, a minor stately home with its origins in the 15th century, though it had been remodelled in the neo-Gothic style in the mid-19th century. It is one of those brooding, over-decorated piles where you can imagine a coach and four arriving at night and an eerie servant saying, 'The master asked me to bid you welcome. Ha ha ha!' The hall stood in 42 acres, mainly woodland, complete with a fishing lake. It had been the headquarters of the US Second Air Division and up to 700 servicemen and women had been stationed there, then during the 1950s it housed a school. It had so many rooms that it was a ready-made design centre and there was also plenty of land on which to build workshops with the compliance of a local authority eager to promote employment. There was also a cross-Channel ferry link to Holland from Harwich, which was not far away, which made life easier when Team Lotus travelled to the Continent, and which would also be convenient when the Europa came on stream because that was intended for export.

Stan Chapman had been out of the ordinary run of publicans, but he could not have dreamed of owning a country estate, let alone two. Colin had a minor stately home for Team Lotus, he had his own mansion not far away from Ketteringham Hall and he could fly his aircraft, of ever-increasing size, from Hethel. Colin was a skilled pilot, though stories abound of his taking short-cuts. According to these tales, he was often too impatient to allow the engines of his aircraft to warm up for the recommended time and there are also tales of foliage lodged in the undercarriage, the result of his clipping trees.

Norfolk was not, however, entirely satisfactory on every score. For a start, new workers would have to be recruited from an area which had no tradition of engineering. To put it at its most kind, the pace of life in Norfolk was on the slow side. The main claim of Norwich, the principal city, was that it had more churches in proportion to its population than any other city in England. Worthy though this claim is, it is not necessarily a selling point. Anyone who knew Norfolk at the time knows why the government had to make grants to persuade businesses to move there. It was not the most exciting part of England in which to live, unless you were wildly enthusiastic about the state of the sugar beet crop, or you wanted your first cousin to bear your children.

That did not matter to Colin – the conditions were right for expansion. It was only ever a base for him. He was either stirring creative mayhem in the works, or he was flying hither and yon. Colin was not one for watching the latest movie or going to the theatre, and he could be self-contained in Norfolk. At the beginning of the war, the Stationers' Company's School had been evacuated to Wisbech in the Fens and Colin actually liked flat country with vast skies – you have to have lived there to understand the charm of the area. He was able to buy the site of the former East Carlton Manor and there build a grand new house, much of it his own design. One thing he insisted on was air conditioning, with the units equipped with pollen filters because of his acute hay fever. Hay fever can be terribly debilitating, yet he managed to work through it and it was not widely known in his lifetime that he was a sufferer. His use of uppers and downers has to be seen in that context.

Colin had been very lucky in the formative years of Lotus, right down to the fact that Williams & Pritchard was close by. The move to Norfolk announced that Lotus was so confident of its reputation that Colin thought that he would have no difficulty in attracting the brightest and the best. However, one person who was not prepared to move was Ron Hickman and his story is instructive:

On 12 June 1964, my service contract said that I was to have five percent of the main Lotus companies, so I had 750 shares in Lotus Cars, 1,000 shares in Lotus Components, 10 shares in Team Lotus, five percent of whatever was in the Bahamas with Team Lotus Overseas and, much to my surprise, I received five percent of Hethel Property, the company which owned the factory site.

It has been written that I didn't want to move to Norfolk because I'd bought a big old house which I wanted to do up. The fact is that I didn't want to be involved with cars any more and I was tired of fighting Colin on a lot of fronts. When Lotus moved to Hethel, the company was restructured and John Standen and I, who had equal shares in the business, were told by Fred Bushell that we would not be on the board of directors. Colin wanted to bring in high-profile people who had connections in the world of commerce.

Colin went out of his way to invite us round for dinner and to assure us that we would both be directors. We went back to Fred with this news and he said it just wasn't the case, he had seen all the documentation. I suppose it was a case of Colin up to his usual tricks, he could be utterly gutless and lie to Olympic standard.

I went to him and said I wasn't prepared to move, indeed, I wasn't prepared to stay at Lotus. I was prepared, however, to remain connected as an independent consultant.

Colin said that I'd kicked him in the balls, that I had been trained by Lotus to be a true Lotus man – there was no mention of any contribution I may have made. We came to the question of settlement and here I was assisted by both Fred Bushell and Bob Webster, who was in charge of Financial Control. Bob told me that I should ask for £50,000, but be prepared to settle for £40,000.

I believe that my five percent in Team Lotus Overseas, the Bahamas shell company, was worth anything between £18,000 and £25,000, so there was up to half a million pounds hidden away which was a great deal of money in 1966. Colin protested that he had never signed an agreement on that, Colin didn't like things in writing, and he said that he had intended it only as a gift. Since I was leaving, he no longer felt inclined to make me that gift.

My contract said that, if I left, I had to sell my shares to anyone nominated by the board. Colin owned 70–75 percent of the shares, so for 'board' read 'Colin'. My shares in Hethel Property, however, did not come under the terms of my contract so I could use them as leverage. When it came to selling the other shares, I had to sell to Colin on his terms.

The one thing that everyone was scared of was if I told everything I knew about Lotus to the press. I was told that I was quite welcome to go to the Bahamas and withdraw my money and then somehow smuggle it back to England. I could not do that, I couldn't risk going through Customs with a bag packed with bank notes, they'd ask a lot of questions and so would the Inland Revenue. There is no way that I'd attempt to smuggle money into the country.

Colin and Fred also assumed that I would do nothing to harm Lotus, and they were right. I wouldn't harm Lotus, I had given too much of myself to the company. Damaging Colin was a different matter, and he knew it. The deal I was offered was £9,000 for my shares in all the companies except for Hethel Property and I would have two 'golden goodbyes' of £7,000. Colin was in the driving seat and I had no bargaining power.

Typical Lotus, these promises were fulfilled in dribs and drabs. I left Lotus on 28 February 1967 and was able to use 'whitemail' (my knowledge of the company plus my shares in Hethel Property) to get the money by late that year. In fact, I was paid £2,000 over the agreement, but I refused to return it because of the way I had been treated over Team Lotus Overseas.

I settled the Hethel Property shares late in 1967 and got stuck into selling early versions of what eventually became the Black & Decker Workmate.

With the move to Norfolk, Team Lotus became separated from the other components of the Lotus group. It was only by a 10 minute drive, but it was enough. Colin's main interest became Team Lotus and though Lotus Cars and Lotus Components continued to reflect his thinking, and his finger was on the pulse, he was delegating more and more. The move to Norfolk also marks a change in the story because Colin became ever more the distant CEO. On the other hand, he rekindled his real passion, motor racing, and that meant Ketteringham. Motor racing itself was becoming ever more professional, and the days of the acetylene mortars were gone. With the move, the story becomes more serious – bland even.

Lotus had become a considerable business which employed more than 500 people. The high jinks of just 10 years previously were a fast-receding memory. Hardly anyone at Lotus had worked in the stable block by Stan Chapman's pub. An indication of the change is that, during 1966, Lotus felt able to take on the design and development of a 5512cc V8 engine for the Argentine entrepreneur, Alejandro de Tomaso, who had plans for a big-banger sports racing car. De Tomaso was the maker of some of the worst cars in history – the competition career of his 1962 Formula 1 car with a de Tomaso flat-eight engine comprised a single lap of a minor race – but he had married an heiress to the Ford empire and no longer held ambitions in Formula 1. He wanted an engine for Group 7 sports car racing. Lotus fulfilled its side of the contract, but de Tomaso lost interest in the project, which was not unusual for him.

Lotus could undertake such a commission because, as part of the move, an engine shop had been established at Hethel. From the middle of 1967, this new department took over the building of the cylinder heads for the 'Twin Cam' engine while also developing an all-new unit which, one day, would power all Lotus models. Concept studies had been instigated as early as 1964 and the concept was fairly firm by 1966: it would be a lightweight four-cylinder 2-litre engine with four valves per cylinder, and its direct descendant would still be made more than 30 years after the first engine was made. Lotus had grown sufficiently large and sufficiently confident to undertake the development of an engine for de Tomaso and, leaving aside the Lotus-Cortina, it was the first of many projects which Lotus would undertake as a consultancy. Colin knew that he had at his command a wealth of talent, united by his philosophy, for which there was a wider demand.

In the future, Lotus would work with other manufacturers on a wide range of projects. There would be engines, work on suspension systems, and joint projects with Vauxhall and Sunbeam for high-performance road cars with 'Lotus' as part of their badge. Lotus would also make a record-breaking bicycle and even develop the infamous Sinclair C5. While Colin was still alive there would also be the development of the DeLorean GT car, and while the car itself would not tarnish his reputation, his arrangements with John Z. DeLorean would.

CHAPTER 17

THE DAWN OF THE COSWORTH ERA

C OSWORTH Engineering had hoped to have its first engine ready for the 1967 Monaco Grand Prix, but it missed its target by a couple of weeks. Team Lotus therefore ran Type 43s in South Africa and Type 33s at Monaco, where their nimbleness and reliability made them a better bet than the heavy 43-BRM. Graham Hill rejoined Lotus for 1967 as joint number one with Clark and he brought his 33 home in second place, though it has to be said that the main reason for that was that others dropped out. It was the last time that Team Lotus ran a 25/33.

Graham had enjoyed a wonderful run at BRM since 1960. He had won the world championship in 1962 and had the series been run to the modern points system, he would have taken the title again in 1964. Then came the 3-litre formula and BRM declined. In 1966, with a reliable 2-litre engine, he had managed three podium finishes, but he had no faith in BRM's H-16 engine.

Ford had sponsored the DFV, but Walter Hayes did not want Lotus to be running effectively a one-car team built around Jimmy. Hayes massaged a deal whereby Graham took the other car on equal standing with Clark. Trade sponsors did such deals all the time, though the general public was usually unaware of the extent of their involvement. Trevor Taylor says that, at the end of 1966, Jimmy told him that Esso was paying him an annual retainer of £100,000. Add that to all the other ways he was earning money and it is probable that Clark was the highest-paid sportsman in Europe, possibly even in the world. For comparison, in 1961 Stirling Moss earned just over £32,000 directly from motor racing. Costs were escalating at a rapid rate and companies began to wonder whether they were receiving a proper return.

At the Dutch Grand Prix, Jimmy and Graham had the Type 49, a full monocoque design with a 10-gallon fuel tank between the cockpit and engine and side tanks each containing 15 gallons. The DFV engine and Hewland gearbox were part of the car's structure. In terms of overall layout the 49 became the model for the modern Formula 1 car, the only difference being that it has long been the practice to position all the fuel between the cockpit and the engine.

Initial testing was carried out at Hethel in secret and the cars made their first public appearance at the Dutch Grand Prix at Zandvoort. Though the new engine had 'Ford' on its cam-covers, most journalists insisted on calling it a Cosworth. In fact the only DFV engines with Cosworth on the cam-covers were those used by Williams when it had sponsorship from Saudi Arabia, because Ford was on a blacklist compiled by some Arab countries since it had links with Israel.

In *Such Sweet Thunder*, their book on the Cosworth DFV, John Blunsden and David Phipps described the scene in the paddock immediately prior to the Dutch Grand Prix:

> Colin Chapman busied himself checking and rechecking everything in sight and shouting orders to anyone who would listen (and several people who wouldn't!); Keith Duckworth tried to convince himself that there was no point in worrying any more, but failed; Jim Clark was easing himself into a state of introversion which so often had proceeded one of his great drives; Graham Hill had long passed through the time barrier beyond which it was dangerous to to attempt to engage him in polite conversation; Harley Copp sought distraction with his movie camera; and Walter Hayes... walked around the paddock telling everyone with a press pass that the engine had already shown its worth in practice, and that if necessary he was willing to wait several Grands Prix for it to win its first race. He was talking good sense, of course, but nobody would believe him!

As it turned out, Hayes need not have shown such reticence. Graham had put his car on pole and he led for the first 10 laps until suffering a timing gear failure, something which was to dog the DFV in its early days. Jimmy had been more subdued, sixth on the grid and fourth when Graham dropped out, but he surged ahead to win at a canter. It was a dream debut, though none could have dreamed even then that the DFV would win 155 world championship races. A Lotus 49-DFV would set pole on the first 11 times it ran. Graham had his fair share of poles, but he was to finish a race only twice in 1967 in a 49. Jimmy, who could be quicker while stressing a car less, took four wins. He had his retirements, but there was no clear pattern to them.

Clark ended the season third in the drivers' world championship behind the Brabham duo of Hulme and Brabham. Denny and Jack each won only two races to Jimmy's four, but Denny scored points in 10 of the 11 races and Jack scored in nine. It was a case of the hare and the tortoise. Dan Gurney and his Eagle-Weslake won in Belgium, but finished in the points on only one other occasion and Gurney's showing was largely due to problems with Ford's other engine, the Weslake V12. Gurney's teammate, Richie Ginther, scored no points at all.

BRM more or less said what it thought of its H-16 engine when its V12, based on its 1.5-litre V8, was ready and the H-16 was consigned to history. Ferrari was going through one of its periodic troughs and, while Cooper had won the 1967 South African Grand Prix, more by luck than anything else, it was clear that the team's decline into oblivion was more or less inevitable.

Brabham was the most successful constructor in Formula 2, which was run to a new 1.6-litre formula. Lotus produced a new monocoque design, the Type 48, and Jimmy managed three wins while Graham could do no better than a couple of second places. Overall, the star of Formula 2 was Jochen Rindt in his Brabham, and he was also in Formula 1 struggling with the unwieldy Cooper-Maserati, but the European Formula 2 Championship was taken by Jacky Ickx in a Matra.

Elsewhere in motor sport, a 'B' version of the Type 41 Formula 3 car was passed over by all save a few optimistic souls since the car had a reputation for fragility. Brabham had become the first port of call for the driver at the start of his single-seater career while Cooper, which had pioneered series production of single-seaters in Britain, found few customers. In 1967, however, a new category was introduced – Formula Ford. The concept was simple: a spaceframe chassis, a Ford 'Kent' 1600cc engine in Cortina GT spec., which could be 'blue-printed' (hand-built to Ford's ideal specification) but not modified, control tyres, a Hewland gearbox which used a VW Beetle casing, and an upper price limit of £1,000, which, like most price limits in motor racing, was soon a fading memory. Formula Ford was an idea promoted by John Webb, who ran Brands Hatch, and was taken up with enthusiasm by the Jim Russell Racing School, which modified some of its existing Lotus 31 Formula 3 cars.

The idea of such a category appealed to Colin's best instincts and he had proven spaceframe designs in his portfolio. He also knew that when you sold a Formula Ford car to a young hopeful, you made a contact which could lead to selling that driver a Formula 3 car, and the driver who bought a Lotus racing car might also buy an Elan. Lotus was one of the first off the mark in Formula Ford with the Type 51, which was actually a 1964 Type 31 Formula 3 car fitted with a Ford engine. The 31 had not been much good as a Formula 3 car, but a poor Lotus was still better than most of the opposition, especially since neither Brabham nor Lola had any interest in the new category.

Compared with other Formula Ford cars, the 51 looked sensational, and it had the unmatched cachet of a Lotus badge. Before long Lotus was offering the 51 for £995 complete with Don Parker trailer, the trailer every serious racer used. Not only that, but you could buy one on hire purchase. Of course, you did not get a hand-built engine for that price, you had to go to someone like David Minister to get an engine which would be competitive. Nick Brittain, a motor-racing entrepreneur, bought a T51 which was fitted with lights and mudguards, so it was street-legal. It being 1967, the car was finished in a 'flower power' livery. Nick was actually trying to promote the idea of a Formula 1 race in Hyde Park. He failed in that, but generated a lot of publicity and Lotus Components even received orders for replicas. A single-seat racing car on the road is many an enthusiast's dream.

In the four years that Jimmy had driven at Indianapolis, he had scored a win and two second places and, had the rules been adhered to in 1963, it would have been two wins and a second. Despite all the evidence against it, Colin cooked a deal with BRM to run 42s with H-16 engines, a repeat of the 1966 proposal, but BRM had still not got its act together. Jimmy drove a 42-BRM at Hethel and managed several laps before the engine decided that it didn't want to play any more. BRM had returned to its old ways of making engines which worked in conversation but not when they were made of metal. Lotus's powertrain section worked on the engine and devised a new exhaust system, which produced a significant increase in power, but the engine was still shy of being competitive.

Even had the engines been delivered on time (BRM offered Lotus its first engine on 27 April, with practice at Indianapolis starting four days later), they would have been down on power compared with the Ford 'quad-cam' Indy engine. They would also have been overweight and too thirsty, while the possibility of their lasting more than a few laps was not something on which you would wager your house. There was, however, a sponsorship deal with Andy Granatelli and STP to fulfil, though Andy had other irons in the fire.

With the BRM engine not looking a possible contender, Lotus went into panic overdrive. Jimmy and Graham were assigned two-year-old Type 38s with Ford engines while the team also took along a 42 which had been made for the BRM unit and that had been designed to be a stressed member so, to accommodate the Ford V8, a spaceframe structure had to be lashed-up. Clark and Hill, the drivers who had won the Indianapolis 500 in 1965 and 1966, were entered in substandard cars in 1967.

The Monaco Grand Prix did not clash with Indianapolis in 1967, so Jimmy and Graham flew to Europe to take part and that took five days out of the month of May, a month which saw a lot of rain over Indianapolis. When there wasn't rain there were high winds.

Jimmy qualified his 38 in only 16th slot, having endured a repeat of the handling problems which had beset him in 1966. Graham struggled, however, but Andy Granatelli watched him carefully and told him that he wasn't being smooth enough – he was driving his Indy car as though it were a Formula 1 car. Andy was a brave man to say that to Graham, but Graham actually listened and his lap times did improve. He even paid tribute to Granatelli in interviews. Graham, winner in 1966, had still not qualified for the race when the final day for qualifying dawned, and he had an engine blow up in his 38 on the final day of practice.

Colin ordered the 42 to be readied and Graham, who had driven the car for only 15 laps, was soon back in the pits with water pouring from the radiator. The seconds ticked away as the mechanics worked then Graham went out for one last attempt.

Despite encountering a bird on the track, which caused him to go off the racing line, Graham qualified. In fact, he did better than just qualify, he actually set a better time than Jimmy. However, since his qualifying had been done on the last day, he had to start from the back row.

Between final qualifying and the race, Colin and Graham had flown to Hethel to test the first Lotus 49-DFV and Jimmy had flown to Zolder to drive in a Formula 2 race. Unlike all the other teams, which were focused throughout the month of May on only the Indianapolis 500, everyone at Team Lotus had other commitments. That might have been fine had the team been running new cars which were as ahead of the field as the Type 29 had been, but lots of people had the latest Ford V8 engine and it was no longer a case of a modern team taking on the hicks. In 1963 Indianapolis had been a huge juicy peach waiting to be plucked, but in 1967 there was serious opposition, many of whom were running copies of Lotus, Lola or Brabham designs.

When the field streamed off for the pace lap, Graham was left behind with a stalled engine. The idea of a pace lap and rolling start is to get everyone under way, so Graham did start and was in last place when, after 16 laps, it started to rain. At Indianapolis, when the rain comes down the racing stops and the race is continued the next day.

Graham had all kinds of mechanical problems during the restarted race, as did Jimmy. The pair of them, each a world champion and each a winner of the Indianapolis 500, were soon out, having lost many laps in the pits. Graham was classified 32nd and Jimmy 31st. It was a far cry from from the days of glory, but Team Lotus would be back and when it returned it would have lost some of its arrogance.

Lotus's move to Hethel must have pleased the local council because, by 1967, the company was employing more than 570 people. Jobs had been created for locals and those who had moved from Cheshunt had bought houses. It was a successful move all round and Norfolk has since become a centre of motor racing as former Lotus men have set up their own businesses in the area. Also during 1967, Lotus introduced two new road cars. One was the Lotus-Cortina Mk II, based on the revised Ford Cortina. It could not be the sensation that the first Lotus-Cortina had been since things had moved rapidly in the motor industry, but it was still a class leader. The other new car was Ron Hickman's legacy to Lotus, the Elan Plus-2. It was an Elan for the driver with a young family since it had four seats, though the rear seats were not for large people. People began to say that Colin built cars which reflected his own needs as a motorist.

With the Elan Plus-2 Ron Hickman did more than just add a bit here and there. The body, which Ron designed, was related to the standard Elan, but it had a drag coefficient of just 0.3, the same as the Europa and streets ahead of any other car in production. It had all the handling characteristics of the Elan, which remained a benchmark, and it was luxuriously appointed. The backbone chassis of the Elan was extended by a foot and the track was widened by seven inches. Many enthusiasts today claim that it handles even more sweetly than the Elan, but it cannot be denied that the interior was noisy.

Though it was to remain only a prototype, work began that year on a new engine. Vauxhall had just introduced a new four-cylinder engine with a single overhead camshaft and Colin saw at once that many of its features paralleled the engine that Lotus was working on. Colin immediately began to negotiate the supply of Vauxhall crankcases and other components so that he could do what Duckworth had done with the FVA, which was to concentrate on getting the cylinder head right. Steve Sanville headed the team working on the new Lotus engine and he was set to work on making a twin overhead camshaft, four-valves-per-cylinder version of the Vauxhall unit. He was joined in the project by Ron Burr, who had joined Lotus from Coventry Climax.

Esso had long supported Lotus and successive competition managers of Esso had influenced the way that Colin operated and even how he chose his drivers. For a company such as Esso, the deal was that they subsidised Lotus and if Lotus was successful, they could then publicise the fact in advertisements. Esso contributed to Lotus's war chest and, if Lotus was successful, Esso then had to pay again in order to spread the glad tidings. When the 3-litre Formula 1 arrived, however, costs soared and dropping a few thousand pounds here and there to support teams and individuals was no long possible. The oil companies made the extent of their unhappiness heard, and underlined their collective misery by threatening to withdraw their support.

Colin was kept informed at every stage. The FIA, motorsport's governing body, was also aware of the situation and announced that, from 1 January 1968, overt commercial sponsorship in European racing would be permitted. Colin had dealt with Andy Granatelli and, being Colin, he had been quick to learn the rudiments of sponsorship. Colin wrote to about 200 companies and hit a brick wall, which is not surprising since sports sponsorship was virtually unknown in Europe in 1967.

At the 1967 London Motor Show Esso made the formal announcement that it was withdrawing support from motor racing. David Lazenby, who headed Lotus Components, intended to run two Type 47s in GT racing. The Type 47 was a Group 4 competition version of the Europa running with a Twin Cam engine. It had won its class in the 1967 BOAC 500 and David was looking for a company to support his 1968 campaign. Someone in David's office had heard on the grapevine that the John Player tobacco company was interested in using motor racing as a promotional tool, and it was as vague as that.

David followed up the lead and discovered that the story was true. He reported to Andrew Ferguson and Andrew was immediately on the case. He visited Player's headquarters in Nottingham and a deal was signed within two hours. Tobacco sponsorship had arrived in motor racing and the amount of money involved was of a different order to that previously seen in the sport. Esso's withdrawal from supporting teams accelerated the decline of Cooper, which struggled on as a makeweight in 1968, while for Lotus it opened a door of opportunity.

Though Ford had sponsored the DFV, all rights to the engine were retained by Cosworth and, naturally, other teams wanted to buy the unit. The only restriction on the number of teams who could use the DFV was Cosworth's own capacity to make and maintain the engine, and in 1968, it took on two more teams, McLaren and Ken Tyrrell, who had stitched together a deal to run Jackie Stewart in a chassis built by Matra.

So began what has become known as the Cosworth Era, when the world and his dog could build a Formula 1 car since the DFV was available off-the-shelf and Mike Hewland could sell you a gearbox. Cynics called it the era of the British Formula 1 kit car.

CHAPTER 18

SPONSORSHIP ARRIVES IN EUROPE

S PONSORSHIP had been part and parcel of American racing for years, but you had to be fairly knowledgeable to know that, say, the 1964 John Zink Trackburner Special was actually a Brabham BT24. Many American fans knew little of Frank Kurtis or J.G. Watson, whose chassis dominated the Indianapolis 500 from the early 1950s until the 'rear-engine revolution'. To this day the official website of the Indy Racing League lists the title sponsor, but not the chassis maker.

The European tradition was different. From 1903, each country was assigned a national racing livery, so Britain had green, France had blue, Italian cars were red, and so on. Even Egypt had a national colour – it was violet. The rule was that the car was painted according to the nationality of the entrant, so a Frenchman who bought an Alfa Romeo would paint it blue and an Englishman who bought a Maserati would paint it his favourite shade of green (there is no such shade as British Racing Green, any shade is acceptable). The notion that a racing team, or individual driver, was competing on behalf of a country fitted the notion of a sporting ideal beloved by the 'buffers in blazers' who were elected to control motor racing. It also fitted the general mood of the first three quarters of the 20th century, which is why 'buffers in blazers' controlled every sport.

The following story may help to illustrate the prevailing attitude among blazered ones' in motor racing. It occurred at Monza in 1967, just 44 days before the running of the last world championship race before display of a sponsor was permitted. Bruce McLaren put his McLaren M5A-BRM on the front row at Monza for the race on 10 September 1967. Alistair Caldwell, who was chief mechanic with McLaren at the time, says:

We painted it red because we had red paint in the workshop.

The Italian organisers came up to us and demanded that we painted the car green because McLaren was based in England. We said 'Yeah, yeah, we'll do it.' They kept on at us, so much so that I sent someone to buy aerosols of the most obnoxious shade of green he could find.

We were going to paint the whole car bright lime green: wheels, tyres, springs, everything. We were about to do it when the organisers turned up. They said, 'The car's still red? Good. Leave it red.' Turns out it would have been the first time since the year dot when there wasn't a red car on the front row of the Italian Grand Prix.

Faced by the collapse or fragmentation of Formula 1, as fuel companies reassessed their commitment, the CSI, the arm of the FIA which regulated sporting procedures, agreed that, from 1 January 1968, a team could advertise a commercial supporter on its cars, provided that the advertisement on each side of the car was no more than roughly one foot square.

BRP had run teams with sponsorship, at different times, from the finance companies Yeoman Credit and UDT. The names of the companies were incorporated in the team's title, so 'Yeoman Credit Racing' appeared on the side of the Coopers that BRP ran in 1960, just like 'Team Lotus'.

On 8 January 1968 at the New Zealand Grand Prix at Pukekohe, Jim Clark put his works Lotus 49 on pole, except that it wasn't a Team Lotus car, it was a Gold Leaf Team Lotus car. On both sides of the car was a one-foot square logo of the bearded sailor, the John Player trademark, and the rest of the car was painted red and white with a gold stripe down the middle.

It was a turning point in motor racing history. It marked the end of cars being entered in national colours as they became mobile billboards. It also marked the beginning of the long affair between motor racing and tobacco. As tobacco companies found themselves being banned from advertising directly on television they switched to sports sponsorship and motor racing has been the chief beneficiary

The arrival of sponsorship, together with the availability of the Cosworth DFV engine, led to the expansion of Formula 1. It also led to an escalation of costs as teams had to add such things as corporate hospitality and public relations to their budgets. There had been a time when a team had to get results in order to attract trade support, but sponsorship meant that a team which could generate publicity for its sponsor could still survive. It opened up all manner of possibilities. For example if a CEO liked motor racing, he could recommend that his company should sponsor a team. Of course, if he was a fan of show jumping, he recommended sponsorship of show jumping. In either case the company's shareholders picked up the bill and the CEO became a celebrity within his chosen pursuit. It was not unknown for such a person to receive some of the sponsorship back. Let us imagine the managing director of a sponsoring company arriving for a meeting and leaving an empty briefcase with the boss's secretary, a briefcase which is heavier when he leaves.

Formula 1 has the potential to present ways of losing money through the books. If you need a new component for your Ford or Volkswagen there is a price list. There is no price list for a works Formula 1 car. If a Formula 1 team says that a pair of wishbones costs £700, that is what they cost even if they actually cost only £500 to make. If a team says that wishbones need to be changed after every race, but in reality they are changed after every two races, that is £1400 in the books, but £500 in reality. That means that £900 has been lost, and every car has four corners. Anyone who introduced a sponsor to a team got a kick-back. Most motor racing journalists have been told by some team manager or other that his cut would be 15 percent of the total sponsorship and that it would be paid in cash, out of the reach of the tax man.

The arrival of sponsorship also put Formula 1 on an altogether more professional footing, and in 1970, for example, March Engineering could come into being from nothing because it had a designer and a sponsor. There was another effect of sponsorship and that was that, by 1973, every team, with March's exception, concentrated on Formula 1. Lotus, McLaren and Brabham had all made production racing cars, but the competition had become so intense in Formula 1 that these were considered a distraction. Besides, there was so much cash coming in from sponsors that constructors did not need the uncertainty of the volatile production racing car business.

Ferrari was in a slightly different position, being subsidised by Fiat, but at the end of 1972 it had pulled out of sports car racing having just won 10 of the 11 rounds of the world championship. For more than 30 years Ferrari had successfully competed in both categories, but the time had come to specialise. The divide between Formula 1 and the rest of racing had begun.

Jim Clark began the 1969 season by winning the Tasman Championship. This was a series for 2.5-litre cars. Most competitors still ran with the Coventry Climax FPF engine, but Jimmy had the Lotus 49 with a DFV engine reduced in capacity. The Tasman series was a bumper pay day for visiting stars and the social life was remarkable.

On 1 January 1968, Jimmy won the South African Grand Prix and set a new record. That win gave Clark his 25th world championship race victory, one more than the great Juan-Manuel Fangio, who had retired with five world championship titles just as Jimmy was on the lower level of his learning curve. Naturally comparisons were drawn between the two drivers, especially since Fangio had an amazing win/start rate. Without getting embroiled in a debate, one has to point out that Fangio was a seasoned Grand Prix driver when the world championship was launched in 1950 and Jimmy made his Grand Prix debut in 1960, in only his third season. The tendency today is to count only world championship races, but both Fangio and Clark turned in some remarkable performances in non-championship events. These are no less worthy than those which carry championship points.

Jimmy's European season began with a Formula 2 race in Barcelona. His race lasted only one lap because he was rammed from behind by Jacky Ickx and retired with suspension damage. A week later he lined up at Hockenheim in another Formula 2 race. His Lotus 48 was off the pace and he was down in eighth place during the first heat when his car twitched, left the track and hit a tree. Jimmy died immediately. No other driver's death has had a greater impact on the motor racing community. Jimmy seemed invincible, invulnerable – he had never sustained an injury – he was the driver that all others acknowledged as the greatest of his era.

When Clark was killed it made every driver uncomfortably aware of his own mortality. Everyone involved in any dangerous activity clings to the irrational belief that other people may get crippled or killed, but 'it cannot happen to me'. Jimmy's death proved that it could happen to anyone and it rocked everyone in the sport. *Motor Sport* magazine did not even attempt an obituary, it merely published a black-edged photograph of Jimmy smiling from the cockpit of a car.

Ever since, it has become usual to say that Jimmy died in an insignificant, piffling little race of no importance. This is nonsense. No race was unimportant to Jimmy because real racing drivers do not grade races, they are in a race or they are not. Jimmy did not line up seventh on the grid at Hockenheim and think, 'Seventh is okay for me, this is a minor race,' he was thinking, 'How can I win from seventh?'

Everyone in the sport was shattered by Jimmy's death, and no one more so than Colin. Colin had lost his best friend, the guy who shared his hotel room, the driver for whom he had created his best work. Jimmy had been Colin's muse. They had an almost telepathic understanding when it came to developing a car. Colin's Formula 1 cars were often not that easy to drive, they tended to have a small area of excellence which only exceptional drivers could explore. Exceptional drivers went straight to that small area and delivered wins. In Jimmy, Colin had a driver who always found the sweet spot. Jimmy's death also haunted Colin for another reason. Lotus racing cars had a reputation for breaking, and the rear suspension of the 49 had collapsed more than once during 1967. Colin was haunted by the possibility that a mistake on the drawing board, or during manufacture or preparation, had caused the death of his best friend.

Besieged by his own demons, Colin missed the next Grand Prix, in Spain. The day-to-day running of the team was neglected. Jackie Oliver was promoted to the Formula 1 team, but things were in such disarray that a car was not ready for him. Bob Sparshott says, 'Nobody knew where Colin was. It was Graham Hill who pulled the team together. After practice on the Saturday Graham took the entire team to dinner at a top restaurant in Madrid. Next day, Graham won the race.'

Among the things Colin was doing, apart from seriously considering his future in motor racing, was commissioning an enquiry into Jimmy's death. It was an unprecedented move, but he had to do it for his own peace of mind. The enquiry was carried out with no obstacles and concluded that Jimmy had suffered deflation in a rear tyre: he had been using tubeless tyres which were new in motor racing. It seems that the deflation was slow, but there came a point when the tyre collapsed completely and then he lost control of the car. A clump of trees was in his way.

Jimmy's young compatriot, Jackie Stewart, had been campaigning against unnecessary risks at circuits. Having trees on the infield with no barrier between them and the track is just such an unnecessary risk. Jimmy was killed because his car had a deflated rear tyre and the organisers at Hockenheim were operating a lethal circuit. The trees were sawn down – hindsight is 20/20 vision – but they could not bring back Clark's sublime talent.

The report exonerated Colin from any blame and yet he did a remarkable thing – he did not have the report published. It was only after Colin's death that Graham Gauld, a close friend of Jim Clark, published the report in full. Colin had satisfied himself, and he did not use the report as he could have done. For years there was speculation that something had broken on the Lotus, because everyone 'knew' that Lotuses were fragile. Colin kept his counsel. A number of Lotus road cars were sold with black replacing the green on the badge. Colin was in deep mourning.

Bob Sparshott recalls Colin's return to the team:

Colin arrived out of the blue at the Monaco Grand Prix as though he had never been away. We had a 49 for Graham with wedge-shaped bodywork. Colin looked it over and then gave us a job list with about 50 points on it. It was nine at night, I was shattered and I made my feelings felt.

Colin took me to one side and said, 'I have been in this business a lot longer than you... ' He was not angry, he spoke to me like a father and when he had finished, I was ready to go a straight 24 hours. He had that effect on people.

Graham won the race, and moved to the top of the world championship table. Lotus had won the first three races in the series, but McLaren had won the curtain raisers at Brands Hatch and Silverstone. Then Bruce McLaren won the Belgian Grand Prix, which followed Monaco. Belgium was the first Grand Prix win for McLaren and it was also the first race in which large wings appeared. People had been playing with aerofoil tabs for years and the American driver/engineer, Jim Hall, had a high-mounted adjustable rear wing on his 1967 Chapparal 2E Can-am cars. It is surprising that people in Formula 1 were slow to catch on, and it is even more surprising that it was not Colin to be first to take up the idea, but Ferrari and Brabham. Ron Tauranac at Brabham had a reputation for conservatism, which was undeserved, while Ferrari had reached 1968 without producing a single original idea. The Ferrari's wing, mounted on the gearbox, was not original, but it was pioneering. Naturally, every car in the pit lane was soon sprouting wings, though the engineering behind many was suspect.

Also at the Belgian Grand Prix was an entry from Anglo-American Racers for Dan Gurney. Dan had almost run out of engines because he had almost run out of money. It was the last time that an Eagle was entered in a Grand Prix, though Dan was able to cut a deal with Jack Brabham to run in the Dutch Grand Prix in a Brabham. It was not Dan Gurney's last Grand Prix, but it was effectively the end of his Formula 1 career. The one driver whose speed Jimmy had feared was side-lined because, though Dan had brought Colin to the Indianapolis 500 by arranging a deal with Ford, he had failed to land a sponsor for himself.

Meanwhile Lotus had come up with something entirely new for Indianapolis. The 56 had a wedge-shaped body (a sign that Colin was thinking seriously about aerodynamics) and was powered by a Pratt & Whitney turbine engine which fed its power through a Ferguson four-wheel-drive system.

The previous year Andy Granatelli had come close to winning the Indy 500 with his beautiful little Paxton car powered by a turbine engine. It had dominated and had come within a few miles of taking a famous victory. When Andy had checked out the turbine engine he had discovered that, while it cost $4,000 more than a Ford V8, it was scheduled to run for 1,200 hours between rebuilds in contrast to 6-10 hours for the Ford unit.

The 56 had originally been designed by Maurice Phillippe to take a 2.8-litre turbocharged version of the Ford V8, but Andy had insisted on a turbine entry. He had phoned Colin to express his viewpoint and, even as he was speaking on the phone, a cargo plane was landing at Heathrow with a Pratt & Whitney unit. Why four-wheel-drive at Indianapolis, the circuit you would think least needed four-wheel-drive? Power had increased and the grip from tyres had not kept pace, though they would soon catch up, and when Colin laid down the parameters for the 56 aerofoils had not become common in racing. Furthermore, Granatelli had been in personal contact with Ferguson since he had been exploring the idea of using four-wheel-drive on all Studebaker models. Studebaker was heading to oblivion, yet its models had outstanding styling, and four-wheel-drive was the sort of feature which might just save the company. The idea came to nothing with Studebaker, but it did take root in Colin's mind. It was one of those ideas he could not let go of and it would lead him down a cul-de-sac.

STP sponsored no fewer than four new 56s, three race cars and a spare. Jim Clark had tested one at the Speedway before his fatal accident, which shows a proper level of preparation, unlike the 1967 rush job. The wedge-shaped bodywork proved to be very efficient at keeping the cars under control in the turns – turbine cars cannot be cornered on the throttle since it is in the nature of the engine to take its time to build power. When Jimmy died, Colin brought in his protégé, Mike Spence, who was then leading the BRM team. During practice, Spence turned in a lap of 169.555mph, the second quickest lap ever seen at Indianapolis, and that by a rookie with no experience of the Speedway. Things were looking good for STP and Lotus and it also shows the level of Spence's talent.

Mike was flying and he was asked to shake-down the car Granatelli had entered for the American, Greg Weld. Though Mike had been very quick, he was still a rookie and Indianapolis is a very subtle track. He lost the car and, knowing he was going to spin, he aimed for the wall at a narrow angle. He hit the wall broadside, which is the sensible thing to do at Indianapolis, and naturally a couple of corners were sacrificed. The front right wheel, however, flew back and hit Mike's head very hard.

Colin's reaction was to demand the telephone numbers of all the leading neurosurgeons in America. If Mike could be saved, he would be saved, that was always Colin's reaction to injury to one of his drivers. It turned out that one of America's most eminent surgeons was in attendance at the Indianapolis Methodist Hospital where Mike had been taken. Even so, Mike died four hours after his crash.

Colin had taken a personal interest in Mike Spence over several years and, at Indianapolis, Mike appeared to be fulfilling all his promise. He had made a mistake, he had done the right thing to minimise the consequences and he had died in a freak accident. It was no fault of Lotus, but coming so soon after Jim Clark's death all the old stories about Colin making dangerous cars bobbed to the surface again. Things were not helped by a press release put out by Carroll Shelby, who had built two turbine cars which were way off the pace. Shelby used Mike's accident as an excuse to withdraw his cars, so as not to be humiliated, and his press release declared that it wasn't possible to build a competitive turbine car which was also safe and reliable. There was no mention of the fact that Shelby's cars had been slow because their chassis flexed. Shelby's press release had the effect of pointing a finger of blame at Colin, who was actually blameless. It was not a move which reflected credit on Shelby.

Soon after Carroll Shelby's political press release came a report from the metallurgist, S.A. Silbermann, appointed by USAC to investigate Spence's accident. Silbermann exonerated Lotus of any structural failure but his report did point out that the steering and suspension parts on the 56 should have been made from steel, or an equivalent alloy, specified by USAC. The Lotus cars did not comply with that regulation, but Silbermann's report noted that the materials Lotus used were probably at least equal, possibly superior, to USAC's specifications.

Naturally, the news story was that Lotus had not complied with the rules, and Silbermann's comment that they possibly surpassed minimum standards was largely ignored. In fact, the British Steel Corporation was able to confirm that the material used was to USAC's specification.

Shelby's press release, followed by the USAC enquiry, devastated Colin. He handed over the running of the STP Lotuses to Andy Granatelli and said that he simply did not have the heart to be involved in the 1968 Indianapolis 500. It was rare that Colin expressed his private feelings in public, but he was being battered on all sides. Everything should have been right for him. The Elan was about to be released in its final form, the S4, with more than 50 detail changes that made it a very serious motor car in the market place. Fred Bushell was preparing to launch Lotus on the stock exchange. Everything should have been looking rosy, but Colin was in personal turmoil.

Jackie Stewart had been signed to drive a 56 at Indianapolis, but he had sustained a hairline fracture in his right wrist as a result of a crash in a Formula 2 race, and so Jackie had to stand down from all racing for a time. Greg Weld was not up to speed and was dropped. Andy Granatelli cast around and picked on Joe Leonard, a 34-year-old former motorcycle champion who had not done a lot in cars.

Colin did return to Indianapolis. He had taken stock and responded with his usual resilience. His appearance at Indianapolis was untrumpeted, he was there just to support his team and he said it was what Jim Clark and Mike Spence would have wanted. 'It's what they would have wanted' is an excuse which is often trotted out, but in this case it was probably true.

Colin arrived to find a dispute on his hands. At the root of it was who should be nominated as chief mechanic, which at Indianapolis is a matter of supreme importance since a lot of money can hang on the title. Andy Granatelli had let it be known that 'Big Vince' was chief wrench and Big Vince's surname just happened to be Granatelli.

Andrew Ferguson tried to patch up the situation by suggesting a deal whereby the Team Lotus men would split 80 percent of the mechanics' share and the temporary STP men would split the remainder. The deal was rejected. Colin was furious and wrote Granatelli a letter which began: 'You now have a very disillusioned friend and if things are not settled very quickly you may have an extremely bitter associate.' According to Andrew Ferguson he went on to point out that he had submerged the identity of Team Lotus under the STP banner for two years (he forgot to say that the Lotus badge was prominent on the nose) and he regarded the ownership of the cars, and hence the responsibility for repairing them, to be Granatelli's. Eventually the two men thrashed out an agreement, which was basically that each side would run their own show.

Just as Graham had pulled the team together in Europe, so at Indianapolis he did the same. He went out and put his car on provisional pole with a four-lap average speed of 171.208mph. Colin simply burst into tears, while Andy Granatelli, true to his Italian roots, planted a big kiss on Graham. After the trauma of the deaths of Jimmy and Mike, Graham had risen to the occasion yet again. There is more to being a great racing driver than winning races, and Graham had shown true greatness in the way he gave his team back its self-belief. Later that day, while Graham was flying back to England, Joe Leonard went out and edged him into second place. It was a remarkable performance for a man with limited experience of racing cars, but it showed that Granatelli did have a good eye for talent. The two 56s sat first and second on the grid while a third car for Art Pollard was in 11th spot.

Granatelli had came up with a contract to have an option to buy, at $80,000 each, one or more of the three race cars plus spares at the value of up to $10,000 per car. Colin must have thought that all his birthdays had come at once, and he signed the deal.

Joe Leonard led the race from pole, with Graham in fourth and Pollard playing himself in, running in the top third of the field. The 56s had been detuned to last the distance and Al Unser took the lead on the eighth lap in his turbocharged Eagle-Offenhauser. The three Lotus cars stayed in contention, but after 111 laps Graham's car shed a wheel when the front suspension broke. At 188 laps, Joe Leonard led when Pollard, in seventh, coasted to a halt with a dead engine. Within a minute or so, Leonard's engine did the same. In both cases the fuel pump drive had sheared and these were engines which were supposed to go 1,200 hours between rebuilds.

What had happened was that there had been a long spell under the yellow flags which caused the engines to run hot. The cars of Pollard and Leonard were fitted with phosphor-bronze drive shafts to the fuel pumps and these were designed to fail when the engines ran too hot. When the yellow flags were lifted, the cars accelerated and the fail-safe system kicked in.

Once again, Andy Granatelli was denied his life's ambition, to be the winning owner at Indianapolis. He fitted his cars with Offenhauser engines and entered them for most other rounds of the USAC series (the Lotus badge, prominent at Indianapolis, was removed) but though the cars took pole positions and led races, they took no wins.

The rules committee of USAC was shaken by speed of the Lotus 56 at Indianapolis, however, and placed a restriction on the size of the air intake on turbine engines for 1969 and announced that, from 1970, four-wheel-drive would be banned and the only turbines permitted would be those originally designed for automotive use. Since there was then no such unit, the brief turbine era at Indianapolis was soon over.

The 56 gave Colin a lot of food for thought and the major themes of the design would appear in his Formula 1 designs. Meanwhile, work was going ahead on the LV220 engine and Colin put it to Ford that it would be possible to make a 4.2-litre V8 version for Indianapolis. No doubt he did not stress unduly the fact that the LV220 used Vauxhall components made by Ford's arch rival, General Motors. Ford listened, pondered, and rejected the offer. They thought that a 2.8-litre turbocharged engine was the best way forward. It would be a further nine years before turbocharging would appear in Formula 1. Meanwhile, in Formula 1, wings were sprouting everywhere and several teams began to explore four-wheel-drive, since the Cosworth DFV was proving too powerful for the available tyres which led to problems with traction.

Jackie Stewart was back in action at the Dutch Grand Prix, which he won. Since Graham spun and crashed and Jackie Oliver had mechanical problems which left him unclassified, the balance of the world championship changed. Oliver crashed during practice for the French Grand Prix and did not start, while Graham was soon out with a broken drive shaft. Neither works Lotus finished the British Grand Prix, which was won by Jo Siffert in Rob Walker's Lotus 49. It was the last time that a car entered by Walker would win a world championship race. Rob's cars won nine championship Formula 1 races, plus umpteen non-championship events, and Formula 2 and GT races.

The Dutch win counted to Lotus in the Constructors' Championship, but Graham's chance of adding another title to his CV seemed to be slipping away. In the wider scheme of things that was not as important as the fact that, when Team Lotus was down and shattered, it had been Graham who had lifted it and stitched it together. Stewart won in Germany, at the Nürburgring, with a great drive in terrible conditions, but Graham was second, so he kept alive his championship hopes, although neither man scored points in the Italian Grand Prix.

At Monza it was Denny Hulme who won for McLaren and it is noticeable that he ran without wings, trading downforce for less drag. This shows how little any team knew about aerofoils: they used them or they didn't, there was no subtle middle ground. Hulme won again in Canada with Hill fourth and Stewart sixth, so suddenly the world championship became a three-way affair. For the United States Grand Prix, Colin entered a third car for Mario Andretti, who put his 49 on pole in his first attempt at Formula 1.

Colin had met Andretti during his trips to Indianapolis and Mario was rare among American drivers from the oval tradition in that he was actually interested in Formula 1. Mario had been born in Italy and he had been 15 years old when his family emigrated to the United States. He had even been a spectator at the 1954 Mille Miglia, where he saw his hero, Alberto Ascari, win in a Lancia. Bob Sparshott recalls:

> Running Mario in a third car meant extra work for us, there were only six
> mechanics on the Formula 1 team. Mario was so confident, he was saying
> things like, 'Tell me when I should go out and set pole.' And he set pole in
> his first Grand Prix. Colin was hugely impressed and was saying, 'This is
> just like things were with Jimmy.'

Mario ran second to Jackie Stewart in the early stages of the race then suffered clutch problems. Colin wanted to sign him, but Mario looked at the deal on offer and considered what he was earning in American racing. He had twice been USAC champion so he could more or less demand a blank cheque. The boy who had grown up in the European tradition had become a man who embraced the American tradition. Andretti was the motor racing equivalent of pizza. Pizza came from Italy, but it was America who gave it to the world. Colin kept in touch with Mario and wooed him assiduously for years, but Mario had business at home. It would be Mario who would, in 1969, give Andy Granatelli his yearned-for win at Indianapolis and also the USAC Championship.

At the final round of the world championship, the Mexican Grand Prix, Hill, Stewart and Hulme all had a chance of taking the title, though Hill led Stewart by three points, with Hulme a further three adrift. Hill qualified third, but he led most of the way. Hulme crashed and Stewart lost fuel pressure and finished a lap down and out of the points. Graham therefore cruised home to his 13th Grand Prix win, his second world championship and Lotus's third Constructors' Cup.

In the formulas below Formula 1, however, Lotus were outclassed. Jackie Oliver's privately-entered Lotus 48 Formula 2 car had an impressive finishing record, 11 finishes from 11 starts, but that was no substitute for wins. Oliver finished a distant fifth in the European Championship and ahead of him were two Matras, a Tecno, and a Brabham. The balance of power was changing and Lotus was not up to speed in Formula 2, but things were slightly different in Formula 3.

John Miles, a fine engineer and a driver whose star was in the ascendant thanks to his performances in an Elan 26R, was handed the one-off 41X Formula 3 car which had revised suspension and a wedge-shaped body which followed, at some distance, the Indianapolis cars. Miles scored wins in four of the most important Formula 3 races in 1968 and since many of them were slip-streaming contests, the efficient bodywork probably played a bigger part than the chassis. The 41X was supposed to have been put into production as the 55, but this never happened.

Colin was distracted during 1968 and who can blame him? The works 47s, based on the Europa, did well in the hands of Miles and Oliver, but Colin knew that Oliver, fine driver as he proved himself to be in sports cars, was not a Jim Clark or a Mike Spence. On the other hand, Jochen Rindt had long ruled Formula 2, though in Formula 1 he had been in the wrong team at the wrong time, first at Cooper, then in 1968 at Brabham.

Jochen's craggy face made him look like an arrogant man, but Ron Tauranac says he was actually laid-back and very friendly. He was a man without side and he was blindingly quick: over a single lap there have been few who could match him. Jochen wanted his own team, built around himself, and he made some progress in that direction, with Robin Herd being the key figure. Robin had designed some excellent cars for McLaren before moving to Cosworth to design a four-wheel-drive for Keith Duckworth. According to Robin, Keith had hoped to sign Jimmy to drive his car but when Jimmy died, the Cosworth F1 car had ceased to be a priority. Jochen's idea had been that Robin would bring the Cosworth car as a stop-gap for 1969, and would meanwhile design a new car for 1970. The project was to be funded by Firestone and BP, but then BP dropped out of the equation and that put the whole project in jeopardy, so the idea was put on ice for a year.

Colin came wooing, but the person Jochen most admired in motor racing was Jack Brabham. Jochen wanted to continue to drive for Jack and Jack would have retired as a driver and built his team around Rindt had a deal been struck. However, Jack and Ron had no major sponsor, they still relied on trade deals, which were diminishing, and the income from their production racing car business. Jochen so admired Jack Brabham that he would have driven for Brabham for a fraction of what Colin had on offer.

Jochen's manager was Bernie Ecclestone and he advised Rindt that he might win a Grand Prix or two more with Lotus but he should look long and hard at the Brabham offer because he was more likely to be killed in a Lotus than a Brabham. Jochen was a close friend of Jackie Stewart, they were near neighbours in Switzerland, and Jackie strongly advised him not to drive for Lotus. However, Jochen was a man who had retirement on his mind and he had to go with Lotus. It was not what he wanted to do, but it was the only deal which made sense from a business point of view. Jochen was preparing for life after racing, he had a television show in Austria and promoted a racing car show bearing his name in five countries. Despite his brilliance in Formula 2, he had yet to win a Grand Prix, and he aimed to be world champion before he hung up his helmet.

Denis Jenkinson, the doyen of motor racing correspondents, was dismissive. He wrote that if Rindt ever won a Grand Prix, he would shave off his beard, and Jenks's beard was his trademark. Jenks believed that Jochen had speed but possessed no subtlety. He was fine in Formula 2, but that was merely a sprint. To win a Grand Prix, Jenks reckoned, needed qualities that Jochen did not possess.

In autumn 1968, Colin put Lotus on the market and offered shares on the stock exchange. A new holding company, Group Lotus Car Companies Limited, came into being on 6 January 1969. Under its umbrella came Lotus Cars, Lotus Cars (Sales), Lotus Cars (Services) and Lotus Components. Team Lotus Ltd remained a private company with the shares owned by Colin, Hazel and Fred Bushell. In this way, shareholders did not face the risk of investing in a company which ran a racing team. By the time that the new company came into being, Cooper Cars, which had been making racing cars for more than 20 years, was finished bar the shouting. Cooper had served motor racing magnificently, but its demise underlined the fragile nature of being a racing car maker.

With the launch of the new company came a new board of directors: there were Colin and Fred, of course, and also Peter Kirwan-Taylor. Dennis Austin was appointed managing director, John Standen (aka John Stand-in because of his wicked impressions of Chapman) headed the service section, while Graham Arnold looked after sales. David Lazenby left Lotus Components to found a new company, Hawke, which made Formula Ford cars. Lazenby was replaced by Mike Warner, who turned a loss-making company into one which made a profit.

So 1968 had been a traumatic year for Colin, and it was small comfort that he had been exonerated for the deaths of Clark and Spence. The fact remains that two leading drivers had been killed at the wheel of a Lotus within a month and that was enough for Colin's detractors. Still, the year had ended on an up-beat note with two world championships and a successful launch on the stock market.

CHAPTER 19

THE YEAR OF FOUR-WHEEL-DRIVE

HE BIG news in Formula 1 in 1969 was four-wheel-drive. Cosworth had poached Robin Herd from McLaren to design a car and Jochen Rindt wanted that car, and Robin Herd, in his own team. It was a case of a car being a sure-fire winner on paper, while being less than good on a race track.

There was a fundamental reason why the Cosworth Formula 1 car never raced: it did not like going round corners, which is something of a handicap for a racing car. The reason was that there was no suitable differential available at the time which would handle the 400-plus bhp which the DFV was delivering. Indianapolis was one thing, the Nürburgring was another, and besides, tyre companies were making rapid strides and that, combined with better understanding of aerofoils, cured the traction problems which had been encountered in 1968.

Despite Cosworth drawing a blank, Matra, McLaren and Lotus all went ahead with four-wheel-drive designs. BRM had already experimented with 4WD and had found no advantage, while Ferrari was not equipped to attempt a 4WD system. At Brabham, Ron Tauranac simply refused to take 4WD seriously. Ron says:

Four-wheel-drive added weight, a lot of weight, and it absorbed horse power. Since you had to connect the front end to the back end, you had to have a propshaft running alongside the driver and that meant a wider car and hence an increase in frontal area. To make a car which was heavier, had more drag, but which had less power, did not make sense.

This was something that McLaren and Matra were soon to discover for themselves. Matra's car raced only four times, McLaren's just once. Colin alone persisted with four-wheel-drive – it was one of those occasions when he got the bit between his teeth – he was determined to pursue the concept and, being Colin, he did so even when all the evidence was stacking up against him.

Maurice Phillippe laid out the four-wheel-drive 63 Formula 1 car, drawing on his experience with the Indianapolis cars, and it was unusual in that the DFV engine was reversed so that the clutch was immediately behind the cockpit, with the Hewland gearbox to the left. Neither Graham nor Jochen liked the car. The driver's feet came too far ahead of the front axle line for their comfort, and it was usually entered as a third car for John Miles, who finished only once, in 10th place at the British Grand Prix. Over the season the front/rear power bias was changed so that it effectively became a rear-wheel-drive car. Mario Andretti drove it a couple of times, but then Mario still shared Colin's faith in four-wheel-drive.

Jochen actually drove a 63 to second place at the Oulton Park Gold Cup in August, but there was a very poor field. It was one of those races where Formula 1, Formula 2 and Formula 5000 cars were on the grid and Jochen finished a distant second to Jacky Ickx's Brabham, the only other Formula 1 car still running healthily. That about sums up the Lotus 63 save for the fact that it was, without serious opposition, the ugliest racing car Lotus ever made.

Jackie Stewart won the opening round of the 1969 world championship in his Tyrrell-entered Matra-DFV, Graham was a distant second and Jochen retired. It was the same scenario at the Race of Champions, the non-championship race which opened the European season. Jack Brabham then won the International Trophy with Rindt second and Stewart third. Stewart won the Spanish Grand Prix and both Graham and Jochen failed to finish because they had identical failures of the rear aerofoil at the same spot. Graham had his wing collapse on the ninth lap and he crashed without injury. He was on his way to the pits to warn the team about the failure, when the same fate befell Jochen, who suffered a broken nose and severe concussion.

While in hospital, Jochen wrote an open letter to European motor racing journalists arguing that aerofoils should be banned altogether, a move which caused friction with Chapman. He also expressed his appreciation for the organisers of the Spanish Grand Prix for fitting an effective guard rail at the point where he crashed by having a silver trophy made for them. Without that guard rail Jochen might have been killed. Jochen also wrote an open letter to Colin, pointing out that during his entire career prior to joining Lotus he'd had only two accidents, and one of those was due to mechanical failure. In the four months and four days since he joined Lotus he'd had three accidents, one in New Zealand, one in the Formula 2 Eifelrennen and the one in Spain, and they were all due to structural failures. He urged Colin to toughen some parts of his cars even if it meant carrying a little extra weight.

In their typically robust way, British magazines did not publish Rindt's letters, apparently fearing Colin's threats of libel action. In fact there was no libel, Jochen had just presented the facts about the number of mechanical failures he had suffered and, like anyone else, he was entitled to an opinion about aerofoils. Colin went ballistic when the letter was published overseas. His relationship with Rindt went off the boil, but Jochen was clearly the quickest driver of his generation. Colin needed Jochen, but Jochen still thought that he had other options and the idea of his own Formula 1 team had not gone away.

Jochen continued his attempts to put together his own team throughout 1969, but Robin Herd decided that since everybody was after him, it would be silly to sell his talent to Rindt for a salary and so, with some of his friends, he formed March Engineering and offered Jochen a drive. Rindt was not impressed and predicted that the project would never leave the ground. March would be launched however, and the name was an acronym of its founders: Max Mosley, whom Robin had known from Oxford University; Alan Rees, who had shared a desk with Robin at school; and Graham Coaker, a friend of Alan's. While Robin went to work on designs for the range of March cars, Max was talking to Andy Granatelli. Andy agreed that STP would back the March works team and would buy a March 701 for Andretti to drive in selected Formula 1 races.

Jochen also negotiated with Jack Brabham, but Jack could not raise the money to pay him. The only team which could offer Rindt a Cosworth engine and a proper wage was Lotus. Jochen and Colin needed each other – neither had a serious choice. They were stuck in a shotgun marriage and their best option was to try to make it work.

The FIA responded to the aerofoil failures in Spain by imposing a rule which said that all rear wings had to be part of the bodywork, they could no longer work directly on the suspension. Jochen's injuries meant that he missed the Monaco Grand Prix, which Graham won, as usual. It was to be his last world championship win. Among the entries at Monaco was a private Cooper-Maserati for Vic Elford. It was the last time that a Cooper ran in a world championship race. The first time had been at Monaco in 1950.

Lotus was back at Indianapolis for what would be the final time. Again there was a deal with Granatelli, who had arranged a supply of turbocharged Ford engines. New rules limited the tyres on four-wheel-drive cars to a maximum width of 10in, front or rear, and the 64 was the most complex car that Lotus had ever made.

Mario Andretti ordered one for himself, though Firestone was expected to pick up the tab. Then Firestone cut back on its racing budget and Granatelli moved in, adding a fourth 64 to his shopping list, and with the car came Mario Andretti. Mario was joined in the team by Graham and Jochen, who had recovered from his crash in Spain, though he was still not fully fit. While Mario put in a lap at 171.657mph, Graham was hard pressed to break the 160mph mark and Jochen was even slower due to problems with his car.

Jochen did not like Indianapolis and was only too willing to allow his displeasure to be known. It wasn't just the track he disliked, it was the whole rigmarole of practising and qualifying with what seemed to him to be an interminable amount of time doing not a lot. American journalists could not believe what Jochen was saying, it was like trashing Mom's apple pie, so he received a lot of coverage, none of it favourable.

The first qualifying session was rained off and when qualifying began in earnest, Mario looked invincible. He appeared to be on his way to a record lap of more than 174mph when his car's right side rear hub failed. The wheel was thrown and Mario finished in the wall sustaining minor burns to the face. An inquiry revealed that the hub had not been properly machined. The accident occurred on 21 May, and the race was due to take place on 30 May. A subcontractor in the Indianapolis area was found to make new hubs, but a sudden power cut at the machinist's works caused the hubs to be chewed. Time had run out and all three race cars had to be withdrawn. More bad publicity surrounded Colin and Lotus, but the fact is that the original hubs had been made by a subcontractor. It was seen as yet another Lotus failure, when it was not, and Colin had reacted correctly when he thought that the safety of his drivers could be jeopardised.

The relationship between Chapman and Granatelli had not been the happiest of affairs. Still, Granatelli had been so impressed by the specification of the 64 that he had agreed to buy the cars for $95,000 each. Andy and Colin met in a motel room to finalise the deal. Granatelli affirmed that he was ready to buy the cars at the quoted price, but he questioned the price of the spares, which he thought was unacceptably high. Colin took this as a personal insult and went through the roof. A heated, very heated, exchange followed. Chapman was still smarting over having to withdraw his cars and said that the deal was off. Granatelli insisted that he had a deal and he demanded his cars. The upshot was that Ferguson had to hide four Lotus 64s. Andrew had one very unhappy sponsor on his trail who was an American in America. Andrew also had to return the turbocharged engines to Ford, so he needed premises where he could dismantle the cars.

Granatelli had his feelers out for any race shop which was handling four red cars with STP writ large upon them. Andrew thought laterally, as a Lotus man would, and he phoned the secretary of Lotus's freight agent at Indianapolis Airport. He explained his dilemma and her husband cleared the family cars out of their garage so Team Lotus could move in. Nobody would have dreamed of scouring a suburban neighbourhood 40 miles from Indianapolis, knocking on doors and asking if the householder, mayhap, had four racing cars about his person.

Ford thought that Lotus had made off with their engines and so called in the police, who could not locate the Team Lotus hide-out. The police were called off when Ford's engines were returned, one by one, by hire cars towing trailers which arrived at Dearborn via country roads. For some reason Colin had decided that he wanted nothing to do with Granatelli or STP. He was happy to do business with Mario Andretti, with Firestone, which had also offered to buy the cars, in fact, with anyone except Granatelli.

Meanwhile Mario Andretti, driving a Hawk-Offenhauser entered by Granatelli, won the Indianapolis 500. Granatelli announced that his ambition was to win the race as many times as he'd lost it. Since he'd 'lost' it for 23 years, it is hardly surprising that he was not to fulfil his ambition.

Chapman said to Ferguson, 'Andrew, bring the cars back to Hethel where I will personally put a hacksaw through them. I will personally dig a hole and I will personally bury them!' The cars remained in their packing cases at Hethel for eight years. The racing driver and car dealer, Robs Lamplough, thought that he had made a deal to buy them in the early 1970s, but Colin disagreed. Lamplough took Lotus to court and won, Lotus was ordered to hand over the cars or else pay substantial damages. Lotus complied, but right up to their final sale the 64s seemed to be dogged by ill fortune.

Back in Europe, Jackie Stewart put together a hat-trick of wins in the Dutch, French and British Grands Prix, was second to Jacky Ickx's Brabham in Germany and then clinched the championship with a win in Italy. Both Graham and Jochen had led the Dutch Grand Prix, but each had encountered mechanical problems. In the French race, held on the twisty and undulating Charade circuit at Clermont-Ferrand, the unaccustomed g-forces that the cars were generating caused Jochen to retire with nausea and double vision and he was not the only driver so affected.

Rindt and Stewart had a tremendous battle for the lead at Silverstone but Jochen had to slow when his front wing began to disintegrate and then both he and Graham had to stop to have their fuel topped up. Jochen retired in Germany, where Hill finished fourth having been off the pace for the whole meeting. Italy brought a slipstreaming contest with the first four cars across the line covered by half a second, but it was Stewart who led Rindt to the flag. It began to look as though Jenks's beard was safe.

By the United States Grand Prix, the works Lotuses had scored just one win and two second places. The 49 was clearly at the end of its development, but Colin and Maurice Phillippe did have a replacement on the drawing board. At Watkins Glen, Rindt battled with Stewart for the lead until Jackie retired and Jochen was able to stroke home an easy winner, which left Jenks clean shaven. Jenks sent half of his beard to Jochen, kept half for himself and then grew another one. Historians have ever since argued whether the replacement beard was genuine or a replica.

Team Lotus's joy at the victory was dampened by a serious accident to Graham Hill. Graham had been holding fifth place when he spun his car, which stalled. He undid his seat belts, push-started his car and jumped on board, but naturally he could not do up his belts. As he passed the pits he pointed to his rear tyres, which were badly worn. He intended to stop for replacements but never made it round the circuit, as one of his rear tyres let go suddenly. The car hit a bank and cartwheeled. Graham, unbelted, was thrown out and severely damaged both his knees. Graham would remain in racing until 1975, but the accident spelt the end of his career as a top-line driver, though he would still turn in the odd surprising performance. He never walked properly again. Colin had no option but to sign another driver and John Miles was that driver.

In the Mexican Grand Prix, which closed the world championship, Jochen retired with a broken wishbone. Another structural failure on a car did nothing for the relationship between Chapman and Rindt. Jochen did, however, sign for Lotus again for 1970. In his own mind, he knew he was making a mistake, but if he could win the world championship, it would make all the difference to his planned future enterprises, which included a Jochen Rindt range of sports clothing.

When Alan Rees threw in his lot with March, he recruited some of the key personnel from Roy Winkelmann Racing, which had been running what was effectively the Lotus works Formula 2 team. Roy Winkelmann Racing, which had an unsurpassed reputation for race preparation, collapsed. Jochen was the acknowledged king of Formula 2 and Colin made him an offer which went far beyond mere cash: Jochen could have the Lotus Formula 2 team which would have the title Jochen Rindt Team Lotus. It was a deal that Jochen entered into with Bernie Ecclestone and those of the Winkelmann mechanics who did not fancy the move to March.

So 1969 had been a poor year for Team Lotus at the higher levels. The Indianapolis project had been a washout and while Lotus finished runner-up to Matra (actually the Tyrrell cars) in the Formula 1 Constructors' Cup, it had won only two Grands Prix. There has been many a team which dreams of winning two Grands Prix, but that was short rations for Colin. In the lower divisions, however, Lotus bounced back with the 59. The Lotus 59 was the work of Dave Baldwin, who would, in the future, be the man responsible for an outstanding line of cars for the learning categories made by Van Diemen. Some of the thinking which Dave would apply to his Formula Ford designs was evident in the 59. It had a spaceframe chassis and outboard suspension, which made it ideal for the private owner. It also had the aerodynamics of a brick. The 59 handled well and Jochen Rindt made hay in Formula 2 on the few occasions he ran in it. He made only eight starts, but won four of them and Graham won a fifth race. Only three 59B Formula 2 cars were made – apart from the two works cars the third was destined for Max Mosley, who wrote his car off.

Four wins by Jochen, and one by Graham, meant that Lotus took five Formula 2 races in 1969 and that equalled the five of Matra. which had more cars in the field. The 59 did quite well in Formula 3 but the year belonged to Tecno. The Pederzani brothers, Luciano and Gianfranco, had built some outstanding karts and they had applied the thinking behind their karts to their first racing cars. They had short wheelbases and wide tracks and for a time they were the class of the field. It was a case of one idea hitting the button with the tyres which were available. The Pederzani brothers had only the one idea, and it was a good one, but you cannot move forward on one idea.

That was the wider picture in Formula 3, but in Britain, the Jim Russell Racing School, based at Snetterton in Norfolk, had discovered a young Brazilian of extraordinary promise. His name was Emerson Fittipaldi and he had arrived in

England to race in Formula Ford. He had done well, winning three of his nine races by mid-summer. Jim Russell was able to broker a deal with Mike Warner who headed Lotus Components whereby Fittipaldi sold his Merlyn Formula Ford car and bought a Lotus 59.

Emerson was placed fifth on his first outing, second on his second, behind a works-supported Lotus, then he won third time out, and the fourth time, and the fifth. Fittipaldi won nine races in the latter part of 1969 and secured the Lombank Formula 3 Championship. People scratched their heads to remember the last time that a driver had come from nowhere and performed like that. Colin soon had Fittipaldi's signature on a contract to drive for Lotus in Formula 2 and Formula 3.

Before the end of the year, Lotus produced a new Formula Ford car, the 61, which was based on the 51 but had a wedge-shaped body. The wedge was becoming a Lotus trademark and Colin set Martin Wade to work on a project to build a wedge-shaped car for Formula 5000. The Lotus 70 was completed in just 10 weeks and, after a development programme in England, one was bought by an American team and Mario Andretti was hired to drive it at Sebring in December.

Mario was leading his heat comfortably when his engine blew up. At that point the impetus seemed to go out of the project and just seven examples of the 70 were made. It had appeared to be a good idea at the time, but Lotus was beginning to flounder in the production racing car market. It was building cars for Formulas Ford, 5000, 3, 2 and 1, and on top of that was also dabbling in GT racing with the Type 62, an update of the Type 47, but fitted with the LV220 engine. Considering that Lotus was also making a full range of road cars, it could be said that its resources were being stretched.

CHAPTER 20

POSTHUMOUS CHAMPION

IN 1970, the Cosworth DFV became freely available to all and March Engineering made 10 DFV-powered Formula 1 cars. The March 701 had a body styled by Peter Wright who, in the future, while working for Lotus, would discover the ground effect principle. The March 701 had side fuel tanks shaped to induce some downforce, and it was a foretaste of what Wright was to make for Lotus. The proliferation of the DFV led to a secondary competition as drivers of team transporters raced each other to be first to park outside the Cosworth works in Northampton. The first to arrive had the engines rebuilt first. Cosworth would soon resolve the problem by licensing selected engineering shops to rebuild the engines.

Jackie Stewart in a Tyrrell-entered March 701 set pole position for the opening round of the world championship in South Africa. Alongside Stewart with an equal time was Chris Amon in a works March. Brabham won, Stewart finished third, but down in sixth place was Graham Hill in a Lotus 49C entered by Rob Walker. Graham's recovery had been remarkable and Colin had no problem in supplying Walker with the latest machinery for him to drive. In fact, Rob Walker always reckoned that Colin sold him cars at less than cost when they were for Graham.

March won the next three races: the non-championship Race of Champions (Stewart), the International Trophy (Amon) and the Spanish Grand Prix. Jackie Stewart's win in Spain was the last time that a private entry would win a Grand Prix. Jackie had already decided that though the 701 was quick straight from the box, it had no development in it. Ken Tyrrell therefore contracted Derek Gardner, who had worked on the Lotus four-wheel-drive system, to design a Formula 1 car. Before the end of the season, Ken Tyrrell had become a constructor.

The March 701 was quick right from the start, but had had no development and was obsolete within months. The reverse was true of the Lotus 72, which was the work of Maurice Phillippe in conjunction with Colin. It was initially difficult, but it would have the longest active career of any Formula 1 car (the Alfa Romeo Tipo 158 began life as a Voiturette.) It was yet another landmark car from Lotus and its main aerodynamic feature, side radiators, would become a feature of all Formula 1 cars. The Lotus 72 was not the first Formula 1 car to have side radiators, that had been Louise Bryden-Brown's private Cooper back in 1961, but the Cooper had been a makeweight. It was Lotus that made the case for side radiators, just as Colin had made the case for monocoque construction even though he was far from the first to use it.

The Lotus 72 was an advance on previous Lotus cars in that while machines such as the 25 had been designed to present as small a frontal area as possible, the 72 was a fully-integrated aerodynamic package. Suspension was by rising-rate torsion bars and the front brakes were mounted inboard with articulated shafts to the wheels. The thinking was that by taking the heat from the brakes away from the front wheels, softer tyres could be used. There was a tyre war going on in Formula 1 and Firestone developed tyres specially for the 72. One detail which shows advanced thinking was the fact that when a Lotus 72 came into the pits from a run, extraction fans were placed over the exits of the NACA cooling ducts to the front brakes.

Shown to the press early in 1970, and given a rapturous reception, the 72 was not without its teething problems. It made its debut in the Spanish Grand Prix where Rindt retired, Miles did not qualify and Graham Hill finished fourth in his 49C. Rindt had a scare during qualifying as an insulating spacer in the front braking system overheated and broke. This left braking on only three wheels, a foretaste of future tragedy and another accident Jochen had in a Lotus which was not his fault. Colin was exploring new technology and design, so it is perhaps not surprising that there were failures. On the other hand, Colin had specified solid brake discs when he could have specified ventilated discs. After the failure on Rindt's car, he did just that.

The anti-squat, anti-dive suspension was soon abandoned on Jochen's car, which was given a complete rebuild with a stiffer monocoque. Rindt was still in a T49C when he won the Monaco Grand Prix, which was the turning point in his career. Jack Brabham had taken the lead on lap 28 out of 80 and had a reasonably comfortable cushion with a few laps to go when he was baulked by Jo Siffert's March. Jo was swinging his car from side to side to pick up fuel, but it cost Jack 12 seconds and Jochen was on a late charge. With two laps to go Rindt was within five seconds of Brabham, but even then overtaking was not easy.

Going into the very last corner, Jack went off line to lap a backmarker and braked on the marbles. He slid into the barrier and Jochen nipped by to take the flag by two-tenths of a second. It was the last world championship win that a T49 would take and it put Jochen back in the title race. While Jack cursed himself after the race, the champagne corks were popping in the Lotus camp. Jochen, knowing what his friend and rival was going through, had champagne sent over to the Brabham pit. Jochen was a man with personal values. He was far from being the Teutonic automaton so often portrayed, he was a warm and humorous man. Why else would his best friend in motor racing be Jackie Stewart?

In Formula 2, the Jochen Rindt Team Lotus used a number of drivers including John Miles, Graham Hill and Jochen himself. The Lotus 69 Formula 2/3 car was built around the spaceframe of the T59, but it had a more slippery body and a monocoque central section since bag tanks were about to become mandatory. If Jochen didn't retire or encounter problems, he won. There was no question that he was the fastest driver in the world. In a Grand Prix, however, Stewart had the measure of him, because Jackie was able to be consistently quick over a race distance.

Jochen had a revised Lotus 72 for the Dutch Grand Prix and led almost the whole way to score his second Grand Prix win of the season. In short order he won the next three races, the French, British and German Grands Prix, retired from his home race having set pole, then headed for the Italian Grand Prix, where he could clinch the world championship.

You would have thought that Jochen would have been over the moon with such a season, but he was a troubled man. He had been shaken by the death of his friend, Piers Courage, in a fiery accident in the Dutch Grand Prix. There had also been the death of Bruce McLaren, a man without an enemy in the world, who died while testing a McLaren Can-Am car at Goodwood. There was an air of gloom over motor racing. Jochen was also bothered by the Lotus 72, which was carrying him towards the world championship, his life's ambition. He was uneasy about it, fearing that at any moment it could break, yet at the same time it provided him with the means by which he could achieve his ambition.

At the Italian Grand Prix Jochen was worried by the speed of the Ferraris and so asked that the wings of his car be removed as an experiment. Denny Hulme had run without wings when he won the 1968 Italian Grand Prix. Without wings, it took longer to warm up the tyres, but there was a substantial gain in straight-line speed. Jochen repeated the strategy for Saturday practice then, on one lap, he braked hard for the Parabolica and his car began to weave, then it slammed into the barriers. A joint in the barrier came adrift, the car ploughed on, hit a solid upright and the front of the 72 was utterly destroyed. After the 1969 Spanish Grand Prix, Jochen had had a trophy made for the organisers for providing a a safe barrier, and now his car was smashed into an unsafe barrier.

The reason for the accident has never been established to everyone's complete satisfaction because the car was so badly damaged, but it is possible that one of the front brake-shafts had broken, which sent the car sideways. A brake-shaft had broken on the car of Jochen's teammate, John Miles, in the Austrian Grand Prix, but that had been positively identified as metal fatigue. It is not 100 percent certain that Jochen's brake-shaft broke before his accident, or broke as a result of it. The shaft was new and had been in the car for only 15 laps. Either way the break was not similar to the metal fatigue which had been evident on John Miles's car. Jochen may have died because he had discarded all the aerodynamic aids which made the car more controllable.

Also, despite his support for Stewart's safety campaign, which was controversial, Jochen preferred not to wear the crotch straps on his safety harness and, on impact, the lower part of his body slid forward. It is possible that he might have survived had he been wearing a full safety harness.

Jochen was supposedly still alive when he was removed from his car, but the ambulance sped past the medical unit that attended every race. Under Italian law, a death at a race meeting meant that the event had to be cancelled, which explains why so many drivers apparently left an Italian circuit 'alive', but died in the ambulance. Jochen was almost certainly dead when he was put into the ambulance.

Maurice Phillippe and Colin studied every frame of every film which was available to them, and they could not determine the cause of the accident though they did identify a bolt coming adrift from the barrier which Jochen initially hit. Had that section of the barrier performed to design, Jochen's car should have bounced off into the infield. Even if there had been a breakage on the Lotus, if the barrier had been assembled correctly, the result should have been no more than a wrecked chassis and a bruised and shaken driver.

There were people prepared to point the finger at Colin and declare that he built dangerous cars. Since there was not to be a report into the enquiry into Jochen's death for seven years, that was an easy charge to make. Those who did so ignored the fact that the Lotus 72 was largely the work of Maurice Phillippe, a designer held in the highest regard by his peers, both then and until his death nearly 20 years later. When the report of the official enquiry was published seven years later, it concluded that the brake-shaft did begin the accident, but that the main contributory factory was the Armco barrier, which had not been properly installed.

Friends and colleagues of Colin noticed that Jochen's death, and the finger pointing which followed, changed him profoundly. Colin developed a shell and he distanced himself from his drivers.

During practice for the race at Monza, Colin had insisted that John Miles should run his car without wings. John did so, and scared himself rigid and to this day says it's the only time he's been really scared in a racing car. Colin was adamant that he should drive without wings, and John could not resist. He says, 'When I was driving the Formula 3 and GT cars, if I was sitting in the canteen with the other 'junior' drivers and Colin came in, we'd all look at him with awe.' Jochen's death, and Colin's attitude to the question of whether or not to run with wings, shook John to the core. He had done done a lot of test driving on the 72 and had suffered a number of structural failures. He told Colin that he wanted to think about his future and Colin told him that he had a couple of weeks. Before the time was up, Colin had fired him. It was the only time that Colin ever sacked a driver from his Formula 1 team, but he was right to do so for John's sake. A driver who needs time to consider his future is like a steeplechaser with a broken leg.

Colin had a replacement for Rindt on hand in the person of Emerson Fittipaldi. Fittipaldi had been given a third car, a Lotus 49C, at the British Grand Prix, and he had brought it home safely, if unspectacularly, in eighth place and two laps down. He followed that with fourth in the German Grand Prix, and was 15th, and last, in Austria.

Come the United States Grand Prix and the fortunes of Team Lotus rested on the young shoulders of Fittipaldi and Reine Wisell, a Swede whom many thought superior to his brilliant compatriot, Ronnie Peterson. It was the first time that Team Lotus had lined up for a Grand Prix without a British driver. With five wins to his credit, Jochen still led the world championship by a handsome margin, yet he could still be overtaken by Jacky Ickx. That would have been ironic, since Rindt loathed Ickx with a passion.

Emerson Fittipaldi rose to the occasion, setting third fastest qualifying time, a mere trace behind Ickx and Stewart, and came through after Stewart retired to win the United States Grand Prix in a Lotus 72. It was the first time that 'Emmo' had actually raced a Type 72 and it settled the issue of the twin championships. Jochen Rindt became the first posthumous world champion and Lotus took its fourth constructors' title.

Jochen was a man driven to win the championship, and, when he died, he had it within his grasp and he was just a few weeks away from a new chapter in his life. The fact that he did win it, but never knew that he had, is one of the saddest stories in Formula 1. It was, to use a word which is often misused, a tragedy, because Jochen had made the decision to continue when all his instincts had told him to quit.

In third place in America was Reine Wisell, an outstanding finish for a Grand Prix debutante. Colin had his two drivers for 1971. It hardly matters that neither finished in the points in Mexico. Graham Hill had not been forgotten and Rob Walker was able to take delivery of a brand-new Lotus 72 in time for the Austrian Grand Prix. At the time, Emerson Fittipaldi was still in a Type 49C. Colin had kept faith with Graham.

After the launch of Group Lotus, it was reasonable to expect that the company would go from strength to strength, but a downturn in the economy meant that the sales graph dipped and there was massive overproduction. Advertising Lotus's products had got out of hand and that was sapping the company as well. Then again, the cost of making production racing cars had greatly increased, yet they still had to be sold at a competitive price. Racing car makers generally did not price their cars carefully – they usually looked at what the opposition was charging and priced accordingly. It was probably not until Rick Gorne joined forces with Adrian Reynard at the end of 1982 that any maker of production racing cars had a clear policy based on the reality of the market. Lotus Components was renamed Lotus Racing and that was a PR massage. A company with the word 'components' in its title sounded like an outfit making spare parts.

Still, there were some major moves in the road car business.

The Europa was selling strongly, but to make it more attractive to the home market, it was offered in component form. A fully assembled Europa cost £1,828, but a Jaguar E-type cost only £1,896, which gives some idea of what Lotus was up against. An entirely new model was the Seven Series IV, a more civilised version of Lotus's entry-level car. It had the same basic layout as its predecessors but had a new spaceframe, which was slightly longer and wider than before; front suspension derived from the Europa, and it had more positive location of the rear axle. Its fibreglass body was unstressed and it offered better weather protection and creature comforts. In retrospect it has been perceived as the 'soft' Seven, but the fact that it sold more strongly than any other Seven shows how it was perceived in its own day. Unlike earlier Sevens, it did not require the hardiness of an Arctic explorer, yet it still offered Lotus status and handling for less than £1,000 in component form.

Tony Rudd moved from BRM to Lotus and began his stint as head of the powertrain division by producing a 'big valve' version of the Twin Cam engine which produced 128bhp and could be had in the 'Sprint' version of the Elan.

Finally, the 25,000th Twin Cam unit was built and it was presented, mounted, to Walter Hayes, who had been such a staunch ally over so many years.

For Colin personally, the year entailed a trip to Buckingham Palace to receive from the Queen a CBE (Commander of the Order of the British Empire, one step from a knighthood). At the time it was very unusual for one so young – Colin was still only 42 – to be so honoured. Aged 42, Enzo Ferrari had yet to make his first car.

CHAPTER 21

CHANGE OF DIRECTION

A SEA change for Lotus came in 1971. Production of customer racing cars ceased, yet ironically, the Lotus 69 gave the company its most successful season in Formula 3 for many a year. From double world championships in 1970, Lotus failed to score a single win in Formula 1 for the first time since 1959. For the first time since Lotus entered single-seat racing there was no works, or works-related, Formula 2 team. On the other hand, Colin took over the Moonraker brand of motor cruisers, together with JCL Marine which built them, and also concluded a deal to supply Jensen with Lotus-designed engines.

Like Jaguar, Jensen had been founded as a specialist body maker in the early 1920s and, though it had made cars since 1935, these had only ever been a small part of the business. Jensen made bodies for the large Austin-Healey and also for the Sunbeam Tiger but, in 1967, the Tiger was axed and the Austin-Healey was being phased out because it did not meet the new safety and emission regulations being introduced in America, its main market.

The company changed hands in 1968 and and in 1970 Kjell Qvale, an American West Coast dealer who specialised in sports cars, bought a major shareholding and became president. Qvale wanted a replacement for the Austin-Healey and he appointed Donald Healey and his son, Geoffrey, to the Jensen board. Donald Healey had actually designed a replacement for the big 'Healey, but it was a little too good for the comfort of Sir William Lyons, whose Jaguar E-type was becoming ever more slow in the form sold in America as it was forced to comply with new emission laws. Lyons made sure that the Austin-Healey 4000 was stillborn.

Donald Healey's service contract with what had once been the British Motor

Corporation came to an end in 1971 and was not renewed. By then, through a succession of takeovers and mergers, Austin-Healey had become part of British Leyland and the new boss decided that the name 'Healey' attached to a car did not shift the metal – he had already axed the Mini Cooper because he objected to paying a £2 royalty to John Cooper on each Mini Cooper sold.

Donald Healey was briefed to design a new sports car for Jensen which would take up spare capacity in the works. Healey decided that the day of the big-engined muscle car was over, so he was thinking in terms of a high-performance 2-litre engine and knew that such a unit (the 907) was under development at Lotus. Kjell Qvale, who sold Lotus cars in California, contacted Colin, who flew to America with Fred Bushell to discuss the use of the new engine in the projected Jensen-Healey sport car.

From America, Fred phoned Mike Warner, who headed Lotus Racing, to request an inventory of all the division's stock. This was no more than standard business practice by an accountant, because Lotus Components had been draining money as overheads, which were mainly increased labour costs. Apparently, Fred thought no more of the phone call. Mike Warner, however, added two and two and did not come up with four. He thought that Lotus Racing was being sold to Qvale over his head and he was most unhappy about it. Mike and his team worked under extreme pressure and delivered the goods – the Lotus 70 Formula 5000 car had gone from a request to a running prototype in just 10 weeks, and the 70 had led its first race.

Colin and Fred returned from California, having reached a broad agreement about supplying the Lotus 907 engine to Jensen, to be met with a letter of resignation from Mike Warner. The resignation was refused and Mike was reminded of his contract. Mike was not being paranoid in his belief that Lotus Racing was being prepared for the chop, he simply made the wrong connection with Kjell Qvale. Lotus had no need for production racing cars any more. Team Lotus had won eight world championships in all, so a win in Formula Ford was neither here nor there. Ever prescient, Colin had decided that he did not need the hassle of a highly volatile market. Prescient Colin may have been, but he had not shared his thoughts with Mike Warner, and once again he backed away from breaking bad news. Mike felt himself backed into a corner and he issued a press release on his own behalf which said that, following a profound disagreement with directors of Lotus, he felt he had no option except to resign.

We speak here of doo-doo hitting a rotating cooling device and Colin went through the roof. Unfriendly words were exchanged – a weak term for a discussion which left blood on the walls – and Mike had no option but to leave, but that had been the object of the exercise. He was joined in exile by several other key personnel from Lotus Racing, including the designer, Dave Baldwin. Before the end of the year they were all in a new outfit, GRD – Group Racing Developments. GRD aimed to fill the gap left by Lotus Racing and did so very successfully for a couple of seasons. GRD was also the first off-shoot from Lotus since the move to Norfolk, and was the first of many. Dotted around north-east Norfolk, especially in the area of the Snetterton circuit, have been many racing car constructors and racing teams that have Lotus in their background.

John Standen was appointed as Warner's successor, but he controlled a division with no future. After Lotus Racing had fulfilled existing orders, it was closed. Lotus would make cars for F2 and F3 in the near future, but they would be made only for Lotus works teams and then paid for by a sponsor. During 1971, however, the young Australian, Dave Walker, driving the sole Gold Leaf Team Lotus entry in Formula 3, would win 25 races from 32 starts and mark himself as a star of the future. It was perhaps the finest season in Formula 3 ever put together by a driver, especially since it included emphatic wins in a heat and the final of the Monaco Grand Prix support race.

Lotus had finally got the measure of Brabham and celebrated the fact by ceasing to build customer racing cars. Brabham, then solely owned by Ron Tauranac, would be sold to Bernie Ecclestone during 1971 and, before long, Brabham would also pull out of the production racing car market.

The decision to make Moonraker motor cruisers was an indication of Colin's ambition to be a business entrepreneur. His passion outside of motor racing was flying and he had toyed many times with pursuing aviation projects. Part of Colin's reason for buying Moonraker from David Buxton, a Lotus dealer and the man who had once run Team Elite, was because he believed that boats were hopelessly out of date. 'There has been no development in boats since Noah and the Ark,' he would say. He regarded them as unnecessarily crude and noisy and felt he could transform them into something much more in keeping with the Lotus philosophy. Colin wanted to make motor cruisers which could operate anywhere, in any conditions. It was the engineering challenge which intrigued him – Colin was the last person to spend a week on the Norfolk Broads watching the world go by at five knots. Boats certainly offered him more opportunity than aviation could at the time, since there were virtually no regulations.

The Lotus influence soon became apparent on the inherited range. New materials were introduced, noise and vibration were reduced and, of course, the boats were made lighter, much lighter. Colin had taken over existing ranges, but he wanted to develop his own line. He might have succeeded except for one thing, economics. When VAT arrived in 1973, the British government applied it to boats. Then the Italian market suddenly collapsed in the wake of the global recession of the mid-1970s, and galloping inflation hit a labour-intensive industry like boat-building more than it hit the motor industry. Many people need a car to conduct their business, but nobody actually needs a motor cruiser.

There was also a more fundamental problem, which was that while the Moonraker range, which was founded in 1970, sold well in the first few years, by 1975 JCL was concentrating on a range of Italian-styled cruisers (originating from Versilcraft Cantiero Nautico), substituting fibreglass composites and Lotus's own injection moulding system for the original wooden hulls. These looked the part, they were handsome vessels, but while they were fine for the calm waters of the Mediterranean, they were not suited to the seas around Britain. They soon acquired a reputation for being unstable in rough seas.

Worse, because Colin's team was re-engineering the boats from bow to stern, there were considerable development costs which could not be recouped in a depressed economy. It was typical of Colin, though, that he pressed on regardless. Somehow everything had turned out fine in the past, and he was always driven by the idea that if he could solve the technical problems he set himself, everything would fall into place. It is a small irony that, from 1984, Versilcraft switched from wooden hulls to fibreglass hulls, and the company survives to this day.

In Formula 1, Team Lotus led with Emerson Fittipaldi and Reine Wisell, while Tony Trimmer and Dave Walker were given occasional outings. Firestone introduced new low-profile tyres and they simply did not suit the 72. Firestone had developed a soft compound for the Lotus 72 in 1970 but, when the 72 was asked to perform on the new rubber, it was unhappy. The season was a disaster. Much was expected of Fittipaldi, who had won from only his fourth Grand Prix start, but there was little he could do with the car. Emerson says:

> The problem was that we were getting so much grip from the tyres that the front suspension was distorting and no matter what we tried, we could do nothing to develop the car. Then Maurice Phillippe came up with a stiffer front suspension for the final race of the year, the Tribute to Tyrrell and Stewart event at Brands Hatch. You could say our 1972 season started at the end of 1971.

Emerson was third on the grid, and Wisell languished in 18th slot with a time 3.4 seconds slower. On lap 15, Jo Siffert crashed his BRM and the car virtually exploded, with poor Siffert dying almost immediately. The real cause of Jo's death was not the fire which engulfed the car, but the fact that the fire consumed all the oxygen around him. After that drivers began to have air bottles attached to their helmets.

Emerson finished second in that race: the results were calculated from the order at the end of lap 14. Since Emerson was only a fifth of a second behind Peter Gethin (BRM), who was declared the winner, and had also set fastest lap, the first win of the season was a distinct possibility. Poor Wisell, languishing towards the back of the field, was out on lap three when another driver missed his braking point and took him out.

Reine Wisell had arrived in Formula 1 with a dazzling reputation and a solid background of success, but he joined Lotus at the wrong time and it wrecked his career. There were two things at play: one was that the 72 was not working, the other was that Fittipaldi was usually a shade faster. Reine had never encountered this before and it gnawed at his self-confidence, which made him even slower. It was a classic case of a driver going slower because of his teammate's pace. By the end of the year Wisell was a spent force as a Formula 1 driver though he did have a drive for BRM in 1972 and a few outings for March in 1973 and 1974. The third place Reine took on his debut with Lotus remained his best Formula 1 result, but who knows what he might have achieved had he joined Lotus a year later? Emerson Fittipaldi says, 'Reine had been very quick in Formula 3 but could not cope with the set-up we had on the 72 in 1971.'

During the year Lotus ran the 56B on occasion. Colin still would not let go of the idea of four-wheel-drive and the turbine engine, come to that, though how anyone could have driven a turbine car at, say, Monaco is something to stretch the imagination. New regulations in Formula 1 had produced a sensible equivalency formula between the 3-litre internal combustion engine and the turbine. Colin was about to go down another cul-de-sac.

At the Dutch Grand Prix, Dave Walker was assigned a 56B which he qualified at the back of the grid, four seconds off the pace. The race was run in heavy rain, however, and that suited 4WD, so after five laps Dave was up to 10th and catching everyone. A win even looked to be on the cards, such was his rate of progress, but then Dave missed his braking point into a corner and crashed. It was the closest that a 4WD car, or a turbine engine, came to scoring a significant result in a world championship race.

Emerson Fittipaldi had a 56B for the Italian Grand Prix. It was the sole Lotus entry though it was entered by a team called World Wide Racing. This was a legacy of Jochen's death at Monza the previous year since it was possible for the investigating magistrate to impound any car entered by Gold Leaf Team Lotus on the suspicion of contribution to manslaughter. At the end of 1971, the Lotus 56B was quietly retired. It brought to an end Formula 1's flirtation with four-wheel-drive and its only flirtation with turbine engines.

Colin may have been chasing his own tail in Formula 1, but he forged ahead with improvements to his road cars. The Europa received a 105bhp version of the Twin Cam engine and the rear deck was revised to improve rearward visibility. Lotus did not have the world's best reputation for reliability, but there is no denying that massive effort was put into the cars and this was reflected in the company's turnover. The measures which had been put into place during 1970, which included the closure of Lotus Racing, were effective. Gross profit (£324,000) during the first six months of 1971 exceeded that of the whole of 1970 and nearly half of production went for export.

From the beginning of 1972, Lotus appeared in a new livery, gold on black, which fitted with the new John Player Special brand of cigarettes. It would become perhaps the most effective use of motor racing as a sponsor's marketing tool in history. Marlboro used motor racing to penetrate new markets, but this was a case of a new brand using the sport to establish itself.

Along with the latest version of the 72 in Formula 1, John Player Team Lotus ran a couple of Type 73 Formula 3 cars. These were made only for the works and

Elan, Elan and Elan. The Elan was not intended to be a racing car, but Ron Hickman's design was picked up and raced seriously. Note that none of the cars has 'pop-up' headlights – they were the first thing to go. *(FF)*

The Steering Wheel Club, run by John Morgan, was the social centre of the British motor racing scene. When it relocated to Curzon Street a party was held. Left to right: Colin and Hazel Chapman, Jim Clark, Jack and Betty Brabham, Hazie and John Morgan. *(LAT)*

Jim Clark in the Lotus-Ford, Indianapolis, 1965. Jim dominated the race and broke every record. This is a shot taken during practice. By the time the race began there were many more sponsors on board. *(IMS)*

From 1966, the Lotus Indy car project was funded by STP, a division of Studebaker-Packard. Andy Granatelli, head of STP, is seen here with Jim Clark and Colin. The smiles and optimism eventually gave way to acrimony. *(PN)*

Colin, a Cosworth DFV engine, and its designer, Keith Duckworth. Cosworth was formed while Mike Costin and Keith Duckworth were working for Lotus and Colin was instrumental in obtaining Ford's backing for the DFV. *(PN)*

Jim Clark holds the trophy for winning the Dutch Grand Prix. Front centre is Walter Hayes, a long-time supporter of both Colin and Lotus, and the man who persuaded Ford to fund the Cosworth DFV project. *(FMC)*

Colin, Jimmy and the Lotus 49 at the 1967 British Grand Prix. Jimmy went on to win his home race for the fourth time. *(FF)*

Chris Meek in his Lotus Europa 'Twin Cam', entered under the banner of 'Team Dealer Lotus'. *(FF)*

Jo Bonnier, Jochen Rindt and Colin take time off at a meeting. The relationship between Rindt and Chapman was often troubled, but each man needed the other. *(FF)*

Emerson Fittipaldi in the turbine-powered Lotus 56B at the 1971 International Trophy at Silverstone. 'Emmo' qualified on the front row, retired in the first heat and was third in the second. The car proved to be a cul-de-sac. *(PN)*

Colin with Ronnie Peterson, the brilliant Swede who had two spells with Team Lotus, the first ending on a less than happy note. Ronnie took nine of his ten Grand Prix victories with Lotus. *(FF)*

Colin with Emerson Fittipaldi in 1972. The Lotus 72 in John Player Special livery became an icon among marketing people. It helped that the car not only looked good, but also carried Fittipaldi to the 1972 World Championship. *(PN)*

Colin, Emerson Fittipaldi and long-time team manager, Peter Warr. Colin's shirt can be best described as 'sudden'. *(PN)*

Colin holds aloft the trophy for the 1973 Spanish Grand Prix, won by Emerson Fittipaldi, who seems to want it back. To Fittipaldi's right is François Cevert, who was second in a Tyrrell, and behind Cevert is King Juan Carlos. How confused it all seems compared to later podium ceremonies. *(PN)*

Colin with Mario Andretti and a Lotus 78 in the pitlane at Silverstone during the 1977 British Grand Prix meeting. It was a combination which put Team Lotus back on course. Mario qualified second, but retired with engine problems. *(PN)*

Nigel Mansell reports after testing the Lotus 88 'twin chassis' car. There is no front wing and the rear wing is little more than a stabiliser, smaller than many a rear wing on some road cars. The car was declared illegal, but was actually a victim of the FISA/FOCA war. *(FF)*

John Z. DeLorean poses with the ill-fated DMC-12, developed by Group Lotus. The connection with DeLorean cast a shadow over Colin's final weeks. *(LAT)*

Fred Bushell, who kept Lotus afloat when many a time the company should have gone under, poses with an Excel. The Excel was a superb car, but was blighted by Lotus's poor reputation. *(LAT)*

Colin Chapman,
19 May 1928 –
15 December 1982.
(LAT)

they proved a dismal flop. They were made using some of the design of the 72, so had a monocoque central section, side radiators and inboard brakes. The problem was that they were too complicated for Formula 3. Once again Colin had ignored the shining example set by Brabham.

Tony Trimmer, who had tasted Formula 1, stepped back to Formula 3 and was joined by Bernard Vermilio. They had a frustrating season and the only highlight was Trimmer's second place in the Monaco Grand Prix support race, but that was only after many of the front-runners had been eliminated. The design of the Type 73 simply would not respond to development. A 73B appeared late in the season, but by then John Player had decided that Formula 3 was not for them. That was the end of Lotus in Formula 3 and the irony is that the class of the F3 field in 1972 was the GRD 372, built by ex-Lotus men. As an aside, GRD did not survive beyond the end of 1974. Ralph Firman took on the last design as the Van Diemen-GRD. It achieved little but it did lead to Van Diemen becoming a constructor and a brilliantly successful maker of Formula Ford cars designed by Dave Baldwin.

In Formula 1, Dave Walker found himself out of his depth. Colin had kept faith with his young protégé, but Walker simply wasn't up to it. He finished the year without scoring a single point, while Emerson Fittipaldi became the youngest driver ever to win a world championship. It is the only occasion when one driver has taken the title and his teammate has failed to score a point.

Emmo failed to finish the Argentine Grand Prix, due to a broken rear radius arm. He bounced back to second place in the South African Grand Prix and then took the Race of Champions at Brands Hatch. It may have been a mixed F1/5000 event, but it attracted works Formula 1 teams from McLaren, March, Matra, Surtees and BRM.

Fittipaldi followed that with a win in the International Trophy, another F1/5000 race with a strong Formula 1 entry, and then he won the first European round of the world championship, the Spanish Grand Prix, having led most of the distance. He was third in the very wet Monaco Grand Prix, won in Belgium and was second in France. The British Grand Prix brought another win, he retired in Germany when lying second, then won again in Austria and Italy. The win at Monza, again in a single entry by World Wide Racing, as the Rindt affair had still not been resolved, gave Emerson the world championship and Lotus its fifth constructors' title. The fact that he did not score points in the final two rounds was a matter of no consequence.

Lotus was back on top of the world in motor racing, but Formula 1 was only a very tiny part of Lotus's activities. Looming on the horizon was the introduction of VAT, which would replace the former purchase tax. When that occurred the loophole in the law which exempted customers who bought cars in component form would be closed. That would hit the majority of Lotus cars sold on the home market. In addition there were tough new emission and safety regulations in the pipeline as Britain conformed to European Union rules. The Lotus 907 engine met all the emission requirements but they spelled the end, or at least the beginning of the end, for the Elan, Europa and Seven.

A new car was laid down and it would carry the name, 'Elite'. It was classic Lotus, with a backbone chassis and all-independent suspension, but it was a full four-seater. The joke continued that Colin's cars reflected his domestic circumstances. In fact, it was a shrewd move because the sports car market was shrinking. There had been a time when America would take anything with four wheels and a canvas hood, but America's love affair with the sports car was cooling. New regulations had killed some models, like the big 'Healey, while others were living on borrowed time.

Perhaps 1972 was not the best time for the Jensen-Healey to be launched. It might have succeeded had its style had some of the flair of Healey's earlier cars, but it had very bland lines. There was nothing anyone could object to, but nothing to get the blood racing either. It was a decent car, but every successful sports car has just a touch of indecency about it. It was hard to think of a good reason for preferring a Jensen-Healey to a Triumph TR6, which was flawed but hairy-chested. Apart from scuttle shake and a crude hood, and a tendency to rust, the Jensen-Healey's major problem was its Lotus engine. The 907 unit was noisy and before long there were stories of its unreliabilty.

Under Tony Rudd the quality of Lotus road cars had improved out of all recognition. The cost of rectification under warranty had dipped to less than one percent of the showroom price and that was then considered good by industry standards – it was about the same as the Ford Escort. While Lotus had strived to improve, the Jensen-Healey did Lotus's reputation no good at all, just at the time when Lotus was preparing to go up-market. One thing which the new Elite did not need was prejudice, because there was no question of it ever being sold as a kit and the cost of the average Lotus model was about to double.

One car which did make an immediate impact was a styling exercise undertaken by Giorgetto Guigario. Guigario had been responsible for outstanding styles, notably the Maserati Ghibli, and had established his own studio. While he was working on the original VW Golf, Guigario advertised his work by taking an extended Lotus Europa chassis and creating a body on it. It was widely admired and fired Colin so much that it would become the Lotus Esprit.

Lotus went into 1973 with another two world championships in the bag, a new road model in the pipeline and a lucrative line in selling engines for the Jensen-Healey. It seemed to have all bases covered.

Dave Walker was released from the Formula 1 team and in his place came Ronnie Peterson, an uncomplicated man who was greatly loved by all who knew him. Ronnie had sometimes been overshadowed by his compatriot, Reine Wisell, in Formula 3, but Alan Rees had detected greatness in him and he had been snapped up by March, who had never been able to provide him with a car fit for his talent. Despite that, Ronnie had finished second to Jackie Stewart in the world championship in 1971, and that in his first full season in Formula 1. A maiden win still eluded him, however.

Chapman concluded his successful wooing of Ronnie Peterson. It had been a long courtship because Ronnie was a man who had become friends with everyone at March, and though his initial three-year contract was over, he felt loyalty to them. The team had been teetering on the edge of bankruptcy before the end of its first season and Robin Herd and Max Mosley could neither pay him properly nor give him a competitive car.

Emerson was not pleased by the decision because Ronnie was not only very quick, he was also joining the team as joint number one. It had been Emerson who had picked up Lotus after Rindt's death and it had been Emerson who had patiently conducted the tyre testing which had made Lotus a contender again. Lotus had switched from Firestone to Goodyear and that had made a huge difference.

Emerson had been down the cul-de-sac of the Lotus 56B turbine car. There was no animosity between Emerson and Ronnie, they were friends, but Emmo knew that Lotus was not capable of running two number one drivers. Thirty years on Emerson still speaks of Ronnie with affection: 'He was a lovely guy'. The only bad thing anyone has ever said about Ronnie was that he was tight with money, but that is true of every racing driver.

Fittipaldi and Peterson would have Lotus 72Es for Formula 1 and they were also signed for Formula 2. The F2 cars were 74s, but they were officially known as Texaco Stars since Texaco was picking up the bills. The 74 followed much of the thinking of the 72 with side radiators, torsion bar suspension and inboard brakes, but the headline was the use of the Lotus 907 engine. Units had been sent to Italy for preparation by Novamotor, who claimed 275bhp for them. On paper, the Lotus Formula 2 team appeared very strong indeed, especially when it is remembered that Ronnie Peterson had dominated the category in 1971.

Everything looked bright for Lotus on all fronts but what Colin and nobody else could have predicted were developments in the Middle East. Israel went to war with some Arab states and that restricted the supply of oil. Then members of OPEC, a consortium of oil-exporting nations, woke up to the fact that they had a finite resource on which the West depended, so they increased the price of crude oil four-fold. Oil-exporting nations, mainly in the Middle East, had been underpaid for years. The sudden increase in the price of crude led to an international crisis. In retrospect, it caused a long-overdue shake-up of Western economies and attitudes. In the short-term it meant inflation in even the best regulated economies.

In Britain a 50mph speed limit was imposed to conserve fuel and, when you have a 50mph limit, it is not the time to sell high-performance cars. It was a great time to buy a Ferrari Daytona, but a poor time to try to sell new sports cars, or motor cruisers come to that. It was not a great time to launch a new Lotus which was unlike any previous Lotus.

That was the background against which the season unfolded. A far as the

Formula 2 team was concerned it was a disaster. The team missed the first two races and then failed to show for the first race they entered, the Easter Monday event at Thruxton on 23 April. Neither car was ready for the Pau Grand Prix on 5 June, but they did make the grid at Nivelles on 10 June. Peterson qualified fourth, Fittipaldi eighth, but since the race clashed with Le Mans the field was not of a high order. In any case, both had retired by lap 12 of 56. That was the pattern of the season. Emerson managed second in heat at Misano, and actually led the second heat before going out with a blown head gasket. Ronnie did not complete a lap before his engine let go.

This was the last time that Lotus went racing outside of Formula 1 in Colin's lifetime. Why is it that the 1972 foray into Formula 3 and the 1973 Texaco Star efforts were so feeble? The fact is that the entire culture had changed. Lotus had become a corporation with road cars at its centre. Team Lotus was a separate organisation, it was located apart from the main operation, and while Lotus had once been driven by racing, and the racer's mentality, it had become a mainstream company with Formula 1 as Colin's hobby. It was about the only hobby Colin had, apart from flying and driving fast. Lots of things would take his interest for a while, his mind was always receptive, but nobody can recall him having an interest that most people would call a leisure pursuit.

Peter Warr recalls that the night before Colin died, they went together to see the Chris Barber jazz band. Barber had been a Lotus customer since 1956, and he'd raced his cars for six or seven years. Peter says, 'Chris Barber and Colin were old friends, but I have no idea if Colin wanted to go because of that, or because he was fond of jazz.' Peter Ross says, 'He loved driving fast, and he'd carve up other motorists. He once told me that he dreaded having an accident on the road because for the next 45 minutes everyone who came upon the crash would lay evidence against him.'

In Peterson and Fittipaldi Colin had two young chargers and there were no team orders – Colin had long given up on that idea. Emerson was reigning world champion, and Ronnie has to be included among the greats even though he never won a championship. He was one of those drivers, like Gilles Villeneuve, who often seemed to be beyond the ragged edge, yet he actually made very few mistakes.

Emerson won the opening two rounds of the series, in Argentina and Brazil, and then came third in South Africa, where Jackie Stewart won. Fittipaldi won in Spain, but it was Peterson who took pole by a handsome margin, nearly two seconds ahead of him. Much the same happened in Belgium. Ronnie was on pole and Emerson was in ninth slot. Only Emerson finished, however, in third, while Stewart took his second win. Ronnie had established himself as clearly the faster Lotus driver, but Emerson (31 points) led the championship from Jackie Stewart (27 points), while Ronnie had yet to score.

What should Colin do? Emerson was fighting for the championship and nothing short of a miracle would bring Ronnie back into contention. Should he order

Peterson to line up behind Fittipaldi and help him to win the drivers' championship? That would be the strategy that some team managers would adopt, but there was also the constructors' title at stake and Colin had signed Peterson to win races. Ron Hickman tells a story from the early 1960s:

> I remember Fred Bushell coming out of Colin's office, laughing. It seems that Colin had been trying to impose team orders and his drivers were against it. They'd said things like, 'I'm in racing to win, if I was ordered to do less than my best, I'd feel I'd lost some of my integrity'. Colin had said, 'That's the trouble with drivers, the only thing they care about is to win, win, win.' Fred laughed again at the very thought.
>
> I said, 'What's funny about that?' Fred said, 'Ask yourself, have you ever met anyone more competitive in your whole life?'

Colin did not impose team orders at any time, though at Indianapolis he did impose a rule that said that all the prize money for laps led would be shared equally among all team drivers. It was a move to discourage unnecessary scrapping.

Fittipaldi's lead narrowed at Monaco where he finished a close second to Stewart, with Ronnie third. Peterson had started from the front row and had led some of the early laps, then succumbed to failing fuel pressure. Ronnie set pole in Sweden and finished second. He led all but the last lap and was nursing a car with a deflating rear tyre when Denny Hulme made a move which gave the McLaren M23 its first win. Fittipaldi had been second for most of the race, but he had failing brakes and then a failing gearbox as he used the transmission to slow his car.

When they went to France the score was Fittipaldi 41, Stewart 39. McLaren gave Jody Scheckter his big break and Jody responded by leading the first 40 laps. Then Emerson tried to overtake but Jody would have none of it. The Lotus collected the McLaren, bounced high in the air and retired on the spot, with Scheckter following a lap later. For once, luck smiled on Peterson and he came through to win his first Grand Prix while Stewart's fourth place edged him into the lead in the championship.

A mistake by Scheckter on the second lap of the British Grand Prix caused a multiple shunt which wiped out his own car and seven others. After the restart, Ronnie led from Emerson and then it started to rain soon after half distance. Fittipaldi's gearbox gave up the ghost and the race was won by Peter Revson (McLaren) from Ronnie. Stewart did not finish so there was still just a single point separating him from Fittipaldi. However, if fans thought they were going to be in for a down-to-the-wire championship, they were to be disappointed. Stewart won in Holland and Germany and was second to Peterson in Austria. Emerson picked up just one point from the three races.

During practice for the Dutch Grand Prix, Emmo had crashed heavily when a front wheel broke. His feet were badly hurt and the pain caused him to retire from the race after two laps. He was still in pain at the German Grand Prix, and only his grit saw him finish in sixth place. Though Peterson led the Austrian Grand Prix, he sportingly waved Emerson through to enhance his world championship chances, but a fuel line came away on Fittipaldi's car. There was no repeat of the courtesy in Italy, where Ronnie won by less than a second from Emerson and Fittipaldi's slender chances of the title slipped away. Ronnie won again in the United States Grand Prix and by that time Emerson felt that Peterson was receiving favoured treatment, which is always a comforting idea when one's teammate is quicker. Emerson says:

At the Italian Grand Prix, I still had a mathematical chance of winning the championship. Only the best 12 races of the 15 counted for the title and since I hadn't finished in five races, I could count every result in the last three races, whereas Jackie had points to drop.

At Monza Colin told me that if Ronnie and I were leading with 10 laps to go, and Ronnie was ahead of me, he'd hang out a board telling Ronnie to let me through, but he did not tell Ronnie this. With 10 laps to go, Ronnie was ahead and I was on his gearbox, but the pit signal was not hung out. It wasn't there on the ninth, eighth or seventh lap. I finished right behind Ronnie and Jackie won the championship.

Marlboro had been on at me to to join them for 1974 and the three competitive teams without rival tobacco sponsorship were McLaren (which Marlboro backed), Brabham and Tyrrell. After Colin forgot to hang out the signal to tell Ronnie to let me by, I was interested in Marlboro's offer. If I had gone to Tyrrell or Brabham, they would have been Marlboro Tyrrell or Marlboro Brabham, but I had been impressed by the McLaren M23 so I went there.

Lotus took its sixth constructors' title, while Emerson, with three wins, was runner-up to Stewart in the drivers' championship and Ronnie, with four wins, was a close third. It was the first time that Lotus had won the constructors' series and one of its drivers had not taken the drivers' world championship.

How could motor racing history have been different had Emerson gone to Tyrrell or Brabham, taking Marlboro with him? In 1974, Fittipaldi took three wins and the title, but Brabham also won three races while Tyrrell took one but finished well ahead of Brabham in the constructors' series. What if Fittipaldi had not gone to McLaren?

Colin had eased Emmo into Formula 3 and Formula 2, he had given Emmo his first F1 drive, his first F1 win and his first world championship. Emerson says:

Colin was very special. He was was the best person I ever worked with in setting up a car. He had tremendous intuition when developing a car, he could feel the car. His mind was always on how to make the car work, at the race track, over dinner, he was always asking questions, he was committed to making the car go faster.

I was so lucky to start with Colin, it was the best schooling I could possibly have had. I spent my first four years in Formula 1 with him and I learned everything from him.

During 1973 production of the Elan and the Seven came to an end, though the Europa would continue for another two years. The Seven was picked up by Graham Nearn of Caterham Cars, a Lotus dealer, and Colin was happy to see it continue production. Caterham made the Series IV at first and then reverted to the Series III. Down the years, Caterham has made many more Sevens than Lotus ever did and the Seven Series III has become an automotive icon which has spawned many imitators.

Whatever else it was, the Seven was the last remaining link with the Lotus of the Hornsey days, of the volunteers, of the guys whose passport was de Havilland. De Havilland had anyway disappeared as a separate entity, having been swallowed by mergers. The day of the maverick designer was coming to an end – it was in 1973 that a young apprentice wheeled out the car with which he wanted to go racing. His name was Adrian Reynard and his company survived until 2002. Reynard was the last of the special builders who became constructors. It simply is not possible any more.

The new Lotus Elite was shown before the end of the year, but it generated nothing of the excitement that its namesake had. While everyone had drooled over John Frayling's masterpiece of styling, the looks of the new car, styled by Oliver Winterbottom, left observers largely unimpressed. It was a sorry mish-mash of sweeps, not curves, and the hard-edge 'origami' styling which worked only on occasion. Worse, it had the look of an estate car. The 1970s was a style-free zone. Dynamically, the Elite was fine with 124mph and 0-60mph in 7.8 seconds thanks to a 160bhp version of the 907 engine. It was a real driver's car as well, a car which communicated everything through the steering wheel. Not only that, it would return an honest 25mpg, a consideration which became ever more important as the oil-exporting countries hiked their tariff. At the time, Colin said, 'The objective was to produce a new car which was an extension to our existing range of cars; we wanted to build a four-place, we wanted to aim for very luxurious standards of accommodation, and high performance, but not necessarily with a big engine and high fuel consumption.'

It was as Colin described, plus it had good luggage space. Lotus had also taken the production of composite bodies to a new level. The trouble was that there was no way that a client could associate the Elite with any previous Lotus. You needed a good reason to buy a car which looked as though it could have been made by anyone. Nothing about the Elite spoke of the fact that Lotus had won more Formula 1 world championships than Ferrari.

The Elite was a symptom of Colin losing his way. He never seemed to be able to put himself in the position of the customer, which is why Lotus fell away in the production racing car market. When it came to technical matters, he had imagination to spare, but he never seemed to be able to leap into the minds of other people. The Europa is a case in point. The original was unattractive to many potential buyers for reasons, such as rear vision, which were not only easily remedied, but should not have been a problem in the first place.

Colin's assertion that the Elite was an extension of Lotus's range should be seen against the background that the Elan Plus Two ceased production during 1974 and the Europa followed in 1975. The Elite was not an extension of the Lotus range, it was intended to be the backbone of it. Had he brought in a dozen people off the street to look at it, he surely could not have put it into production. History has delivered its verdict. An Elite goes on the used car market for less than a half the price of a cheap and cheerful MG Midget, which was a third of the price of an Elite when both were new.

The Elite was made at Hethel, along with the 907 engine, while Team Lotus was based at Ketteringham Hall. They were not far apart in terms of miles, but actually they were worlds apart. Lotus had been at its most exciting when the racing guys and the road car guys had bounced ideas off each other, when they had been ingredients in the same pot. The Elite became a canker at the core of the company.

CHAPTER 22

LOSING THE PLOT

THE LOTUS 72 won seven of the 15 rounds of the 1973 world championship, and had worked splendidly on the tyres that Goodyear supplied. There seemed little wrong with the overall concept of the 72 and Colin asked Ralph Bellamy to draw what was, in effect, a 72 with 100lbs shed from its weight. Maurice Phillippe had been lured by a new American F1 team, VELS-Parnelli, which had the special attraction of Mario Andretti as its driver. The new car was to be called the John Player Special Mk I, but it was only ever called the 76 except in John Player press releases. Colin asked journalists to call it a John Player Mk I, and he asked nicely, but he was ignored. The Lotus 76 was first shown to the world on a turntable at the London Theatre and it looked the business.

The headline was that it had four pedals and a button on the gearknob for operating the clutch, a system developed by Automotive Products. Long before anyone else, Colin had realised that every time a car changed gear, it lost time. The pedal on the far left was to be used for leaving the line, after which the button on the gearknob would be used to shift gear. The remaining pedals allowed the driver to use left-foot or right-foot braking. Left-foot braking has since become the norm in Formula 1, but it was then a novel idea. Ronnie, who had served his apprentice-ship in karting, loved the idea, but it was another Lotus queerbox, the chimera which Colin had pursued for years. His thinking was sound, however: every gearchange then cost about a 10th of a second, 10 of those make a full second and 60 seconds over a 60-lap race equals a minute. The trouble was that Colin's thinking was ahead of contemporary technology.

With Fittipaldi off to McLaren, where he won a second world championship in 1974, Colin signed Jacky Ickx. When one thinks of Ickx, the word 'imperious' is never far behind. Jacky had put in some fabulous drives in Formula 1, especially in the wet, but he seemed not to be fully committed. He came into his own in sports car racing, winning that category's world championship twice and taking a record six wins at Le Mans.

It is hard to imagine Chapman and Ickx rubbing along easily in the best of circumstances, and the Lotus 76 did not create happiness. The long and short of it is that the Lotus 76 did not work. All manner of pedal arrangements were tried, but the design was flawed from the start because it was designed for tyres which were no longer being made. Worse, when it was put on the scales it weighed exactly the same as a Lotus 72. The lighter, brighter, 72 was a whimsical dream with a lot more problems. Doug Nye recorded Colin's comments in *Theme Lotus*: 'When we got the 76s the trouble was that their systems didn't work – fuel, oil, cooling and brakes didn't work – and the steering wasn't very good. Nothing very serious...! We got stuck-in and did an awful lot of work until Ronnie got impatient and said, "drag the old ones out."'

Peterson put his 72 on pole for the Argentine Grand Prix, and he led, only to have a misfiring engine. Peterson was fourth on the grid in Brazil, despite a disagreement with the local food, and he trailed in sixth, with Ickx third and lapped by Fittipaldi's McLaren. Ronnie was supposed to drive a 76 in the Race of Champions, but his car was not ready, and Jacky Ickx won in the obsolete 72 having overtaken Niki Lauda's Ferrari on the outside of Paddock Bend in a downpour. It is a move still spoken of with awe by all who saw it and, unusually for the time, the race was televised.

Both drivers had 76s for the South African Grand Prix, but they need not have bothered turning up. After Monaco, which Ronnie won in a 72, the 76 was usually a T-car. Jacky and Ronnie raced them on occasion but it was in a 72 that Peterson won in Monaco, France and Italy. Not bad for a car in its fifth year of competition. The Lotus 72 was an outstanding machine, but Team Lotus had run out of ideas. The Type 72 would become the longest-serving design in Formula 1 history, but that was through necessity, not through planning.

Peterson and Ickx were retained for 1975 and the John Player Special Mk I was quietly dropped. The Lotus 72 soldiered on into its sixth season and Ickx left the team after the French Grand Prix. Goodyear was making tyres to suit the leading teams and Lotus was not among them. At the British Grand Prix, which followed the French race, Colin brought in two young British drivers, Jim Crawford and Brian Henton. Henton did not endear himself to Colin by declaring, after a test run, that the car was 'crap' and the worst racing car he'd ever driven. Colin was not used to such bluntness, but Robin Herd rates Henton equal with Niki Lauda as the best test driver he's ever encountered.

The team's best result all year had been Ickx's second place in the Spanish Grand Prix, a race dogged by controversy over safety. After an accident involving fatalities to spectators, it was stopped after 29 laps of a scheduled 75. By any standards it was a freak result. Colin had an obsolete car and a brilliant driver whose career was going nowhere. Ronnie was a potential world champion, yet he finished the season with just six points. Lotus finished seventh in the constructors' series with just nine points and with no new ideas on the horizon.

Lotus was more active on the road car front and, in 1975, launched the Eclat, which was basically a fastback Elite and shared that car's chassis and drive train. The new style did not limit rear passenger space, but Lotus liked to call the Eclat a 2+2, possibly to make the Elite seem larger. The Eclat, not the prettiest of cars, sold in very small numbers. Lotus was in decline as a maker of road cars.

The Esprit was also shown in 1975, but did not reach production until mid-1976. Early cars were not as quick as Lotus hoped – the works claimed 138mph but *The Autocar* could get only 124mph with 0-60mph in 8.4 seconds and other road test figures were similar. This suggests problems with the engine installation, since the Esprit was slower than the Eclat. There were also vibration and cooling problems which were not sorted out until the Esprit S2 of 1979. Launching a car which fails to deliver what is claimed for it is not the brightest thing to do. Lotus was in a mess.

Despite that, in 2002, Lotus celebrated the building of its 60,000th road car and fully a third of that number were variants of the Esprit, which was still in production, though with probably not much more than the odd washer interchangeable with the original model. The Esprit was the last Lotus road car in which Colin took any real interest.

Lotus did not stride confidently into 1976, it lurched in. It had one very unhappy star driver in Formula 1 and endless problems with the road cars against a background of spiralling inflation. Colin took stock and decided that he was really interested only in Formula 1, so he moved his office to Ketteringham Hall and more or less left the Hethel section to be run by Mike Kimberley, who found himself with his hands full.

During 1976 the Jensen-Healey project came to an end, so Lotus was no longer selling engines there. Jensen-Healey had been taking up to 3,000 engines a year, while Lotus itself would take about 800 engines in a good year, if it was a very good year. One of the main original selling points of the Jensen-Healey was that it had a Lotus engine. When the 907 unit got a reputation for poor reliability, the reputation rubbed off on Lotus itself. Customers had put up with poor quality control on the Elan and Europa, so many cars in the 1960s had poor quality control and, besides, the Elan and Europa were bought by enthusiasts who were prepared to suffer for their pleasure. When Lotus moved its range up-market it encountered a different sort of customer.

There was even the case of problems with some of the composite body panels not being cured properly. Then it was discovered that some of the workers had been opening the autoclave during their lunch break to heat their pies and pasties. It was just one of the problems of moving a car factory to an area where people were more used to lifting sugar beet than making cars.

Colin put together a new Formula 1 design team at Ketteringham Hall. Heading it was Peter Warr, the team co-ordinator, and other key elements were Mike Cooke, Geoff Aldridge and Martin Ogilvie, all engineers. The Lotus 77 had, as its thrust, the idea that its dimensions could be changed to suit any circuit. The idea was that it could have a short wheelbase on tight circuits and a long wheelbase on circuits with wide open sweeps, and the track could be adjusted as well. Furthermore, the rear anti-roll bar could be adjusted from the cockpit.

A car for all seasons seemed sensible in theory, and the 77, or John Player Mk II, was soon dubbed the 'adjustacar', but it was a sign of desperation. In the CART series it became common practice to run cars with a combination of long and short wheelbases, and high and low downforce bodywork, but CART runs on one-mile ovals, super speedways, town races and road races and even in 1976 Formula 1 circuits, were being homogenised. At the time, data acquisition came mainly through driver feedback and that was rarely accurate enough to fine-tune the concept behind the Lotus 77.

Stories abound of engineers listening to a driver, nodding sagely, and saying things like: 'I've worked with a lot of drivers and not many could have told me with such accuracy what you've told me about the behaviour of the car. We'll tighten the front roll bar a couple of notches and loosen the rear a couple. Fine.' Nothing would actually be done to the car, but the driver would immediately be quicker. It happened time and again.

The 77 had a very slim profile. When it was launched it had outboard suspension with the brakes, on shafts, mounted close to the body but in the air-stream. The springs were outboard as well. Nobody said so at the time because it was, after all, a new Lotus, but it looked a mess. Ronnie Peterson and Jim Crawford took on the early testing and it was soon apparent that the new car did not deliver what it promised. Ronnie had been down that route before and he did not want to do so again. Jim Crawford was not offered a drive.

The scheduled opening round of the world championship was the Argentine Grand Prix, but that was cancelled for financial and political reasons so the actual start to the series was the Brazilian Grand Prix, where Mario Andretti, finding he had a spare weekend, took over the second Lotus. Mario put his car 14th on the grid with Ronnie 16th, and the Lotus 77 did not look promising. Ronnie had made firm friends at March and Robin Herd knew what was going through his mind. At the Brazilian Grand Prix Ronnie crashed his 77 when the water temperature sensor came undone and water splashed on to one of the rear tyres at a critical moment. Before the cause was discovered the driver blamed the car and the designer blamed the driver and relations between them hit a new low. Ronnie was ripe for courting. Robin Herd remembers:

> Ronnie's car was off the pace while the March 761 was going well, Chapman was rubbishing him, the relationship had gone sour and he wanted to join us.
>
> There was great politicking going on and we were trying to keep this

away from Chapman. I was in Ronnie's hotel bedroom, telling how March was going to dominate the world and there was this knock at the door, it was Chapman. There were two single beds in the room and I dived between one and the wall so it finished up with Ronnie sitting on one bed, Chapman on the other, and me on the floor just behind Chapman.

There was Colin telling Ronnie that we were a load of thieving bastards who didn't have any money, (we actually had all of £50,000) and Lotus was going to be doing this, that, and the other. He went on for an hour outlining all his plans with me dying for a leak, but hanging on to his every word. I often wonder what would have happened if I'd got up and gone to the bathroom. A good talker was Chapman, very convincing.

Ronnie switched to March, and won the 1976 Italian Grand Prix. Meanwhile Colin signed Peterson's compatriot, Gunnar Nilsson, and took on Bob Evans in the second car on a race by race basis. Ever since he had made his Formula 1 debut with Lotus in 1968, Mario Andretti had dabbled in Formula 1, doing a few races each year. He'd even won the 1971 South African Grand Prix for Ferrari. In 1975 he had competed in 12 races for VELS-Parnelli (8 retirements, three championship points) and shortly before the 1976 Spanish Grand Prix, the Parnelli outfit folded. Colin was on the case like a flash. Mario was looking for a drive and Bob Evans was shown the door.

The main problem with the Lotus 77 was that it had massive braking power, but heat from the brakes was not getting to the front tyres. Len Terry, who had always had a difficult relationship with Colin, recalls:

I felt sorry for Chapman and I phoned him with a suggestion. I thought he needed a more conventional set-up, with the brakes inside the wheels, where their heat would warm the tyres. He agreed to let me try.

I went to Ron Tauranac, obtained Ralt uprights and we designed the suspension round those. It worked. Gunnar Nilsson qualified it fourth at the British Grand Prix and a Lotus 77 won the last race of the year.

It was a long haul, but the programme was helped by the appointment of Tony Southgate, who had been with Lola, Brabham, BRM, Eagle and Shadow. His first job was to trouble-shoot, to sort out the car's many reliability problems. In the meantime work was in hand on the Lotus 78, the first 'wing car'. In 1975, with Team Lotus struggling, Colin had sat down and drawn up a design specification which he then handed over to Tony Rudd, who headed a new research and development team at Ketteringham Hall. Colin did not just write down what he thought should happen, he wrote a lot of pertinent questions. It was Colin at his creative best. At the top level, Formula 1 had become far too complex for one man to embrace. Colin had the sense to realise that, but he was sufficiently on the ball to ask all the right questions. Not everyone in Formula 1 was asking sensible questions. Much of the time they were scratching their heads and the most profound question they asked was, 'What the hell do we do now?'

Colin had concluded that the 76 and 77 had not been using their front tyres properly, which is why drivers complained of excessive understeer. The aerodynamics of the next car (78) should be such that, under braking, the downforce should load the front tyres and so give more bite. Ralph Bellamy and Peter Wright were given the brief to explore that area. During a wind tunnel test, Wright discovered what he had long suspected, that ground effect could be achieved. He had experimented with the concept on the body he had designed for the March 701. Robin Herd says, 'Every team gets daft ideas from fans. One of the daft ideas we got was that if we blanked off the aerodynamic sidepods on the 701 we would have a car which was sucked to the ground. Just as well we ignored such suggestions!' Frank Costin said:

> Of course we knew about ground effect, it was a well-known principle in aviation. It was what allowed certain aircraft to fly very slowly. Racing car aerodynamics are basically the reverse of those in aviation, on aircraft the wings are there to keep the machine up, on racing cars they are designed to keep the machine down. What I could never work out was a way to seal the air between the car and the ground.

As it happened, Peter Wright and Tony Rudd had sketched ideas for a wing car in 1969 when they had been together at BRM. That had been all too clever for BRM at the time, which partly explains why they left.

It can be argued that the Lotus 78 represents the last major breakthrough in Formula 1 design. Prior to the 78, attention to a car's aerodynamics had concentrated on the shape of the upper bodywork, and the only attention paid to undercar airflow had been the fitting of smooth undertrays to eliminate such obvious interruptions to the airflow as a prop shaft. The 78 set a new agenda.

As work on the 78 progressed, so parts were tried out on the 77 and the 77 improved. It became ever more strong and towards the end of the season the 77 sprouted the first skirts seen in Formula 1, thin strips of stiff nylon brushes attached to the underneath of the outer wall of each sidepod. It was soon apparent to the R&D team working on the 78 that the proposed aerodynamics would work most effectively if the car's behaviour could be accurately predicted. That meant that there could not be flexing or deflection on major components.

A test rig was constructed by Mike Cooke. It was a Heath Robinson affair, using cables, pulleys and oil drums filled with concrete, but it proved very effective. It was enough to ensure that components such as wishbones did not flex. If one did, it was sent back to be redesigned. Such attention to detail has long been common practice in Formula 1, but nobody bothered to do it before the Team Lotus R&D team. It was not as spectacular a breakthrough as the very concept of a wing car, but it was an important breakthrough nonetheless. The new components helped to turn the Lotus 77 from being a desperate measure into one which became ever stronger and, eventually, a winner.

At the last Grand Prix of the year, in Japan, all the attention was on whether

James Hunt (McLaren) would win the world championship or whether it would be Hunt's great pal, Niki Lauda (Ferrari). To call the race dramatic is to use litotes. On the one hand you had the dashing young Hunt, Mr Good Time, while on the other you had the apparently cold and calculating Lauda. The race for the title was given added spice by an unprecedented number of disqualifications, disputes and reinstatements. On top of that, there was the drama of Niki's amazing recovery from a near-fatal accident during the German Grand Prix. The media had a field day. In fact, it was probably the first time that the international media had a really good hook on which to hang a motor racing story.

The Japanese Grand Prix was run in a deluge and Lauda demonstrated his character by refusing to carry on after the second lap, because to drive in such conditions, he believed, was madness. Hunt came third and took the title, by a single point from Lauda. Against that backdrop, the fact that Mario Andretti actually won the race in a Lotus 77 tended to be lost. Mario had always been in contention in Japan, indeed he had set pole position, but attention throughout the season had been on the Hunt versus Lauda battle, so it was not immediately picked up that the 77 was a car under serious development. Mario Andretti had committed himself to Lotus, and nobody has ever bested Mario as a development driver.

The end of the 1976 Japanese Grand Prix had been a time for celebration for Colin, but not so Christmas 1976. Colin's grandfather had recently died, aged 96, and Stan Chapman had very been extremely busy doing all the things that have to be done in such circumstances. He was pretty well exhausted. Stan left his home in Torquay to drive to Norfolk to spend Christmas with Colin, Hazel and the three children. Torquay to Norfolk is a long haul, probably best undertaken by train, but Stan not only chose to drive, but to drive in his Mini and not the Bentley S3 that Colin had bought for him. On the journey he appears to have fallen asleep at the wheel and crashed, fatally.

Not even Colin's schoolfriends can remember much about his mother, but they all have something to say about Stan. By all accounts, Stan had been the dominant force in Colin's early life and Colin appears to have been a chip off the old block. His father's death must have come as a bitter blow.

For Colin, though, there was always the diversion of work and on 9 January 1977, two Lotus 78 'wing cars' were on the grid for the Argentine Grand Prix with Andretti in eighth place, which boded well for the new car. It was not a false omen because the 78 would take five wins during the season. Mario Andretti says that he could have been world champion in 1977 had it not been for two gallons of fuel: 'Colin insisted on pumping out an imperial gallon of fuel on the starting line in South Africa. He was always keen on cutting things to the bone.' In point of fact, Mario qualified sixth on the grid and never ran above fourth until crashing on lap 44 of 78.

Mario is on firmer ground when he says that an extra gallon would have seen him take victory in the Swedish Grand Prix. Vibration in his car caused the engine to switch from 'lean' to 'rich' and he began to run out of fuel having led most of the race from pole, and he finally finished sixth. Even had Mario won that race, he would still have trailed 20 points behind Lauda. It's funny how drivers rarely say, 'I should never have won the Liechtenstein Grand Prix, but poor old Harry Hotshoe ran out of fuel. That night I cried myself to sleep.'

The Lotus 78 was not only a remarkable concept, it also put Lotus back on top, though Ferrari took the 1977 constructors' title. During the 1970s, the balance of advantage went back and forth between Ferrari and the teams which used the DFV engine. Most designers had worked out that the most important parameter of the aerodynamic package of a car was airflow to the underneath of the rear wing, so the size and height of the rear wing became critical, as did the airflow over the rear deck of the car. The DFV, though compact, was a tall engine, whereas Ferrari had a flat-12 unit. In the mid-1970s, the rules governing the size and height of the rear wing gave a flat engine an aerodynamic advantage over a V8, which is why Alfa Romeo converted its V12 engine into a flat-12. Why the rules should be framed to allow Ferrari its first consistent winning streak since 1961, itself an unusual event, is a mystery.

A flat rear deck which allowed a free flow of air to the rear wing or, more particularly, to the underside of the rear wing, works fine when you are only concerned with the air flowing over the car. The genius which drove the Lotus 78 was that it exploited the air between the ground and the underside of the car. The DFV may have been a tall engine, but it was narrow, and that is what Lotus exploited. With a V8, air had more space in which to move at the sides and beneath the car. Colin's team realised that not only could the Type 78 use that air to pull the car to the ground, but it could also direct that air to squirt under the rear wing. 'Squirt' is used because the effect was roughly the same as adjusting the nozzle on a garden hose.

To reduce it to basics, what happens when you adjust the nozzle of your garden hose? At one extreme you get a light shower, at the other extreme you get nothing but a dry nozzle and trouble building at the tap end of the hose. The trick is to adjust the nozzle to your requirements and to direct the flow of water where it will do the most good, which is usually on the flower beds and not on the garden shed.

In the case of the wing car, air rushing under the front of each sidepod was directed to a space where it expanded and that caused air pressure to drop. A low pressure area on each side of the car caused it to be 'sucked' to the ground in popular journalese. In fact, it was pushed to the ground because the air pressure on top of the 78 was greater than that beneath. This gave downforce without the usual penalty of increased drag, or 'something for nothing' as Colin was fond of saying.

There was a great deal of trial and error at first. For a start, spring rates increased far beyond what had ever been encountered before. The loading on components such as wishbones was greater than ever before, but most had been tested on the 77 throughout 1976. What seems extraordinary is that the Lotus 78 shot to the front of the grid and no rival appeared to notice why, even though pit garages were Liberty Hall. Engineers, mechanics and members of the media could wander around more or less as they pleased. People simply did not notice and this gave Lotus a clear lead of a whole season.

There were several reasons for the opposition being slow on the uptake. Chief among them was the fact that people were used to looking at aerodynamics only in terms of airflow over the visible surface of a car. Another factor was that hardly any team did serious wind tunnel testing. Even the few that did were at a primitive stage, and that includes Team Lotus. The typical wind tunnel, which in Britain tended to mean either Southampton University or Imperial College, London, allowed only a relatively small-scale model, which tended to be run in four configurations: high ground clearance, low ground clearance, nose up or nose down. The first sophisticated wind tunnel programme was was not begun until John Barnard and Alan Jenkins tackled the problem for McLaren in the 1980s. Of all the teams based in Britain – which at the beginning of 1977 meant everyone save for Ferrari – only Lotus had access to the full-scale wind tunnel operated by MIRA (Motor Industry Research Association), because only Lotus was a mainstream car manufacturer.

Formula 1 was still a minority interest sport which was rarely televised. This meant that there was a very small coterie of journalists and all the regulars were on first name terms with everyone else. If Colin told a journalist that the secret of the Lotus 78 was finding an ideal weight distribution then that became the secret ingredient. As it happens, the 78 did have weight distribution which was radically different to any other contemporary Formula 1 car. Once weight distribution had been identified as the secret ingredient, it was the story accepted by everyone.

Teams had small workforces. Having as many as two designers on the staff was a luxury so response time was slow. McLaren, for example, was committed to proving its new M26, which had a monocoque that featured aluminium honeycomb, then a new departure. Besides, many a team was too occupied with trying to balance the books to take much notice. March would be gone by the end of 1977, as would Penske. Shadow was going down the tubes, as was Surtees. It was a time of transition, indeed 1977 was one of the turning points in Formula 1: most teams were either struggling to stay afloat or else were pursuing their own technical breakthroughs.

Walter Wolf Racing (formerly Wolf-Williams) sprung a surprise at the opening round of the 1977 season, in Argentina, when Jody Scheckter won. The Wolf WR1 was a simple, nimble car ascribed to Dr Harvey Postlethwaite. What most people did not notice was that the assistant designer on the project was Patrick Head, who had joined with Frank Williams to start a new team.

Mario could qualify in only eighth position in Argentina, but he was in second place when, with two laps to go, he retired with a broken wheel bearing. At least Lotus was pointing in the right direction. In fact it probably helped to disguise the new concept that, after four rounds, Team Lotus had scored only four points (equal sixth in the Constructors' Cup) while Ferrari seemed unassailable with 22 points.

At Mario's suggestion, the driver had control over how he emptied the tanks in order to trim the balance of the car. There was also a rear anti-roll bar, adjustable from the cockpit. During the season Mario fine-tuned his car in a race to a degree never before seen in Formula 1. Colin believed that he had found the only driver who might replace Jim Clark, at least in a working relationship.

Mario won the fourth round, the United States Grand Prix (West) at Long Beach, but Niki Lauda was second, and then Mario won again in Spain. After that the season settled into its usual pattern of wins, places, crashes and retirements. Mario ended the season with four wins, which was more than any other driver.

Gunnar Nilsson improved throughout the season, he was Mario's eager apprentice, and he won the Belgian Grand Prix. Alan Rees, who had head-hunted Ronnie Peterson for March, was one of the founders of the new Arrows team and he signed Gunnar to lead the new team. Towards the end of 1977, however, Gunnar had bouts of feeling unwell and then was diagnosed with terminal cancer. He never drove again but he refused pain-killing drugs so that he could think clearly in order to set up a campaign to to raise funds for research into the disease.

Gunnar's illness had nothing to do with Colin's next move. There was a seat to fill at Lotus and he turned to Ronnie Peterson, whose career was in the doldrums. For 1977 Ronnie had signed for Tyrrell, and the Project 34 six-wheeler, and the Tyrrell simply did not work on the compounds that Goodyear provided that year. One of the most naturally gifted drivers ever seen in Formula 1 needed a seat and Colin, as shrewd a negotiator of a driver's contract as he was a judge of a driver's ability, signed Ronnie. There was a condition, and that was that for 1978 at least, Mario was to to be given every assistance to take the world championship. As it worked out, Mario needed little assistance, and in fact it was his skill at setting up cars which revived Ronnie's flagging reputation.

At the road car plant, the Lotus press officer, Don McLaughlan, had his lap filled with problems. No car was selling in sensible numbers and the Esprit had failed to live up to expectations. Despite that, Don managed to place an Esprit as the vehicular star in the James Bond movie, *The Spy Who Loved Me*. Through the legerdemain of film directors, the Esprit turned into a submarine and, when it emerged on a ramp, Roger Moore (as 007) was able to pass a wriggling fish to a startled bystander.

Q. How did a fish get inside a sealed vehicle?

A. Do not ask such things, ask instead how Don McLaughlan managed to turn the Esprit into one of the tiny number of movie cars which has star status. In later years, BMW paid millions of pounds for Bond to drive its cars (the bad hats drove Mercedes-Benz) and nothing that Bond has done in Bavaria's fine cars compares with the sub-aqua exploits of the Esprit.

CHAPTER 23

ENTER JOHN DELOREAN

COMMON lore has it that Ronnie Peterson was quicker than Mario Andretti during 1978, but faithfully played his part as number two in return for a clear crack at the title in 1979. A look at the details casts some doubt on this story. Ronnie was prepared to ride shotgun to his team leader, no doubt about that, but during qualifying Mario was often the quicker driver, especially in the early part of the season. It panned out like this: the team's best effort was behind Mario. That went without saying, but Mike Cooke's work with his test rig had probably resulted in more equal quality between components than had ever been achieved in Formula 1 before. The great thing about the driver line-up was that there was no tension between Mario and Ronnie. For a start, they liked each other. They both knew what the position was and accepted it. It was going to be Mario's championship in 1978 and then Ronnie would be let off the leash.

If this sounds like team orders, it was not. It was an agreement. The cornering forces generated by the Type 78 were higher than had ever before been experienced in motor racing and Mario had spent two years developing the wing car concept. Ronnie knew that Andretti had learned how to fine-tune the car during a race and, for his part, Mario was prepared to share what he had learned. That had always been his way, he was a team player, and besides, Mario had never been paired with anyone as quick as he was. For all his brilliance, Ronnie was not a development driver and he needed Mario to set up the cars. Once Mario had explained his thinking, Ronnie could drive the thing. Andretti has recorded driving behind Peterson and being astounded at what Ronnie could do with a

Lotus, but Ronnie could not have tuned the car to allow him to do that. Andretti and Peterson was a case of symbiosis. Colin had been very shrewd in his choice of drivers and each man was sufficiently honest to recognise that. It was a 'dream team'.

At the start of 1978 nobody quite realised how strong Lotus was, though Mario set pole and led to the flag in Argentina. Lotus did not show particularly strongly in Brazil, though it was Ronnie's turn to set pole. In the early races of 1978 the flat-12 engines from Ferrari and Alfa Romeo pumped out much more power than a Cosworth and the very rigid monocoque of the McLaren M26 had its own advantage. For all the many good points of the Lotus 78, the fact remains that the monocoque was not that special and nor was the roadholding. The car's superior aerodynamics disguised these basic flaws.

Ronnie won the South African Grand Prix by overtaking Patrick Depailler's Tyrrell at the very last corner. It was the last Grand Prix win for the Lotus 78. It had put Lotus back into contention and had won seven Grands Prix. There was still the odd non-championship race left, and the International Trophy at Silverstone attracted a small, but quality, grid. Colin was particularly ebullient at Silverstone where a Lotus 79 was entered for Mario. In essence, it was a development of the Type 78 with an inch added to the wheelbase and the front and rear track, but whereas the 78 looked functional, the 79 was one of those rare racing cars which combine function with aesthetic appeal. Journalists rushed to be the first to call it 'Black Beauty' and it figures on most people's list of the most beautiful racing cars ever. Handsome is as handsome does, however, and the main point of interest was the sliding skirts in the sidepods which sealed the air passing under the car and so allowed the areas of high and low pressure to be calculated with more precision, since they remained constant under most circumstances.

It was Ronnie in a 78 who set pole at Silverstone with Mario third in the new 79, but the race was run in a monsoon and both men crashed out after two laps. They each drove a 78 for the United States Grand Prix (West) at Long Beach, where Mario was second and Ronnie fourth. The 78 was used at Monaco, to no effect, and it was not until Belgium, in late May, that Mario debuted the 79 in a world championship race. He led from pole to the flag and Ronnie, in a 78, came second.

Both drivers had 79s for Spain – they occupied the front row of the grid and came home an easy 1-2. By this time, the message was clear, all other cars were obsolete. Brabham and McLaren both revived an idea pioneered by the American, Jim Hall, on one of his Chapparal sports racing cars: a rear-mounted extractor fan to create a low-pressure area under the car. Brabham had its version in time for the Swedish Grand Prix and, in the hands of Niki Lauda, it won. This caused general consternation, and although the result was allowed to stand, the concept was immediately banned, which is why the McLaren did not run in public, though it was tested. Brabham was owned by Bernie Ecclestone, who did not protest at his car's exclusion, but then Bernie had been working on a reshaped Formula 1 Constructors' Association (FOCA). His 'fan' car was a small sacrifice in the context of his wider vision.

In the French Grand Prix it was another Andretti-Peterson 1-2. They dominated the British Grand Prix until they both retired with mechanical failure. They filled the front row in Germany and Austria, Mario won the former, Ronnie the latter, and in Holland they filled the front row again and finished in close formation with Mario ahead. Then, at Monza, came tragedy. During qualifying, the engine blew in Ronnie's 79 so he had to revert to the team spare, a 78. While Mario set pole, Ronnie was back on the third row. At the start there was mayhem. A collision between Patrese and Hunt started a chain reaction which caused Hunt's car to smash into Peterson's. Ronnie sustained severely broken legs and his car was on fire, but James sprinted over and hauled him out. Ronnie was taken to hospital, but it seemed to be no more than an accident which would sideline him for the rest of the season.

The race was restarted and Andretti won from Gilles Villeneuve's Ferrari on the road, but both were judged to have jumped the start and were penalised a minute each, which dropped Mario down to sixth and Gilles to seventh. Mario could not be caught in the championship, however, and Lotus had tied up the constructors' series long before. Naturally Team Lotus celebrated with its usual vigour, tinged with regret for Ronnie's injury. During the night, however, marrow from Ronnie's broken bones seeped into his bloodstream and put him into a coma. He died in the early hours of the Monday morning, one of the most gifted and popular drivers of his day. The rest of the season fizzled out for Lotus, which failed to take a single point from the last two races. It seemed almost as if the stuffing had been knocked out of the team. For all its revolutionary nature, the Lotus 79 was destined never again to win a Grand Prix.

An end came to an era when John Player told Colin during the year that it would not renew its sponsorship deal for 1979. Sports sponsorship overall had developed during the 11 years of the partnership and the company wanted to spread its image over a much wider area. Motor racing was growing in popularity year on year, thanks largely to FOCA's promotion of it through television, but Formula 1 was still far from being a major sport. That left Colin with a headache, but Team Lotus would go into 1979 with even more sponsorship than before.

In terms of Group Lotus, the only bright spot came with the launch of the Esprit S2, which featured a number of detail improvements. The good news for the customer was that the cooling and vibration problems which had beset the first attempt had been sorted out. It also achieved the sort of performance that had been projected for the original: 135mph and 0-60mph in eight seconds. In other words, it had taken two years to get the Esprit right, which must have cheered the 718 purchasers of the original no end. It is little wonder that the road car division of Group Lotus was in trouble. Lotus was kept going largely through a contract with Chrysler to put a 2.2-litre version of the Lotus engine into the Sunbeam hatchback to make a car suitable for rallying.

During 1978, into Colin's life came John Zachary DeLorean or John Z., as he liked to be known. It was a fateful meeting and one which cast a dark shadow over the last weeks of Chapman's life and was to brand him, posthumously, as a criminal.

DeLorean was tall, stylish and charismatic, and had a much younger wife, his third. Christina DeLorean was a 'trophy wife' before the phrase had been coined. She was John Z.'s junior by 25 years, just as wife number two had been. Christina was was a successful model and an aspiring actress with movie experience. They made a glamorous couple.

DeLorean held a master's degree in automotive engineering and had studied for credits for a master's degree in business administration. He promoted himself expertly as the 'golden boy' of Detroit who had quit a $600,000 a year job to realise his dream of starting his own car company. It was not just any car company, it was to be the first to be based on 'ethics', and wasn't 'ethics' just about the most hip word to use in the 1970s? His angle was that he was the only man in history who had sacked General Motors. Wow! Journalists queued up to repeat the line. Unfortunately, it was a lie, but the bigger the lie, the more likely it is to be believed.

DeLorean had a deep streak of dishonesty. It showed itself in little ways, such as the fact that he talked up the grinding poverty of his childhood, whereas in reality it was as nothing compared to what millions of Americans suffered in the Depression. DeLorean liked to claim French ancestry, French-Alsatian, whereas his father was in fact an immigrant from Romania. More seriously, according to *DeLorean*, a meticulously researched book by Ivan Fallon and James Sprodes, when he was aged 23, DeLorean became involved in a criminal scam. He took two copies of Detroit's 1948 Yellow Pages and clipped out 2,700 advertisements. He then registered a company with a name that closely resembled the company that owned Yellow Pages and he sent the advertisements to all the companies who had advertised in the 1948 edition together with an invoice for their inclusion in the 1949 Yellow Pages. The police were on him within hours and he was lucky that Yellow Pages did not press charges. A criminal record would have wrecked his career. Another lucky break was that the only newspaper to publish the story, the *Detroit Times*, was on its last legs and went out of business shortly afterwards, so no subsequent journalist had access to the clippings files that all newspapers maintain.

DeLorean went through a number of jobs until he was head-hunted by General Motors. By all accounts, he was a fine automotive engineer and he was also a man who asked all the right questions. DeLorean had exceptional talents for an executive in a large corporation. He was soon promoted within the Pontiac division of General Motors and he was quick to take all the credit for introducing exciting models such as the Pontiac GTO, but then it is always the general that wins the battle, never the men under him. By the age of 40 he had become general manager of Pontiac and was a colourful figure in Detroit.

He dyed his hair, he wore trendy clothes and he was always available to the press. He portrayed himself as a maverick, a different type of corporate executive, he was the hip guy who did not wear a suit to work. He aligned himself with fashionable causes such as a drive to increase the number of black and Hispanic workers in the motor industry, a hot issue in the 1960s. All in all he portrayed himself as a 'happening' man. People close to him, however, recall that he was actually a racist who feared black people, and the campaign for an increase in workers from ethnic minorities was no more than cynical exploitation of a social problem. It worked, though, and the news media swallowed it.

Having been made a vice-president of General Motors, the man in charge of Chevrolet, the General's largest division, DeLorean resigned in April 1973. He spread the story that a large corporation was too stifling for a man such as himself. He hinted that he had been groomed for the presidency of the company, and General Motors was the largest industrial corporation in the world, but that it was not for him. The fact is, however, that DeLorean had been forced to resign.

Detroit newspapers and the motoring press had been receiving a lot of inside information about General Motors, all of it slanted from DeLorean's perspective. An internal investigation showed that one particularly damaging document had been leaked by DeLorean himself, and it was suspected that it had not been the only one. DeLorean's version, naturally, was different. His story was that he had quit to pursue a dream, that there was more to life than pushing paper around. Hey, he was the hip guy in the shades and flares, even if, at 48 years old, he was a little old for the pose. As usual, the media swallowed his side of things and General Motors maintained its usual policy of corporate silence.

DeLorean was given a handsome leaving package and set loose on the world. Why General Motors was so generous remains a mystery, since DeLorean had managed to upset a lot of people and there were rumours of grave financial misdemeanours. His job had included overseeing top television shows, which were made with corporate sponsorship. Though he was often gauche in social contexts, DeLorean loved the showbiz element, if only because it gave him names to drop. Part of his leaving package was a $200,000 a year job as the president of the National Alliance of Businessmen, which was for one year only. Much of his duties consisted of addressing black and Hispanic audiences and, apparently, he was rather good at this. He lifted the hearts of his audience, though he couldn't care less for them, and he conducted press conferences which were unusual in their candour. The media loved that because it was such a change from the cautious men who wore suits and followed the corporate line. The DeLorean legend grew, even though, after 12 months, he was unemployed.

DeLorean was a high roller with lots of connections and a well-oiled publicity machine. He decided that what the world needed was an 'ethical' sports car, and he began work on a prototype, the DeLorean Safety Vehicle, which, he hoped, would be a genuine sports car, with all the fun that that implied, but would be constructed to protect passengers in the event of a crash. There had been some well-publicised examples of Detroit accountants calmly considering that a modification to make a car more safe would cost more than compensation paid to families of people killed in an unsafe configuration. Ralph Nader had published a best-selling book, *Unsafe At Any Speed*, which had taken Detroit to task. Nader had been sued, and Nader had won. Nader became a hero of the consumer throughout the world, and he inspired many a consumer-led movement. By almost, but never quite, aligning himself with Nader, DeLorean was making all the right noises. Central to Nader's book was the Chevrolet Corvair, which Nader claimed was inherently unstable because of its rear-mounted engine. John Z. DeLorean's 'ethical' sports car, his DeLorean Safety Vehicle, had a rear-mounted engine.

DeLorean sketched out his concept and had Giorgetto Guigario create a body for his car. The body itself was based on a 1970 design exercise, the Tapiro, which Guigario had built on a Porsche 911. A body styled in 1970 is perhaps not the best start for a car which would not be launched until 1981, but DeLorean was on a roll.

On three points DeLorean was firm about his car: it should be rear-engined (the engine should be behind the back axle line), so that passengers should be protected in the event of a rear-end shunt. It should have gullwing doors, because that was both a good marketing ploy and would allow high door-sills to provide side-impact protection. Finally, it should have a stainless steel body, which would never rust. The 'stainless steel' body grabbed headlines, but it was never more than a metal veneer over a plastic composite shell.

It requires a leap of imagination for many people to put themselves in the position of a motorist in the mid-1970s. You bought a car and it could rust before your eyes. Stainless steel sounded positively sexy. There were two inherent problems with the idea, which only came to light after the car was in production. One was that anyone who touched a DeLorean DMC-12 left a fingerprint, and it was a nightmare to keep clean. A second problem was that all DeLorean DMC-12s looked identical. Most Ferraris, about 85 percent, are red, but Ferrari makes no more than 4,000 cars a year and Ferrari has a range of models and there are colour options. DeLorean proposed one model, which would be made at a rate of 30,000 units annually, and nobody could have a finish other than the stainless steel veneer.

As soon as General Motors learned that John Z. DeLorean intended to market a car which would compete with its own Chevrolet Corvette, it ceased to pay him the rest of his severance package. That left DeLorean with no option but to press ahead with his dream. All the media stories had said that John Z. had his pick of jobs, but the word was out and no serious company would employ him. This was not known in Norfolk, however, or was it? Colin had excellent connections to the motor industry, and not only Ford. In 1978 Lotus was in league with the Chrysler Corporation as they developed the 'Sunbeam-Lotus' hot hatchback.

It would have been unusual if Colin was not fully briefed about DeLorean before they met. By 1978, when Chapman and DeLorean met, Colin had contacts within the motor industry at a level which was a fast-receding memory for John Z.

DeLorean, whose reputation rested on what he had done within General Motors, but he was only ever an employee. Colin headed Lotus, on all its fronts, and Lotus was on its way to winning yet another brace of Formula 1 world championships.

DeLorean attempted to persuade various legislatures and governments to back his project. His sales pitch was that it would bring employment and prestige to any state or nation and there would be a tangible cash benefit in the form of a royalty on each car sold. The car itself was proposed to have a price of $12,000 (hence the name, DMC-12), which would make it a very attractive proposition, but it actually hit the market at $25,600, which was more expensive than the Chevrolet Corvette and Datsun 280ZX Turbo, both of which were significantly quicker. $25,600 was pushing into Porsche 911 territory.

DeLorean first tried various towns and states in America, then he tried Puerto Rico, and drew a blank. Next he tried Spain and then the Republic of Ireland and drew more blanks. Finally he struck lucky with the Northern Ireland Development Agency (NIDA). Northern Ireland was going through a very bleak patch with civil unrest, terrorist bombings and sectarian murders a common occurrence. On top of that, there was large-scale unemployment, at 35 percent more than twice the rest of the United Kingdom, as the province's traditional industries, such as ship building, declined.

NIDA was attracted to the prospect of a factory which would create an initial 1,300 jobs, with more promised in the future. A committee assembled by the then Labour government rejected the proposal as unworkable, but the government desperately wanted to make a gesture to the people of Northern Ireland. According to one member of the committee, 'It took us no time at all to reject the project, but we were told in no uncertain terms to mind our own business. I believe that the message came from the highest level of government.'

The upshot was that the British government agreed to fund the DeLorean project to the tune of £53 million, a figure that would rise to £85 million. John Z. DeLorean would claim that he had a personal stake in the company of $4 million, but in fact he put up just $750,000 of his wife's money. DeLorean himself did not invest a cent, but he flitted across the Atlantic on Concorde, using British taxpayer's money, and accumulated a collection of art in his penthouse suite in Manhattan. His suits were not bought 'off-the-peg', Lobb made his shoes (at $300 per foot) and he stayed at only the best hotels.

Even at the time, the government received criticism for its backing of DeLorean. An injection of £12 million could have saved Triumph, one of the greatest names in motorcycles, which had been forced to close mere days before the announcement of Westminster's largesse to DeLorean. A grant of £4 million would have seen Bob Jankel move his established company, Panther Westwinds, to Northern Ireland. Panther Westwinds had an unmatched reputation for quality and had a much-admired prototype sports car, the 'Equus', ready to go into production. The Equus made extensive use of Vauxhall components, so British money could have supported British workers not only in Northern Ireland, but on the mainland. The Panther Equus oozed flair, and its development had even been commissioned by General Motors, but DeLorean sang a better song: he could have been president of General Motors.

NIDA swallowed the DeLorean legend, but one thing that John Z. did not tell his benefactors was that he despised the Irish. His visits to the factory, on a 70-acre site at Dunmurry, an area of Belfast between Catholic and Protestant enclaves, would be infrequent. It seemed to have escaped everyone's notice that DeLorean's dream was a long way from being ready for production and it had been a long time since a new motor company had leapt fully-formed onto the market. Lotus had taken years to become established and by the time the original Elite went into production, Lotus had an international reputation in motor racing which made ownership of an Elite desirable. Furthermore, DeLorean talked airily of sales of 30,000 a year, all in America, which then had a 55mph blanket speed limit. Porsche dreamed of selling 30,000 cars a year in the States and they had been established there for a quarter of a century. Porsche had enormous 'badge', whereas the DeLorean Motor Corporation had only its chief executive's fading image.

Thus DeLorean secured his money, but he still had the problem of engineering his car. He had a body style, an overall layout, but no actual car. He knocked on the doors of BMW and Porsche, but discovered that they wanted sensible money for the work and eventually he turned to Colin Chapman. At the time, Group Lotus was not doing very well. There was the Chrysler Sunbeam-Lotus in development, which would take the Lotus engine, but Lotus was preparing to withdraw from the American market. DeLorean grabbed Colin's attention with a proposal to buy to Group Lotus outright, a plan which Colin was not keen on, but he took the view that if someone wanted to talk, he was prepared to listen. One reason that Colin never considered selling Group Lotus was that it would have meant opening the books to scrutiny.

DeLorean's idea of buying Lotus was really only a kite being flown, as he would have had to use part of his grant from the British government to buy a British company, an implausible scenario. In 1978, Group Lotus was valued at only £3 million on the London Stock Exchange, but it was recognised as one of the jewels of British engineering and in 1978, with the British-owned motor industry falling apart, this meant something.

A relationship between Chapman and DeLorean was never going to be easy. Both were automotive engineers, but DeLorean's skill had been in 'making the numbers'. He was sharp when it came to rationalising production. He had rejuvenated the Pontiac marque by offering such items as optional suspension kits, but it was not that difficult to improve Pontiac's products, which had been mediocre. DeLorean did not push back the boundaries of design as Chapman did. He had only one idea and that was a 1970s sports car to be made in the 1980s. Both men were restless and difficult to pin down. Neither man had much time for the details of administration, but at least Colin recognised that and he surrounded himself with people who could look after the details. Colin wanted to know the effect of the details, he was on top of everything, but he did not need to know the details themselves. DeLorean appears to have been too lazy to have bothered.

Chapman, Bushell and DeLorean met in a hotel in Switzerland and DeLorean advanced on two fronts: one was the purchase of Group Lotus and the other was the idea that Lotus should engineer what became the DMC-12. Colin was not taken with DeLorean's concept of his dream car. For a start, he thought that the 2.85-litre V6 Renault engine was not the right choice, as it was not powerful or exciting enough. Colin was right. DeLorean spoke of a 130mph car, but no road test ever saw more than 120mph, except in European specification, and there were precious few of those. Every Lotus, even the four-seat second-generation Elite, could comfortably exceed 120mph with an engine of two-thirds the size. Colin also questioned the use of gullwing doors, which were unnecessarily complicated and expensive. He felt that they would be be no help at all in selling the car.

The big sticking point for Colin, however, was the rear-engined layout. Putting the engine behind the rear axle line frees up space in the interior and offers more luggage space, but makes a car difficult to balance. The engineers at Porsche only tamed the layout through years of careful development, and for competition cars they had long pursued the mid-engined route. DeLorean flattered Chapman. 'If anyone can make it work, Colin, you can,' he said. Charmer and chancer met charmer and chancer and there was a challenge. The idea was to build the car around a fabricated steel backbone chassis, something with which Lotus was completely familiar.

Fred Bushell had meantime been considering the economics of the deal. Lotus was not selling many cars, and DeLorean was looking to make considerably more cars in a fortnight than Lotus was making in a year. Furthermore, John Z. had the approval of the British government and was offering millions of dollars to develop his car. It was the money up front which grabbed Colin's attention.

Colin liked the idea of paying income tax no more than most of us, so he had a network of off-shore companies designed to avoid paying a penny more than necessary. One was GPD (General Product Development) Services Inc., a company registered in Panama in 1977 (as ILC Inc.), which was operated from Geneva by long-time friends of Chapman's, Jaroslav 'Jerry' and Marie-Denise Juhan. Neither appeared on the board of directors, but they were granted power of attorney by the three Panamanian nationals who did.

GPD had been set up ostensibly to obtain contract work for Lotus, with the advantage that it did not have to post company records in either Panama or Switzerland. Lotus had enormous expertise and had contracted that to the motor industry since the Ford Lotus-Cortina. GPD's official role was to commission Group Lotus to undertake development of the DeLorean DMC-12, but all the money disappeared, and then the British government paid a second time, as money for the development of the car was paid to Group Lotus through regular channels. Group Lotus submitted invoices in the normal way and was paid in the normal way.

In other words, the British government paid twice over for the development of the DMC-12. The difference is that none of the money paid to GPD was spent on developing the car. Regardless of the scandals which later gathered around Chapman, Bushell and DeLorean (and DeLorean's accountancy firm, Arthur Andersen) the work of Group Lotus has never been been doubted. The company did its work, did it well, and submitted proper invoices which were settled. In fact, the engineers at Lotus deserve massive credit because they turned John Z. DeLorean's half-baked dream into a viable proposition. Chief among them was Colin Spooner.

DeLorean had his own network of companies, which included DeLorean Research Limited Partnerships (DRLP). He had persuaded friends and associates to invest $18.5 million in DRLP to develop the car. From DRLP and from DeLorean Motor Cars Ltd a total of $17.67 million was transferred to GPD Services in late 1978, ostensibly to pay Lotus for its work on the DMC-12. In fact the British government, through DMC, paid for this work to the tune of £12 million ($20.4 million at the then exchange rate). The $17.67 million paid to GPD Services disappeared from the books and would ensure that the British government, under Margaret Thatcher, would mount an exhaustive enquiry.

John DeLorean, it is alleged, received $8.5 million; Chapman's share was alleged to be $8.39 million; and Bushell, allegedly, received one-tenth of what Chapman received. The figures are those given at Bushell's trial in 1992. Though DeLorean had promised NIDA that he would work for no other company except DeLorean Motor Cars Ltd, he used his share of the 'missing millions' to gain control of the Logan Manufacturing Corporation. Logan made machinery that prepared snow runs for ski resorts and had 80 percent of the market. DeLorean broke his bond with the British government, while Chapman merely salted his share away.

It probably seemed a good wheeze at the time, but the scheme was to rebound. It was to cast a shadow on the last weeks of Colin's life.

CHAPTER 24

ESSEX MAN

URING 1978, Colin became involved not only with John Z. DeLorean, but with another interesting businessman, David Thieme, head of Essex Petroleum. Nobody has ever seen a filling station selling Essex fuel, because there weren't any. Thieme was actually an oil broker who operated from an office in Monte Carlo and who bought and sold crude oil without ever seeing any. It was one of those arcane business practices which few laymen understand, but which make some people vast sums of money. It all depends on the fundamental principle of profit, which is that if you sell for more than you pay, you are ahead in the game. Bearing in mind the capacity of a modern oil tanker, a fraction of a penny on each gallon of the stuff soon adds up.

David Thieme had become very wealthy – he was rumoured to have made $70 million in 1979 alone – and he liked to make conspicuous displays of his wealth. In the movie *Superman* the Man of Steel flies Lois Lane over the Atlantic and over a tanker with the Essex logo on its funnel. In *Superman II*, one of the vehicles caught in a multiple pile-up in Metropolis is a tanker with the Essex logo on the cab door.

Sponsorship of a Formula 1 team appealed to Thieme for all manner of reasons, including the fact that he simply liked motor racing. He and Colin had known each other for only a short time, but they got on famously. They were two of a kind and each greatly admired the other, though for different reasons. Essex Petroleum bought the space on the sidepods of the Martini Team Lotus cars (Martini & Rossi was the title sponsor) and the world awaited the Type 80 which, Colin promised, would make the Type 79, 'look like a double-decker bus'.

The Type 80 had the same wheelbase and track as the 79 but as first shown it had no front wings at all while the rear wing was little more than a spoiler. Practically the entire downforce of the car was to be generated by under-car aerodynamics. It had the longest sidepods ever, and there were even miniature sliding skirts beneath the long, tapering nosecone. It looked sensational in Lotus green and it seemed that Colin had made yet another quantum leap.

The trouble was that the car did not work and Lotus would end the season without taking a single win. Meanwhile every other designer in Formula 1 had been busily working away on ground effect aerodynamics. Patrick Head at Williams had taken a long hard look at the Lotus 79, had understood what made it tick and his 1979 car, the FW07, was in essence a Lotus 79 carried a stage further. It was far from being a copy, as the Tyrrell 009 was, it was the Type 79 redesigned by Patrick Head. The Williams did not actually appear until the Spanish Grand Prix, the fifth round of the championship, but from mid-season on, the FW07 was the class of the field.

A problem with the Type 80, which nobody had ever before encountered, was 'porpoising', with the nose of the car rising and falling if the car went over a bump. Once Mario saw the front wheels lift from the track at Silverstone. The only way a driver could bring the car under control was to brake. The sliding skirts in the nose soon gave way to conventional aerofoils and the rear wing grew larger. A feature of the Type 80 was that all the skirts were curved and these had a tendency to stick. In the event, though development was continued, the Type 80 raced on only three occasions, each time driven by Andretti. For the rest of the season, Team Lotus depended on the Type 79 and that had become obsolete.

The Type 79 did not actually have that good a chassis, it merely had ground-breaking aerodynamics. Though Mario and Ronnie had usually managed to fill the front row of any grid, it was never by very much. By contrast, the Williams FW07 had an excellent chassis as well as full ground effect aerodynamics. Mario Andretti says:

If you look at Colin Chapman's career, it was all peaks and valleys. Once Colin felt he had achieved something, as with the Lotus 79, he wasn't interested in refining it. His mind was on the next step.

I remember being at scrutineering in Spain with Nigel Bennett, who was then the team manager. We were looking at the new Williams, shaking our heads, and saying, 'That's what our car should be.'

The Lotus 80 had so much downforce, but the chassis...! Colin never did anything about stiffening the chassis. The car needed much stiffer springs but every time you put in stiffer springs, the chassis flexed and rivets would pop everywhere. It was a car you could not understand because it gave you a different message on every lap.

Every time I tried to talk in technical terms, Colin hit the ceiling. He did not want technical advice from me. He knew, I didn't, and that's when we started to drift apart...

For 1979, Colin had signed the Argentine Carlos Reutemann, who had led Ferrari the previous season. Reutemann was a driver who could be absolutely brilliant, he had set pole in his very first Grand Prix, but if things were not going right, he could be moody. Things did not go right for Lotus in 1979. In the first couple of races, the Lotus 79 was a front-runner and Carlos took a couple of podium finishes. It was clear, however, that Ligier had leap-frogged Lotus in aerodynamics and for all that Ferrari could not exploit full ground effect, it had a sweet chassis and lots of power. Then, in the French Grand Prix, Jean-Pierre Jabouille gave Renault its first world championship race win, which was also the first for a turbocharged engine.

At Silverstone, Clay Reggazoni gave the Williams FW07 its first win and Williams continued to win, with Alan Jones taking four of the remaining six races. The Lotus 79 had been a front runner at the beginning of the season, with a reasonably good finishing rate, but from the eighth round on, its highest finish was fifth. In the 15 races of the season, Andretti retired nine times while Reutemann retired six times, plus once when he was classified in the results but had actually retired. The opposition had streaked ahead and the Type 79 had very little depth beneath the aerodynamic package. It was being stressed in a way had been unnecessary in 1978.

Lotus had gone from double world championships to 'team shambles' in one effortless bound. Some insiders will say that the DeLorean project had become so important to the financial health of Group Lotus that energy which could have gone into motor racing was diverted. A strange argument, this, since the DeLorean project was paying everyone's wages at Hethel and Team Lotus was a separate entity.

Reutemann left at the end of the season to drive for Williams. Andretti stayed on for another year, but was becoming increasingly disenchanted.

During 1979 the Chrysler Sunbeam-Lotus was launched. The Chrysler Corporation had bought a number of European motor manufacturers in the 1970s and had tried to weld them into one profitable group. Then the cars were marketed under the name 'Talbot', which had historical resonance with both Britain and France – if you had a very long memory. One of the models was a hatchback called the 'Sunbeam', which was actually based on the floorpan of the old Hillman Avenger, through shortened by three inches. Lotus was contracted to develop this into a high-performance car. It was launched as the Chrysler Sunbeam-Lotus, but it soon became the Talbot Sunbeam-Lotus.

Chrysler, Hillman, Talbot, Lotus and Sunbeam: it was not a case so much of brightening an image, as a case of trying to create one out of a mish-mash. In standard form, a 2.2-litre Lotus engine, which produced 150bhp, was mated to a five-speed ZF gearbox, and it received all the other usual tweaks, lowered suspension, fat tyres, alloy wheels and so on. Bare shells were delivered to Lotus, who undertook assembly at a facility about 20 miles from Hethel. It was quite a good little car, 121mph, 0-60mph in 7.4 seconds, but it had no presence at all, even though the works team of Guy Frequelin and Henri Toivenen took the 1981 World Rally Championship for Makes. By then, Peugeot had bought Chrysler's European interests and the Sunbeam-Lotus did not live to see 1982. Nevertheless, the 2,308 units which Lotus made in 1979–81 outnumbered cars sold under the Lotus name and played a significant part in keeping Group Lotus afloat.

Despite a very disappointing 1979, Essex Petroleum became the title sponsor of Team Lotus in 1980, while most of the team's previous backers took their money elsewhere. When the new Type 81 was launched, David Thieme hired the Royal Albert Hall, the champagne was Dom Perignon, and the leading chef in Britain, Michel Roux, supervised the lunch. To entertain everyone, Ray Charles had been flown over from America. Motor racing had never seen a launch like it, though some journalists began to feel uneasy about David Thieme. The occasion was used to launch two 'special edition' Lotus Esprits. The entire Lotus road car range received 2.2-litre engines for 1980 and there was also the new Esprit Turbo. It was more than just a standard engine with an AiResearch turbocharger bolted on, the engine, designated '910', had been thoroughly reworked, with a longer stroke than the 907. With 210bhp, the Esprit Turbo would top 148mph and sprint 0-60mph in 6.1 seconds.

The 'special editions' came in the garish blue, silver and red livery of Essex Petroleum. Normally aspirated or turbocharged, customers were assured that no more than 100 examples would be made of each. In the event only 80 customers wanted to buy an Esprit S3 in Essex livery and there were only 57 takers for the turbocharged version. Chapman and Thieme each fed the other's ego and each had an ego with a voracious appetite.

The Type 81 Formula 1 car was supposed to combine the best elements of its immediate predecessors, but it did not. Andretti was joined in the team by the personable and gifted Elio de Angelis. Elio was rare for a racing driver in that he was a cultured man, interested in the arts, and one who played classical music – he had studied the piano to a very serious level. A world champion and a young charger sounds like a good team combination, and so it might have been had the car been any good. In the first round of the championship, Team Lotus occupied third row on the grid, and both cars retired. In the second round, Brazil, de Angelis managed the fourth row and finished a fine second, and that was to be the highlight of the season. By the third round, de Angelis was on row seven and Andretti was on row eight.

Mario became more and more disheartened as the season wore on. A newcomer, wanting to make an impression, may drive out of his skin to move from 11th to 10th, but there was no need for Mario to do that, he had nothing to prove. It was not until the last race of the season that he scored his solitary world championship point. Off the track, the relationship between Mario and Colin fell apart and Andretti moved to Alfa Romeo at the end of the season.

At the Austrian Grand Prix, Colin entered a third car for Nigel Mansell. A number of people had urged Colin to give Mansell a test (a large number of people thought Mansell had no future). Nigel did well and only afterwards did it emerge that he had discharged himself from hospital, where he was recovering from a heavy racing accident, to attend the Lotus test session. That degree of grit and determination appealed to Colin. His initial judgement of Mansell was confirmed when it emerged that Nigel drove in Austria sitting in petrol from a spillage when the mechanics topped up the fuel tank on the grid. He was in considerable pain but gave up only when his engine blew after 40 laps. Colin decided that Nigel was made of the right stuff and signed him to drive alongside de Angelis in 1981.

The feeble effort of Team Lotus during 1980 was over-shadowed by what became known as the 'FISA/FOCA War'. Bernie Ecclestone had organised the leading teams into the Formula 1 Constructors' Association (FOCA). FOCA had negotiated wide-ranging television coverage, and television rights, and this would lead the sport to unprecedented popular appeal and make some people very wealthy indeed. Furthermore, members of FOCA would have their cars and equipment flown to races outside of Europe by chartered aircraft, a deal worth the best part of a million pounds even in 1978. Since only 10 teams (the top 10 based on the previous season's performance) would be eligible for membership, it widened the divide between the professional teams and the amateurs who would enter a few races.

FOCA negotiated with race organisers and guaranteed to present a core of 20 cars of the highest standard, with other teams being allowed to make their own way to the races to see if they could fight their way into the top 10. With the negotiating skills of Ecclestone and Mosley at work – they played hard cop, soft cop – teams received more for competing in a race, although for the first time they were obliged to compete. Ecclestone was trying to make Formula 1 into a thoroughly professional sport.

In late 1978, Jean-Marie Balestre, an autocratic French publisher, was elected president of the Fédération Internationale de l'Automobile (FIA) and also the Federation Internationale du Sportive Automobile (FISA), and he saw FOCA as a threat to his authority. It was a classic case of a traditional ruling body not keeping up with the times and the same thing has happened in other sports. Balestre, it should be noted, always wore a blazer.

Balestre believed that FOCA was creaming off too much money, money which should be invested in the sport as a whole. The FOCA side, largely teams using the Cosworth DFV engine, argued that the performers should be the ones to benefit. Balestre argued that all decisions should be made by FISA, and he was backed by constructors such as Ferrari, Alfa Romeo and Renault. Late in 1979, Balestre started to say that he wanted to ban sliding skirts from 1981. The Cosworth teams were appalled because ground effect aerodynamics had kept them competitive, while Ferrari and Renault, looking after their interests, were all for the ban.

Colin was with Ecclestone, but he could play no particular part in the war except to stand firm with other members of FOCA.

Ferrari, Alfa Romeo and Renault withdrew their entries from the Spanish Grand Prix, having taken part in the first free practice session. FISA declared the race illegal, but the FOCA teams went ahead and so an all-Cosworth Grand Prix took place. De Angelis was third, but it was excluded from the world championship. The war seemed to overshadow everything in Formula 1 and it would rumble on for some time.

During the year, Colin's boat businesses went into liquidation. By all accounts, considerable progress had been made with the two ranges of boats which Colin had bought, but the economic climate was not good and the cost of developing the boats was rather more than the profits they generated. Late in 1980, a new company, Lotus Engineering and Technology, was formed with the brief to seek consultancy work from the motor industry, something which Lotus had actually been doing since the Lotus-Cortina. It was this element of Group Lotus rather than the road cars it made which would ensure that every time the company went to the brink, there would be a saviour.

CHAPTER 25

ONE CHASSIS
OR TWO?

I N SOUTH Africa early in 1981, the FOCA teams ran a non-championship Grand Prix and all the cars had sliding skirts, which FISA had banned from 1 January. The race was boycotted by the grandees, a group which now included Ligier since it had officially become Talbot-Ligier. The South African Grand Prix proved that Formula 1 needed the grandees and the grandees realised that they were hurt by missing out on the television coverage, which was the reason why most of them were in Formula 1. The approach of the race at Long Beach really got through to Renault since it intended to enter the North American market, and it needed the exposure.

These factors focused the minds of everyone and both sides signed the 'Concorde Agreement'. In very simple terms, FOCA agreed to FISA's ban on sliding skirts, and FISA agreed to allow FOCA to continue to negotiate the television rights and other aspects of the commercial side of the sport. On the face of it, there was give and take on both sides, but the matter was not quite finished. Ecclestone, for FOCA, had negotiated with a fifth ace up his sleeve. He knew that his team, Brabham, had a system that would drive a coach and horses through the regulations. The new rules said that there had to be 6cm between the bottom of the car and the road, but this could only be measured in the scrutineers' bay, when the car was at rest.

Brabham had a hydro-pneumatic suspension system whereby a car could be legal at rest but, once it was under way, it could be lowered so that the outer panels of the sidepods formed a seal with the road and so produced the same effect as sliding skirts. As a result, suspension movement was minimal and the cars virtually became karts, at least those entered by teams which were exploiting the new loophole. Lotus had come up with a more elegant, and safer solution, the soi-disant 'twin-chassis' Type 88. This was entered at the beginning of 1981, but it was never allowed to race.

Peter Wright has written:

> It was actually while I was contemplating how one might apply ground effect to a high performance road car, such as the Lotus Turbo-Esprit, that a possible solution occurred to me. Unconstrained by any performance regulations, there was no reason why a ground effect underbody could not be connected directly to the outboard ends of the lower suspension.

Peter read the regulations thoroughly, highlighted the relevant sections and went to see Chapman.

> One of the wonderful things about working for Colin Chapman was that as soon as you took an idea to him, he picked it up (if it was any good) and extrapolated where it might take one, while at the same time scrutinising it for weaknesses, it was sometimes hard to keep up with his fertile mind. Within hours Martin Ogilvie (Chief Designer) and I moved upstairs to a locked office in Ketteringham Hall, and a veil of secrecy was drawn over what we were doing.

In broad terms, the body and chassis were two separate entities. The chassis was a conventional monocoque and instead of being attached directly to it, the body was a single unit joined to the chassis by springs. At rest, the body was the required 6cm clear of the road, at speed downforce would compress the secondary springs and lower the body to the road. This allowed the chassis to have conventional suspension rather than the near-solid suspension which resulted from lowering the whole car. It sounds simple in theory, but was actually very complex. To take just one of the problems: the springs between the body and the chassis needed to compress very quickly but be released at a slower rate to ensure that there was no sudden loss of downforce when, say, braking for a chicane.

To call the 86 and 88 'twin chassis' cars is to stretch a point, though the body did have its own frame. 'Twin chassis' was a term created by Lotus as a snappy way of describing the concept, but it was to hang about its neck like a dead albatross. The Italian coachbuilder, Touring, had been famous for its Superleggera bodies in which lightweight panels were attached to a lightweight frame, which could itself be termed a chassis since the word merely means a frame which supports, and Ferraris had been fitted with Superleggera bodies. Besides, the word 'chassis', like 'sheep' or 'deer' is both a singular and a plural. Initially, the bare chassis of a Type 81 was used to test the concept and an exclusive test was booked at Jarama in Spain. The tests proved sufficiently promising to progress the project further. The fact that Lotus booked Jarama for an exclusive test was enough to crank up the rumour mill.

One rumour said that the car had no suspension, Lotus had built a giant kart, whereas the concept allowed for normal suspension travel. Among those who believed the story about a car without suspension was Enzo Ferrari. Such was the animosity between FISA and FOCA that Enzo Ferrari insisted on a new rule which demanded that cars should have suspension and so FISA added that rule, which has remained in the book ever since. It shows the partisanship which FISA displayed: Ferrari demanded a rule, Ferrari got his rule. Some cynics maintain that FIA stands for Ferrari's Internal Agency.

The bodywork of the Type 86 was made in CFRP/Nomex honeycomb sandwich and Martin Ogilvie suggested that the Type 88's chassis could be made from that as well, since a conventional aluminium monocoque was not up to handling the very high forces which the Type 88 would generate. Colin latched on to the idea immediately. The glory days of 1977–78 were a distant memory, but an entirely original concept, plus a new material, was manna from heaven. He embraced the Type 88 with a passion which bordered on fervour, a fervour which perhaps diverted him a little too much.

It had long been known that the McLaren MP4 would have a monocoque made from carbon composites. When the car was launched at the beginning of 1981, there was both a story and a photo-opportunity. The story was that the monocoque of the MP4 was the largest object yet made from carbon composites, and the photograph showed the new joint MD of McLaren, Ron Dennis, holding an MP4 monocoque. A few weeks later Lotus could show a car with a carbon composite monocoque combined with Kevlar and Colin could say, airily, that it rendered the McLaren tub obsolete. Further, while McLaren had gone to an American aerospace company to make its tub, Lotus had made its tub in-house.

Both McLaren and Lotus were thought to be taking something of a gamble, because the use of carbon composites in the fan blades of the Rolls-Royce RB211 aero engine had been a disaster and was the main factor in the company going into liquidation. It was even said that if a McLaren received an unfortunate impact, the body of the driver would end up amid a shower of carbon dust. Andrea de Cesaris, driving for McLaren, proved the sceptics wrong as he crashed a McLaren more than a dozen times during 1981 and single-handedly proved the case for carbon composite construction. De Cesaris has never received due credit for this pioneering achievement.

Had the 88 been launched against a normal background, it might have been accepted without controversy. As it was, the FISA/FOCA power struggle was ongoing. Then there was the FOCA-only South African race and the signing of the Concorde Agreement, which was more of a cease-fire than a formal end to hostilities.

By the time the 88 was ready to race Colin suspected that he would have a fight on his hands, so while the 88 was the Team Lotus entry for what had become the official start to the world championship, the United States (West) Grand Prix at Long Beach, he also sent three examples of the 81. At Long Beach the scrutineers passed the 88, it practised and then was black-flagged. The same happened in Brazil. In Argentina it was passed by the scrutineers, who were then forced to reverse their decision when delegates from FISA arrived and it was not allowed to take to the track. A battle was brewing and Chapman and Wright had their case well prepared.

It is against the background of an uneasy truce in the FISA/FOCA War that the history of the 88 needs to be seen. Max Mosley, later Balestre's successor as president of the FIA, says:

> When Lotus discovered ground effect, more or less by chance, everyone else thought, 'Lucky old Colin', and they were happy with that. They all thought they could be that lucky, that they might stumble on a special advantage. The Lotus 88 was different, everyone thought that Colin was being too clever by half.

So far as the FISA/FOCA War is concerned, it amounted to FOCA showing willingness to hang out to dry one of its own in order to bring the situation under control. For once in his life, Colin was not a major piece on a chess board, he was a pawn, and the 88 was to be sacrificed for the greater good of FOCA.

Look at an 88 today and its seems remarkable how compact it is. The sidepods, like those of an 80, run the whole length of the car but, like the 80 as originally shown, there are no front wings to interrupt the overall dynamic and the rear aerofoil is not much more than a spoiler. It is much less obtrusive than on, say, a Ford Sierra Cosworth.

Before the case concerning the 88 was heard by the FIA, Lotus was struck by another blow. On landing in Switzerland, David Thieme was arrested following a complaint, by Credit Suisse, of financial malpractice. He was held for two weeks and released, on bail of £70,000, without a single charge being laid. However, it was enough to finish Essex Petroleum. In the world in which Thieme operated, the fact that he was arrested at all finished his career, because we speak here of Switzerland and a Swiss bank. The Swiss authorities arrested him on suspicion, and suspicion alone. Nowhere else in the West can someone be be held in prison for two weeks because a bank has suspicions which it cannot substantiate. Thieme later sued Credit Suisse, claiming damages of £100 million, but best information is that he received not a penny.

On 23 April, the FIA ruled against the 88 and it was a stitch-up. No independent engineer or scrutineer found the car to be illegal. Nowhere in the rules did it say that a car could have only one chassis, but then Colin was always ahead of the rule book, as all the best designers are. Team Lotus withdrew from the San Marino Grand Prix on the grounds that the cars it had prepared for the race had been branded illegal and there was no time in which to prepare race-worthy substitutes. It was only the second time since 1958 that no works Lotus ran in a Grand Prix and only the third time that Colin had missed a race.

Lotus returned at Monaco, still in Essex livery but, in Spain, John Player was back on board, having realised that sponsoring tiddlywinks, darts, or whatever was no substitute for Formula 1. From loyalty to Thieme, whose company could no longer pay its bills, some sort of Essex signwriting remained on the sidepods. In essence, however, Lotus was back to the gold on black livery.

Using the monocoque of the 88, Lotus created the 87 and the designation suggests that it must have been in the back of Colin's mind. It arrived in time for the Belgian Grand Prix, where Mansell finished third and de Angelis fifth. The Lotus 87 was a conventional Formula 1 car in that it had a Cosworth engine, but it came at a time when rivals were arriving with the latest in turbocharged technology.

Sharp on his feet as ever, Colin began to woo Toyota. The proposal was a successor to the Elan which used Toyota components. Toyota made a fine dohc engine which had done well in Formula 3. Toyota was also conducting a Formula 1 feasibility programme, which had resulted in three distinctly different engines, one of which had recorded a peak of 1500bhp in testing. So far as Colin was concerned, a tie-in with Toyota was the answer to all his cares: there could be a turbo engine for Formula 1 and exceptionally good components for a born-again Elan to revive the road car part of the business, which was down to making fewer than 400 cars a year.

Toyota was prepared to listen and, though it would not enter Formula 1 until 2002, Toyota components began to be used on Lotus road cars from 1982 onwards. After Colin's death, Toyota became a significant shareholder in Group Lotus for a while. A least one Toyota-based sports car prototype was made by Lotus.

Colin had not revolutionised motor cruisers through the Moonraker range, but his fertile brain was active. He had been intrigued by, and bought, the first microlight aircraft. Colin began to conceive of a stage between a microlight and a conventional light aircraft: an ultra-lightweight aeroplane. He commissioned a design from Bert Rutan, an American who specialised in lightweight aircraft and who would build *Voyager*, still the only aircraft to make a non-stop circumnavigation of the globe. Colin also set a small team on the design of an engine for such a machine, an air-cooled flat-twin of 480cc. At least one aircraft was made, and flown in 1983, and the engine was displayed on the Lotus stand at the 1983 London Motor Show, but both events took place after Colin died and the impetus behind the project died with him. It had been a Chapman, rather than a Lotus, enterprise.

Since 1977, Peter Wright had often turned for advice to David Williams, Head of Flight Instrumentation at the Cranfield College of Aeronautics. Cranfield, a world-class establishment, was founded in 1946 as a postgraduate institution and was therefore was beyond the orbit of most people in motor racing. Peter discussed the problems he had encountered with the Lotus 80 and those discussions informed his thinking when considering the 88. Peter has written:

> One day he [David Williams] said to me, 'What you need is an Active
> Suspension,' and he took me into the laboratory to demonstrate an
> artificial-feel control column for a fly-by-wire research aircraft. He

demonstrated how the control computer could provide any spring rate, mass and damping for the system, and the technology could provide a suspension system with unique properties.

Peter reported back to Colin, who was on the case at once. During 1981 an Esprit fitted with Active Suspension was undergoing regular tests. In motor racing terms, and at its most simple, Active Suspension meant that if a car went over a bump on-board sensors would adjust all four corners to the optimum, and it would be done immediately, whereas a conventional coil spring takes time to compress or be released. A conventional spring is made to a particular specification: an 800lb spring operates at that rate, it cannot be changed, second by second, from 700lb to 900lb, whereas a computer-controlled hydraulic system could do so. This was just the sort of development that was guaranteed to fire Colin. He did not live to see a Lotus 99, fitted with Active Suspension, win two Grands Prix in 1987, but his spirit of innovation was behind those wins.

Active Suspension provides a model for how he operated. Colin chose Peter Wright, he did not go to the local Job Centre. One of the things that Peter brought to the job was a broad view. David Williams at Cranfield was the person who suggested Active Suspension, because he was involved in a parallel programme. Peter knew David because he did not have a narrow view and Peter knew how to report to Colin in the right way. It was Colin, and he alone, who grasped the concept and who authorised the money to explore it. Colin did not take Active Suspension on board solely for racing – he knew that it could have a significant application for up-market road cars.

As for the 1981 season, races were won by Williams, Ferrari, Brabham, Ligier and Renault. It was a mix of wins by the best Cosworth teams and those using turbocharged engines. The DFV users were assisted by a high rate of attrition among the turbo engines and by other ploys, such as cars running underweight in qualifying. Brabham favoured ballasted bodywork when the weighing machine loomed, and Williams switched tyres. Much weight can be added when tyres are filled with water.

Down in seventh place in the constructors' series was Lotus. Mansell's third place in Belgium had flattered to deceive. The 87 was better than most Cosworth cars, but it had been built in a rush. Lotus had not had the time to put in place the strategies used by Brabham and Williams to disguise the fact that they ran underweight, illegal cars in qualifying. The Lotus 88 was finally declared to be illegal, but it had been presented above board. There was no subterfuge involved with the 88. It is fair to say that Colin Chapman could stray beyond the usual bounds of conduct in business, but nobody has ever been able to accuse him of misconduct in racing, apart from the Lotus 15 at Le Mans in 1959, that is. It was not until this book was published that the scam was known..

The only two occasions when a Team Lotus entry was declared illegal were the wheel bolts on the 1962 entries at Le Mans and the 88. In neither case was anything hidden. Tyres filled with water had little appeal for Colin who, in 1981, was involved with ultra-light aircraft and Active Suspension. Not even whispers and rumours ever linked Colin Chapman to a misdemeanour when it came to technology. He was not interested in breaking the rules, he was only interested in being ahead of the rules, but lurking in the background was a major scandal centred on Chapman's relationship with DeLorean.

The DeLorean DMC-12 was launched early in 1981 and the contribution made by Lotus was widely admired. Also during 1981, the Talbot Sunbeam-Lotus works team won rallying's world championship for Makes due to consistently high finishes by Guy Frequelin and Henri Toivenen rather than complete domination. The works cars had 240bhp, rather than the 150bhp of the standard car, and while this was not an unusually high output for a Group 2 rally car, where the Sunbeam-Lotus scored was through the exceptional torque of the Lotus engine.

As a reward for winning a world championship on what was a very small budget, Talbot's new owner, Peugeot, slashed the programme so that Sunbeam-Lotus rally cars appeared only in British events in 1982, and then were seen no more. The association did, however, lead to Lotus's development of the 2.2-litre Chrysler Turbo III engine. Lotus may not have been making many cars (345 in 1981) but it was becoming ever more important as a consultant to the motor industry.

CHAPTER 26

THE FINAL YEAR

T HE LAST year of Colin's life was 1982, and one reason why his death came as such a shock was that he was still a comparatively young man and he was firing on all cylinders right up until the end. There was no falling off in performance, no reaching for the carpet slippers, his light was extinguished not as a candle burns but as a switch is snapped.

He had his Active Suspension programme, the ultra-lightweight aircraft project and Lotus Engineering and Technology steaming ahead. He continued to woo Toyota but also conducted a charm campaign on every other possible front because a turbocharged engine had ceased to be a desirable option in Formula 1: it had become a necessity. McLaren had the right idea when it persuaded a sponsor to underwrite an exclusive engine. Porsche was contracted to make the basic lump which, it was hoped, might become a helicopter engine. It did not, but the line of thought was sound. Without the degree of backing which McLaren enjoyed, Colin went to existing makers and his advances to Renault were not rejected. However, he would not live to see the result of his wooing of Renault.

On the Formula 1 front, 1982 was the most odd of years. Keijo 'Keke' Rosberg took the title in a Williams with just one win and that was in the 'Swiss' Grand Prix, held in France because the fun-loving Swiss banned circuit racing in 1955. It was a time of transition, the last year when a DFV engine would be competitive because, though clearly out-gunned in terms of power, it was reliable. During 1982, 11 drivers won a Grand Prix, but no driver won more than two. Among the 11 was Elio de Angelis, who gave Lotus its last win in Colin's lifetime.

Ferrari won the Constructors' Championship despite losing both its star drivers. Gilles Villeneuve was fatally injured during practice for the Belgian Grand Prix. Didier Pironi crashed during practice for the German Grand Prix and sustained injuries so severe that he never raced again.

Lotus began the season with Type 87s for de Angelis and Mansell and the 91 arrived in time for the second round, in Brazil. The 91 was a stronger, and lighter, version of the 87 and the carbon composite monocoque weighed just over 40lb. During 1982 the DFV exceeded 150 world championship race wins, and while that achievement, which may never be surpassed, is to the credit of Keith Duckworth, Mike Costin, Dick Scammell and Benny Rood, it was Colin who instigated the DFV. Only Colin had the connections which could find the funding and it was Lotus which had won five constructors' world championships with the DFV.

The 1982 season largely depended on which turbo engine went pop, and when. In 1983 the DFV challenge collapsed with a rapidity which surprised many people, including everyone at Cosworth Engineering. Colin lived to see the DFV in the last season when it was a frequent winner. He also lived to see Elio de Angelis score his maiden win and a welcome return to form for Team Lotus.

Of all the Cosworth runners, Williams was clearly to the fore. Lotus might have been there except for being diverted by the 88, which cost Colin a lot in terms of emotional energy. Lotus could not be considered a top team in 1982, but at the Austrian Grand Prix Elio de Angelis held on to win by less then a 10th of second from Rosberg's Williams. It was one of the closest finishes in Formula 1 history but it was just that, a finish.

Elio had done well to qualify seventh, which equalled his best grid position of the season. There was a multiple pile-up just after the start which had wiped out some of the quick guys and had eliminated others because shards from the crashed cars caused punctures. Then the top turbo cars blew up. Elio seized his advantage and held it, lap after lap, despite the best that Rosberg could do. It was a popular win. Everyone liked de Angelis and was pleased to see the civilised young man become a Grand Prix winner, having withstood the pressure of having Rosberg a fraction of a second behind in a Williams FW08, which everyone knew was the better car.

They were pleased for Colin as well. However anyone regarded Colin as a man, when it came to design every engineer in the pitlane admired him. Colin had been the dynamic force who had been part of the landscape of the life of every engineer. Men like Gordon Murray (Brabham) and Patrick Head (Williams) had come into motor racing with Colin as their example.

The date of the Austrian Grand Prix was 15 August 1982. It was the last time that a Lotus, supervised by Colin Chapman, would win a Grand Prix. Within 10 weeks Colin would be part of 'The DeLorean Scandal' and investigative teams from newspapers and television, with the assistance of government agencies on both sides of the Atlantic, would be targeting him. It would be alleged that he was part of a multi-million pound conspiracy to defraud the British government, and he was guilty of that.

At the core of the scandal, as it involved Chapman, was the $17.67 million paid to General Product Development Services Inc. to commission Group Lotus to develop the DeLorean DMC-12. That money was split between Chapman and DeLorean, with Fred Bushell taking a cut of Colin's share.

The DeLorean DMC-12 had been launched at the Geneva Motor Show in March 1981. It was well-received and most press reports which spoke of the 'stainless steel sports car' were too deferential to point out that it was actually a plastic-bodied sports car with a stainless steel veneer. Lurking behind the glitz, however, was a a major problem to which no journalist was privy. Only two pre-production cars had been subjected to durability testing. DeLorean's original plan had been for a thousand test cars running in all climates, but economic reality had brought the figure tumbling, if 'tumbling' is a word which can adequately describe a fall from 1,000 test cars to two.

The two pre-production cars were each scheduled to cover 50,000 miles, a ridiculously low mileage by automotive industry standards, but one crashed before it reached that mark. The other passed the test, but all 50,000 miles were undertaken in the temperate climate of Ireland and the car was not exposed to extremely hot and cold weather, which is normal practice. One effect of this was that in sub-zero temperatures, which are not unknown in many parts of North America, the car's target market, the throttle cable could freeze solid. The inability to slow in moving traffic from, say, 60mph is nobody's idea of fun.

Condensation caused water to drip on the throttle cable overnight. The water froze when the car was driven in cold conditions on a steady throttle, which is the norm on an American freeway. The addition of a small plate to prevent water dripping on the cable was all that was needed but, by the time it was fitted, the damage had been done. Proper testing would have eliminated the problem before it appeared on production cars.

Lotus had done the engineering of the chassis well, everyone agreed that, and despite the unpromising engine layout, the DMC-12 handled pretty well. The problems lay with the DeLorean Motor Company. For a start, the workforce had no experience of car construction and there were severe problems with the build-quality of the product. A huge problem was that the alternator had a maximum output of 75 amps, but with all systems on, up to 90 amps were needed. There were soon reports of cars stopping because the electrical system could not take the strain. Other reports had people trapped in their cars when the doors wouldn't open. Dealers who had orders for 20 or 30 cars found that customers were cancelling. From a back-log of 20 or 30 orders, they were down to one or two, if they were lucky. Where once the DMC-12 exchanged hands at a premium, dealers were being forced to discount cars.

Three Quality Assurance Centers had to be established in America to rectify faults and, in the first three months alone, $2.5 million was spent fixing substandard cars. That was 2.5 million bucks straight out of the window. Worse than that, the economy in the West went into recession. DeLorean's response was to increase production, which meant taking on more workers, and those workers had to be trained on the job. This did not improve the already questionable build quality, though the company's wage bill rose substantially. John DeLorean managed to wheedle ever more money from the British government while making ever more cars for a market that did not want them.

Then DeLorean's former executive secretary, Marian Gibson, an English woman resident in New York, became disturbed by what she saw as financial irregularities at DMC's headquarters in New York. DeLorean was buying works of art for his offices while not investing a single cent of his own money in his factory. In late September 1981, she had confided her fears to a Conservative MP, Nicholas Winterton, and soon afterwards she passed on copies of files and receipts. Those who defend John Z. DeLorean point to the fact that Gibson had been effectively demoted within DMC and had a personal axe to grind. They also say that Gibson was only able to get her hands on sensitive documents because of DeLorean's policy of openness. On 3 October, the British Prime Minister, Margaret Thatcher, ordered an inquiry into DMC. Word got out and by 5 October the media had the story. It made headlines and they marked the beginning of the end for DeLorean.

DeLorean had been hoping to float a new company, DeLorean Motors Holding, which would exchange shares, one for one, with the Belfast company. Had this happened, it would have netted DeLorean $120 million, while NIDA would have received less than $8.5 million. This launch was always problematic, but Marian Gibson's revelations made it impossible. Further, the news media sniffed a deeper story. On 11 January 1982, DMC put its workforce on a three-day week. This was a terrible blow to the people of Northern Ireland, but nobody there could fail to notice that there were fields filling up with DeLorean cars which had no buyers.

One curious omission from DeLorean's business plan was a proposal to sell the car in its country of origin, the United Kingdom. Fewer than three dozen were made with right-hand-drive and then late in the day. Some had to be broken up because the quality was so appalling. DMC closed before the remainder could be sold, though the receiver disposed of them later. More than 50 countries drive on the left and they include Australia and Japan.

John Z. DeLorean, who knew that his ethical sports car needed more oomph – as Colin had said from the outset – had instigated a twin-turbo conversion programme. Work was done on it, but everything fell apart before it could be offered to the customer.

The cars which did not have to comply with American emission controls, which strangled the engine, were considerably faster than those built for the US market. Though not a large country, Britain is most car companies' third largest market for sports cars. Then there was the rest of Europe. The DMC-12 had a French engine and gearbox, but was not sold in France. Germany is a strong market for sports cars, but DeLorean never quite got around to selling cars there. Japan loves sports cars, and in the early 1980s Japan had what appeared to be a bullet-proof economy. DeLorean did not think it worthwhile to fly to Japan.

The British government called in the late Sir Kenneth Cork to run an eye over the books of DMC. Sir Kenneth was a forensic accountant who had been Lord Mayor of the City of London 1978-9, a man who had been showered with honorary doctorates and whose portrait is in the National Portrait Gallery. Lord Mayor is a position which dates from 1189 and you are not elected to it unless your peers have measured you and found you not wanting. It is a position above politics. Sir Kenneth's autobiography, *Cork on Cork,* is not recommended as light bedtime reading, but it has been a valued source when considering the Chapman/DeLorean affair.

Sir Kenneth had a direct line to an old friend, the Secretary of State for Northern Ireland, James Prior. Prior had inherited the DeLorean factory from the previous government and his patience with DeLorean was running short. Prior was one of those rare men, a politician who was trusted by politicians of all shades of opinion – he was so trusted that Margaret Thatcher, who loathed him, had to include him in her cabinet.

Prior indicated to Sir Kenneth that there would be few further handouts. The DeLorean Motor Company was, after all, a wholly-owned subsidiary of an American corporation, and it had only one customer, the DeLorean Motor Corporation, which distributed the cars in the US.

Sir Kenneth records that DeLorean spoke confidently, but vaguely, of a rescue package. An Arab head of state was interested, so was a West Coast millionaire, and so on. In mid-February 1982 Sir Kenneth was appointed joint receiver with instructions to try to save the company if at all possible. DMC had become very important to Northern Ireland. It was doing more than just employing people, it was a symbol of a more optimistic future for the province.

Eventually a company called Minet Financial Management agreed to make a loan of $100 million. Minet specialised in high-risk, high-yield investment outside the reach of the Inland Revenue. Sir Kenneth told DeLorean he would consider Minet's proposal provided that DeLorean invested $20 million of his own money. DeLorean said that he had only half that, but he found a company willing to lend him the other $10 million for 90 days at 12 percent interest. Sir Kenneth set a deadline of 20 October, but DeLorean never got round to signing the papers to secure the loan. The factory was closed on 20 October and that same day, in Los Angeles, DeLorean was arrested when buying cocaine, which he intended to sell at a profit to use the money to keep afloat his dream.

DeLorean's arrest had nothing to do with Chapman. Lotus had completed its work for DMC more than two years earlier, but the arrest would be the beginning of a nightmare for Colin because it uncovered the money paid to GPD Services. It was was to be a brief period because Colin would be dead of a heart attack, aged just 56, days after DeLorean was caught in a sting operation.

By the time of Chapman's death, speculation was rife in the news media that he and DeLorean had conspired to defraud the British government of $17.67 million. The speculation proved to be true. Even before he died, it was clear that Chapman would go to prison and his glittering career would be over. No motor racing insider was unduly surprised that Chapman was involved in a scam, because stories about his business practices had been circulating for years. The fraud with DeLorean, however, was a different matter, since it involved the British and American governments.

What follows is sourced from *The Times* newspaper and the dates refer to the issues in which the stories appeared. The actual events took place within the previous 24 hours.

21 October 1982: The British government announces that the Belfast factory will close. Within hours, John DeLorean is arrested on a charge of conspiring to possess 100 kilos of cocaine. DeLorean is filmed holding a pack of cocaine in his hands. On the film DeLorean suggests that the cocaine will save his dream. DeLorean will later claim that the British government asked the American authorities to set him up to destroy him. In fact, he had not met the deadline set by Sir Kenneth Cork, who had been trying to save DMC.

The sting had begun in early March when Paul Lydick, chief of police of the small town of Ventura, California, began surveillance of a local resident suspected of transporting large sums of money out of the state. Lydick called in the Inland Revenue Service and the United States Customs Service. They discovered that there was already an investigation going on into the activities of a pilot, William Morgan Hetrick.

Hetrick was running an air charter business, Morgan Aviation, with six aeroplanes but not many customers. As it happens, Hetrick had been known to DeLorean for some years. It was mere coincidence, but Hetrick had regularly piloted Christina DeLorean, when she had been the significant other of a friend of DeLorean's called Fletcher Jones. Jones liked to party. DeLorean liked to party. California in the early 1970s? It would have been an odd rich man's party if there were not starlets around and if nobody was stuffing white powder in their nostrils or taking a drag on a roll up and discovering the 'meaning of life'. One of the other people invited to these parties was James Hoffman, a man who dealt in substances which make the world go away. DeLorean met Hoffman at Fletcher Jones's parties. Hoffman was part of the scene.

On 11 July 1982, DeLorean and Hoffman met in a hotel in California. Hoffman had been caught with drugs but was able to cut a deal with the authorities and become a 'CI': a confidential informant or co-operating individual. He had also been a business associate of Morgan Hetrick, though the relationship had ended in litigation. DeLorean later claimed that Hoffman had contacted him, while Hoffman would claim that the reverse was true. At that first meeting the subject of narcotics, apparently, was not raised – so why did they arrange to meet? Hoffman reported to his controllers that DeLorean was desperate for cash and that he could be used in a sting to catch Morgan Hetrick.

Hoffman and DeLorean met again in a hotel, this time in Washington DC, on 4 September, where DeLorean was introduced to an agent posing as a 'Mr Vicenza', who passed himself off as a drug dealer with connections to organised crime. DeLorean offered to invest $1.8 million dollars (Mr Vicenza was to put up $3 million) to buy 220 kilos of cocaine at $50,000 per kilo. Distribution was to be carried out by Mr Vicenza, while DeLorean was to launder the money through the DeLorean Motor Corporation.

Another meeting was conducted, in Los Angeles, on 20 September, and this time Morgan Hetrick was present. Hetrick boasted of his prowess as a smuggler and claimed it was possible to make a profit of $120,000 on each kilo of cocaine, if you could fly it straight from Columbia.

Briefly, that is the background to the 'sting'.

22 October 1982: *The Times* mentions GPD Services Inc. for the first time. America's Inland Revenue Service (IRS) is the source of this news, and the IRS claims that it had first asked DeLorean for information about GPD Services 21 months earlier.

The fact that the IRS made a public statement within hours of DeLorean's arrest is unusual, especially since the statement contained information about GPD Services, which gave the media a direct link to Chapman. It seems reasonable to assume that the IRS was working in conjunction with its British counterpart and had been doing so for the best part of two years. Sir Kenneth Cork wrote: 'GPD has been described as a "shelf corporation" and a "cash laundry". It appeared to have no assets and no office premises... It was evident to me that GPD's only role was to launder the money.'

Some have suggested that DeLorean was set up at the behest of the IRS to gain access to the accounts of GPD. Sir Kenneth Cork records that he interviewed Marie-Denis Juhan before Chapman died. He confronted her with evidence that she had siphoned money paid into GPD and passed it to an account connected to DeLorean. According to Cork, she denied everything and claimed that her signature had been forged.

The Swiss authorities have traditionally turned a blind eye to movements of money, but forgery is another matter. Much of Swiss banking depends on signatures because so many clients are not seen in person. A forged signature which is allowed to pass is like introducing a virus.

Once Cork had the cooperation of the Swiss authorities, he was able to trace the money as it was shunted from bank to bank, and they included Rothschild's in Zurich, the Chase Bank in New York and the Pierson Heldring Pierson Bank of Amsterdam.

Sir Kenneth interviewed Chapman, who denied any impropriety. Cork described the interview as 'uphill work' and made an appointment to interview him again. Before a second interview could take place, Chapman flew himself to Paris on 15

December, to attend a meeting of the FIA. He flew himself home and then suffered a massive heart attack. A post mortem was performed on his body.

John Z. DeLorean eventually came to trial and was acquitted. The jurors, who explained their decision after the trial, were in no doubt that DeLorean had indeed intended to buy cocaine and sell it for profit. They concluded, however, that his entrapment was so blatant that, according to the guidelines laid down by the judge, they had no option but to acquit him.

Christina DeLorean, who had played the supportive wife throughout the legal proceedings, which had dragged on for two years, immediately filed for divorce. John DeLorean never remarried and became a virtual recluse though, from time time, there have been rumours of a new DeLorean automotive project.

DeLorean later went on trial charged with fraud in a federal court in Detroit, but was again acquitted. Attempts by the British government to extradite him to face trial with Fred Bushell failed.

12 July 1989: Fred Bushell, Chapman's right hand man for more than 30 years, is arrested and charged that he conspired with Chapman, DeLorean and others to defraud the DeLorean Motor Company of $17.67 million. John DeLorean, it is alleged, received $8.5 million; Chapman's share was $8.39 million; and Bushell received one 10th of what Chapman received.

20 June 1992: Bushell is sentenced to three years imprisonment and a fine of £2.25 million at Belfast Crown Court. In sentencing him, Lord Justice Murray says that if the other people named on the charge sheet with Bushell had stood in the dock – Chapman and DeLorean – they would have received at least 10 years imprisonment.

It is most unusual for a senior British judge to make such a statement. Lord Justice Murray did not say that Chapman and DeLorean, had they stood before him, might have received sentences of 'up to' 10 years, he said that they would have, not might have, received sentences of 'at least' 10 years. Colin would have ended his days in disgrace. As it was, nearly 10 years passed between DeLorean's arrest and Lord Justice Murray's remarks. It had become stale news, a short item on the inside pages of some newspapers, and Colin's glittering reputation remained, more or less, intact.

There is one other intriguing twist to the tale. In 1997 a firm of solicitors, Morganroth and Morganroth of Detroit, sued John Z. DeLorean for millions of dollars owing over more than 10 years. An account of the trial is available on the Internet. The matter of GPD Services came up in the trial and DeLorean's former lawyers used the misappropriation of that money against him. They were awarded $5 million compensation and $5 million punitive damages. DeLorean could have kept his former lawyers at bay when he sold the former Logan Manufacturing Corporation, the company he bought with his share of the GPD scam, for $5.7

million, but instead he counter-sued claiming malpractice – hence the punitive damages.

At the trial, Christina Thomopoulous, the former Mrs DeLorean, testified that she had witnessed John Z. practice forging the signatures of Colin Chapman and Sir Kenneth Cork. She had seen him steam open envelopes, handle documents while wearing rubber gloves and had also seen him 'age' documents. Further, she had seen forged documents with the forged signatures of Chapman and Cork on them.

This evidence emerged five years after Fred Bushell's trial, and after his release from prison, and 10 years after Christina had filed for divorce and, to judge from the name, remarried. Why would DeLorean want to forge the signatures of Colin Chapman and Sir Kenneth Cork, both of whom were long dead by 1997? There is no evidence that DeLorean ever used these documents, but what was in his mind when he was going to so much trouble to make them look authentic?

What if Colin and DeLorean had stood in the dock alongside Fred and these documents had been produced in court? What if Christina Thomopoulous had been called as a witness? Would Lord Justice Murray have made the remarks he did?

EPILOGUE

WHEN Colin died, Team Lotus had achieved 72 Grand Prix wins, 88 pole positions, six drivers' world championships and seven constructors' titles. In addition there were countless wins in (non-championship) Formula 1, Formula 2, Formula 3, Formula Junior and Formula Ford, plus Indianapolis and sports and GT cars. Unlike other team owners, Colin had either personally designed, or had overseen the design, of every single car. Every modern racing car owes something to him.

He had also been an inspiration to many people. Cedric Selzer said, 'Colin used people, but he also motivated them. He could detect in people qualities they didn't know they had and he could draw out those qualities. As a result, you finished up having more confidence in yourself.'

More fine engineers and drivers passed through Team Lotus in the Chapman era than through any other team. Graham Hill won his first world championship for BRM, but it was Colin who provided Graham with the means to start racing. From Len Terry on, Lotus bred fine designers. People like Nigel Allen, Peter Ross and Mac Macintosh made their marks elsewhere, but all look back on their days in Hornsey with affection.

Colin left an astonishing legacy, but he also left behind him a mess and Fred Bushell had to pay the price for it. Fred was branded as a criminal and he had to endure being in prison while his wife, Hilda, was dying. Fred could not comfort her in her last days. It was a cruel punishment. Fred may have been embroiled in shady financial dealings, but his contribution to Lotus was immense. Keith Duckworth says, 'The only reason why Lotus survived was Fred Bushell. He had an absolute genius for running companies which were actually broke. Lotus never went into receivership. Fred was a genius.'

From the moment that Fred Bushell came on board, Lotus was saved. Colin Chapman could not have done it by himself, he had no time for the plodding detail which is the reality of running a business. Colin expressed himself, and Fred gave him the means by which to do it.

When Colin died, he faced disgrace and a prison sentence, but Keith Duckworth says:

> Colin had often sailed close to the wind, but I think he really went off the rails when he saw the British government give DeLorean huge pots of gold. The whole DeLorean venture was sheer stupidity. Lotus was a proper company and the government didn't give money to Lotus.
>
> I have a great deal of sympathy for Colin. I'd say that virtually anything he did was justified by the sheer stupidity of the British government.

Whatever the moral implications of Keith's opinion, it is a fact that the Labour government of Jim Callaghan threw tens of millions of pounds at DeLorean and the only time that Lotus received grants was to persuade the company to relocate to Norfolk, and those grants were open to almost any company which could create jobs there.

Colin was unique in the history of motor racing. He ran a car company as well as a team, but unlike, say, Enzo Ferrari, he was a designer as well. Ferrari's only practical experience of engineering was as a conscript during World War One when he had to shoe mules. Ferrari would attend race circuits only during practice for the Italian Grand Prix, whereas Chapman missed only three races between 1958 and 1982. Ferrari employed people to design engines for him, while Colin instigated the DFV, and Keith Duckworth and Mike Costin first met at Lotus. Without Colin their paths would never have crossed. During the lifetime of Enzo Ferrari, his Scuderia produced not one original idea, whereas Colin set landmark after landmark. The Lotus 25 was a long way from being the first monocoque car, but it was the one which everyone else copied. People did not join Ferrari and go on to other things unless it was to join the mainstream car industry. Lotus spawned countless outfits, including Progress, GRD, Hawke and Van Diemen. Colin showed people what was possible at a time when Britain was still a rigid, deferential society.

Colin left more than a record of remarkable achievement – he left a spirit, a philosophy, particularly in the consultancy department. Lotus road cars made during Colin's lifetime were often of indifferent quality, but today the world beats a path to Hethel. These days Lotus makes more cars a year, and of a higher quality, than ever was the case when Colin was alive. They have succeeded because they have, at their hearts, the qualities which Colin espoused. The Lotus Elise is an Elan for its day. Mazda may have used the Elan as the model for the MX-5 but, fine car though it is, the MX-5 does not have that indefinable quality which the Elan had. It was almost as though Colin gave a piece of himself to each of his cars. Even today an engineer at Lotus, who may not have even started school at the time of Colin's death, will wonder whether his work would pass muster with Chapman.

Colin and Hazel's three children, Jane, Sarah and Clive, have recorded what fun he was, when he was at home. He was the sort of 'sparky' dad that Roald Dahl held up as an example in his stories for children. In fact, since the children were at boarding schools and their holidays mainly coincided with the busiest time of the racing season, the family was not often together. When they were together, however, Colin would devise some exciting project for them to undertake. Colin could not do anything without enthusiasm, so when he was in 'father mode' he brought to that the energy which he applied to everything he did.

Clive Chapman was just 20 when Colin died and only really learned about his father's achievements in later life. Colin did not often bring his work home with him, though he did keep a drawing board at home. Clive has written, 'One of his [Colin's] sayings was, "Those who can do, and those who can't talk about it."' Colin did not give many interviews, he simply got on with the job in hand, with his mind on the next one, and the one after that.

He was no saint. He exploited people shamelessly, he was an accomplished liar and he was a philanderer. From the earliest days of Lotus, he had an unenviable reputation for dubious business ethics. Also from the earliest days, he was intent on building his own legend – look at the way he ripped off Derek Jolly's Austin Seven engine and then invented a story about having inspiration after a Christmas party.

After Colin died, rumours began to circulate that he had faked his own death to avoid further implication in the DeLorean Affair and was sunning himself on a tropical beach. There were stories of mysterious faxes, suggesting suspension layouts, which arrived at the works. On the day after Fred Bushell was sentenced Ross Benson, writing in the *Daily Mail*, claimed that a friend of Colin's had told him that he'd met up with Colin in South America just three years previously. So widespread were the rumours (believed by at least one Formula 1 team owner) that a German magazine offered a substantial reward for a recent photograph of Chapman, whose body had undergone a post mortem.

A doctor had to sign Colin's death certificate and according to a senior Lotus designer, the doctor soon closed his practice and moved to Portugal, where he died soon afterwards. According to someone who worked for both Lotus and DeLorean, the doctor was invited to Florida by a Mafioso colleague of John Z. and the doctor died in a hit and run accident ordered by the Mafia. It's a rare trick to die on two continents.

Plenty of former employees will swear that Colin was murdered by Mafiosi friends of DeLorean who had invested in DMC. In an article in the May 1995 edition of the magazine *Business Age*, Tom Rubython and Anil Bhoyrul claimed that Colin was prevailed upon to take two strangers to Paris and, during the flight, they drugged him and administered a fatal dose of digitalis. Fred Bushell was actually the only passenger on that flight. Besides, most people would not think it a very good idea to drug the pilot.

If DeLorean actually knew members of the Mafia, what use would he have had for 'Mr Vicenza', whose main attraction was that he claimed Mafia connections? Mr Vicenza was only able to entrap DeLorean because John Z. was desperate for money to save his dream and had nobody else to turn to.

There is more. According to one theory, the Conservative government discovered that Lotus was using VARI injection moulding, which was covered by a Hungarian patent, so the British government was paying royalties to an eastern bloc country. Margaret Thatcher prevailed on Ronald Reagan to persuade the FBI to set up a sting to trap DeLorean and hence entangle Chapman. A fine tale, except that the VARI system was developed by Peter Wright and Lotus held the patents.

These are some of the less fanciful stories and most came from senior figures at Lotus. The stories are of no value in themselves but they are valuable for another reason. Conspiracy theories spring up only around the deaths of a very few exceptional people. Elvis is still spotted in supermarkets and the assassination of JFK has spawned a minor industry. Colin had played so important a part in the lives of so many people that some were reluctant to believe that his life was snuffed out by something as mundane as a heart attack. Thousands of people die from heart attacks every day, but they do not engender stories involving a Prime Minister, a President, the Mafia, the FBI and, in one story, MI5.

The most popular of the Chapman legends has him faking his own death. This is partly because people did not want to believe he had just keeled over and died, and partly because Colin was always a step ahead of everyone else, and had so often found a loophole. People assumed he had the whole situation under control, that somehow up his sleeve was a 'Get Out Of Death' card.

Legends accrue only around heroes. Colin Chapman was an imperfect human being, but he was a hero. A hero in Greek legend always had human imperfections, but was possessed of extraordinary powers. That more or less sums up Colin Chapman.

SELECT BIBLIOGRAPHY

Balfe, Chris *Mario Andretti* (pitpass.com), 2002

Blunsden, John and David Phipps *Such Sweet Thunder* Motor Racing Publications, 1971

Clarke, R.M. (ed) *Lotus Sports Racers, 1953–1965* Brooklands Books (Compilation of magazine articles)

---*DeLorean* Brooklands Books (Compilation)

Cork, Sir Kenneth *Cork on Cork* MacMillan, 1988

Crombac, Gérard 'Jabby' *Colin Chapman, His Life and His Cars* Haynes, 1986

Fallon, Ivan and James Sprodes *DeLorean* Hamish Hamilton, 1983

Ferguson, Andrew *Team Lotus – The Indianapolis Years* Patrick Stephens Limited, 1994

Hodges, David *A-Z of Formula Racing Cars* Bayview Books, 1990

---*A-Z of Grand Prix Cars* Crowood Press, 2001

Nye, Doug *The Story of Lotus, 1961–1971* Motor Racing Publications, 1972

---*Theme Lotus* Motor Racing Publications, 1978

Read, Robin *Colin Chapman's Lotus* Haynes, 1989

Smith, Ian H. *The Story of Lotus, 1947-60* Motor Racing Publications, 1970

Wright, Peter *The Lotus 88* (grandprix.com), 2002

INDEX